Y0-AGH-786

". . . television problem plays are so representative of general American difficulties that they will undoubtedly prove far more interesting to future sociologists and historians than to literary scholars. Serious television drama, nevertheless, is literature, if not in its purest sense. It is more elliptical and swift-paced than written forms, of course, and it relies more upon skillful acting, expert direction and special effects than upon the beauty and texture of language. But it serves many of the same functions as novels and short stories and depends on some of the same elements, such as imagination, invention and characterization."

From the Introduction by
NED E. HOOPES

WILLIAM I. KAUFMAN worked in national television for 17 years in many capacities. He has written and compiled 12 books about television.

NED E. HOOPES has taught at Pace College, Hunter College High School, Evanston Township High School. He is the television columnist for *Media and Methods* and was formerly host of the television show *Reading Room*.

GREAT TELEVISION PLAYS

SELECTED BY
William I. Kaufman

INTRODUCTION BY
Ned E. Hoopes

LAUREL EDITION

Published by
DELL PUBLISHING CO., INC.
1 Dag Hammarskjold Plaza
New York, N.Y. 10017

Laurel ® TM 674623, Dell Publishing Co., Inc.

ISBN: 0-440-33207-9

Printed in the United States of America
First printing—April 1969
Second printing—July 1969
Third printing—October 1969
Fourth printing—August 1970
Fifth printing—November 1970
Sixth printing—August 1971
Seventh printing—January 1972
Eighth printing—October 1972
Ninth printing—July 1974
Tenth printing—January 1975
Eleventh printing—October 1975
Twelfth printing—September 1976
Thirteenth printing—October 1977

CONTENTS

GREAT
TELEVISION
PLAYS

INTRODUCTION

Television drama is an effective barometer of contemporary attitudes and values. In fact, television's original plays, those which are indigenous to the new electronic medium of communication, have assumed the major responsibility for exploring the social reality and domestic problems of a majority of Americans.

Drama is, after all, one of the most social of all art forms, reflecting the tenor of the times and commenting upon the nature of man. A playwright selects topics of special concern to him and deals with issues and conflicts that engage his imagination because of their immediacy and urgency. Consequently, in examining any form of drama, one must not ignore the values of the playwright or the assumptions he has made about his audience. This is especially true in analyzing television dramas of the last two decades.

If one can trust any form of literature as an index of prevailing attitudes, then television's problem play is, perhaps, the most accurate measure of today's so-called average American. Indeed, the special province of television has become that large middle area of common experience which has been abandoned, or certainly neglected, by the other art forms.

Television drama is, of course, derived from a long and honorable literary tradition, though it still lacks status and stature itself. The sentimental novels of authors like Samuel Richardson and Charles Dickens and the problem plays of Ibsen and his descendants Sidney Howard and Arthur Miller all dealt with the moral universe of "the common man." Novelists and playwrights alike set out to instruct people in the management of their lives, and they argued pretty much on behalf of a generalized middle-class ethic. Then television playwrights took on the job of treating domestic difficulties. In fact, they have been almost doggedly homiletic in doing so.

Paddy Chayefsky was to television drama what Ibsen was to social drama. His "small masterpieces," such as *The Big Deal,* were about unexceptional people in unexceptional situations. He explored in intimate detail the agonizing problems of "small people," and (for millions of home viewers) he tried to elevate both the people and the problems from which they suffered.

Rod Serling, also dedicated to realistic problem plays, offered marginal and oblique challenges to accepted values in plays like *Requiem for a Heavyweight.* The key to "television drama," he said, "is intimacy. The facial study on a small screen carries with it," he argued, "a meaning and power far beyond its usage in motion pictures."

While most modern novelists and major playwrights have shifted their focus from sociology to metaphysics, television dramatists continue to dwell on the emotionally handicapped, the distressed and alienated, and upon the hostility that exists between man and woman, and children and their parents. Whereas legitimate theater and even movies have almost completely abandoned domestic drama and have stopped trying to be social engineers, television still tries to teach viewers not so much *how* to live as how to put up with the kind of lives they are forced to live in this tense and distressing era.

In fact, television problem plays are so representative of general American difficulties that they will undoubtedly prove far more interesting to future sociologists and historians than to literary scholars. Serious television drama, nevertheless, is literature, if not in its purest sense. It is more elliptical and swift-paced than written forms, of course, and it relies more upon skillful acting, expert direction and special effects than upon the beauty and texture of language. But it serves many of the same functions as novels and short stories and depends on some of the same elements, such as imagination, invention and characterization.

Television drama is, however, a special visual form of literature with its own characteristics and its own technical and artistic limitations imposed by the medium itself. Almost any television play will lose some of its power and initial impact when it is encountered in a book rather than upon the screen, because, of course, it was designed to be seen and not read.

Television drama must appeal to a special kind of mass audience made up of individuals watching at home, either alone or in small groups. The other visual literary forms—movies and stage plays—appeal to a collective paying audience who participate in a contagious experience in a theater. Rather than attempting to elicit a unified response, playwrights in creating television plays must think of viewers as individual participants with a wide variety of attitudes and with fragmentary reactions. The audience, consequently, has a definite effect upon the style, subject matter, language and range of themes possible for television plays.

Because the television industry is less able to keep commercial interests distinct from literary interests, sponsors must also be taken into consideration. Their influence on television drama is considerable. Time must be allowed for advertising breaks and no potential customer can be offended.

A television performance is, perhaps, the most ephemeral of all literary forms because, if it is not seen at the specific scheduled time, it may not be seen at all. Transmitted simultaneously to millions of viewers, a video performance is an opening and a closing at the same time.

Because of the size of the screen, the focus in most television plays is upon people rather than plots, or places or even complicated ideas. It is more of a psychoanalytical medium that best evokes a single mood or makes a dominant impression in a highly compressed form. Mob scenes and expansive crowds must be avoided; in fact, the smaller the cast, the more effective the play, usually, for television.

Even within its limitations, however, a substantial body of serious television dramatic literature has been developed. Like most literature, it is inconsistent and uneven in quality. At its best, a television play is artistic and truthful and at its worst is trivial, formless, obvious and distorted.

Some of television's finest moments were those 52-minute plays (eight minutes for commercials) produced live on such weekly series as *Kraft Theatre, Philco-Goodyear Playhouse, Studio One* and so forth during the 1950s. Such television drama began with adaptations of classics and established contemporary novels and short stories. Slowly the emphasis shifted from adaptations to original plays. Alvin Sapinsley, for example, experimented with poetic drama. In his *Lee at Gettysburg*, presented on ABC's *Omnibus*, he was able to carry over effectively to the new visual medium some of the suggestiveness, the rhythm and the compression achieved in earlier poetic radio plays.

It was a period when writers had a real opportunity to learn their craft. Television was a new medium and playwrights didn't really know what to do with it, but they learned. Out of the liabilities and assets of television a new kind of play was developed—a type that had never existed in any other dramatic form. As Tad Mosel, one of the early television playwrights, said, "It was a play in which the writer closed in on one hour, one day, one week in someone's life and in so doing implied a neighborhood, a community, a world." These early television plays were not always successes—indeed there were more failures than successes—but some of the best of them are worth studying. For a time, such drama almost disappeared on television, except for original plays, such as *The Merry Jests of Hershel Ostropolier* by Ernest Kinoy, which were written especially for the major networks' Sunday morning religious and public affairs programs.

With plays like Ronald Ribman's *The Final War of Olly Winter*, produced on *CBS Playhouse*, however, there has begun a kind of revival of those early days of live television drama. But now the dramas are video-taped. This new process allows more editorial comment without denying the dynamics of a continuous, concentrated performance.

This book contains some of the most exciting achievements of television drama and should provide a rich opportunity for comparison with other literary forms.

NED HOOPES

PREFACE

This collection of television plays contains some of the finest drama that has appeared on television over a span of many years, beginning in the early days when outstanding live drama was performed on a regular basis.

When I speak of the "early days" I refer to the 1940s and 1950s. It is a sad commentary on the television industry of today that, despite technological innovations, we are seeing fewer and fewer high-quality original plays.

Although scions of the television industry keep talking about the lack of original materials, they cannot justify the dearth of good drama. Today's outstanding American television dramatists—Tad Mosel, Paddy Chayefsky, Alvin Sapinsley, Reginald Rose, Rod Serling and many others—began their careers as writers of television plays during a period when the television industry permitted writers to work on a trial-and-error basis. Their early dramas, furthermore, brought to public notice for the first time the talents of men who are now the outstanding producers and directors of the theater and of films.

I do believe that, along with the disappearance of live television drama, came the exodus of fine television writers and fine television writing.

I often ask myself why this has happened and I keep coming up with the same answer time after time. The plain fact of the matter is that the current television leadership has not provided a climate in which future Paddy Chayefskys can develop. A lack of people in high places with taste and a lack of men who have the ability to work with the creative writer have created this poverty of material.

There are more young people studying creative writing today than at any other time in the history of education. The book-publishing industry continues to be concerned with the discovery of new writing talent. It is with dedication to the new writer that the publisher devotes much of his own creative energies in an endless search for high quality. While a great many inferior first books are published, the book industry believes the only way one develops new talent is to give it an opportunity for creative expression, a chance to be read.

Perhaps someday the television industry will learn from the book industry the lesson that it once knew so well and we shall once again have the opportunity to view outstanding drama on a regular basis. Television will once again be concerned with raising the level of the public taste as it educates and informs and we shall once more be the discoverers of American writers who have a medium through which their works may have the hearing and the viewing they deserve.

It is my wish that students of the television play will learn and enjoy while reading this anthology and perhaps some will take the courageous step toward becoming a creative writer with something to say, something that will bring joy and knowledge to other young people just as the authors whose works appear here have done.

WILLIAM I. KAUFMAN

THE MERRY JESTS OF
HERSHEL OSTROPOLIER

by Ernest Kinoy

NARRATOR: This is the story my grandmother used to tell me Friday afternoon while the kettle of fish simmered on the stove . . . and the sabbath bread baked in the oven. This is a story of the old days, in the old country. Of Hershel Ostropolier . . . the wise fool. The Jester.

[HERSHEL *is poised motionless in an extravagant posture. He wears a sort of neutral black basic leotard and tights, with an extravagant cap, a sort of Mittel-Europa variation of the stuffed cap and bells of the traditional jester. Around his waist is knotted a shawl, which dangles to one side ending in the traditional ritual fringes.* [*All of the characters wear some version of this basic costume, for the women a leotard top and long skirt. Their individuality as characters is expressed in some piece of dressing, a hat, a cape, a gold chain, etc.*]

NARRATOR: At this time Hershel served his Magnificence the Grand Parness of Miedziboz. [HERSHEL *sweeps into an exaggerated burlesque of a courtly obeissance, ending up tied up in pretzel knots, his hat swept off in his low bow.*] But his Magnificence was not always pleased with his jester, for Hershel aimed his shaft at high places . . . as well as low. .
[HERSHEL *unwinds with a snap.*]

HERSHEL: Tell me, my Lord Parness, wherein lies the difference between poor Hershel Ostropolier and his excellency the Grand Parness of Miedziboz?

NARRATOR [*As the Parness*]: A riddle? Hershel . . . the answer quickly, I'm a busy man!

HERSHEL [*With a flourish*]: If it please you, sir . . . whereas his Excellency the Parness is paid two thousand guldens a year for being good . . . poor Hershel is good

. . . poor Hershel is good . . . for nothing! [HERSHEL *cuts a caper, ending with his cap over his heart, and his hand outstretched.*] My Lord, my salary for the week?

NARRATOR: But the wealthy jurist with his full purse had a habit of taking the jester at his word . . . and Hershel . . . was good . . . for nothing! [*During this, the realization that he is not to be paid creeps over* HERSHEL'S *face and body muscle by muscle. Jamming his cap on his head, he turns and walks "home," in place, a picture of dejection. Directly in front of* HERSHEL *his* WIFE *suddenly appears in the light, her arms akimbo in classic position of the folktale "shrew."*] But Hershel had a wife . . . and she was never known for a soft and velvet tongue.

[*The wife,* BRONKE, *has a wooden ladle in one hand.* HERSHEL *stops when he sees her, there is almost a little dance as he feints to one side, then to the other, then with a quick movement she swings with the ladle,* HERSHEL *ducks under her arm, she whirls twice around to find him, and by the time she stops,* HERSHEL *is comfortably stretched out on a bench . . . one leg crossed over the other, his toes wiggling.*]

BRONKE: Well . . . did he pay you?

HERSHEL: With compliments . . . yes. With guldens . . . no!

BRONKE: I've had enough. Too much! Here it is almost time to prepare for Passover. Do we have wine in the house?

HERSHEL: No.

BRONKE: Have we money for new clothes?

HERSHEL: No.

BRONKE: Money to buy matzos for the holiday?

HERSHEL: No.

BRONKE: Have we made any preparation at all for Passover?

HERSHEL: Yes.

BRONKE: What!

HERSHEL [*Swinging upright*]: Bronke, my wife, we're half-ready for Passover now.

BRONKE: Half-ready?

HERSHEL [*Leaping up on the bench to lecture*]: Certainly. What do you have to do to prepare for Passover? First—

clean out every crumb of leavened bread in the house,
and second—buy matzos to eat instead.

BRONKE: And how will we buy matzos with no money?

HERSHEL: Ahh . . . but that's the *second* half! The first
half we've already done. There hasn't been a crumb of
bread in the house for a week! See . . . we're half-ready
for Passover.

[*In irritation* BRONKE *swipes at him with the ladle, once
forehand, once backhand.* HERSHEL *skips over it lightly
each time with an extravagant classic entrechat, coming
down finally with a grin.*]

BRONKE [*Giving up, sighing.*]: It's all very well to laugh
. . . but it's no joke to have to serve a funny story for
supper instead of a chicken.

HERSHEL: Well, it's not my fault. Consider, dear wife.
You've caused me more trouble than ten good-for-
nothing relatives.

BRONKE [*Whirls on him.*]: What's that?

HERSHEL [*Dodging.*]: Oh . . . I can prove it. Once five years
ago a millionaire wanted me to marry his daughter.

BRONKE: But how could you? You were married to me.

HERSHEL [*Waving her off.*]: I know . . . I know. Everything
was arranged . . . so I went to the rich man and I said:
"In my family there are drunkards, cardplayers, sinners,
good-for-nothings without number." [HERSHEL *quickly
changes over, plays the very fat rich man.*] "Makes no
difference . . . no family is perfect! You can marry my
daughter!" [*As* HERSHEL *again.*] "But my dear father-
in-law-to-be—I've already got a wife!" So what does he
do? [HERSHEL *takes himself by the scruff of the neck and
throws himself out in the character of the rich father.*]
"Out . . . out . . . no-good . . . out."

[*Then dropping the character, he sums up sweetly.*] You
see? He was willing to swallow all the others but you.
That proves you must be worse than all the good-for-
nothings in my family rolled into one. [BRONKE *stares at
him . . . then sits down and dissolves into tears.* HERSHEL
flutters behind her, trying to console her.] Wife . . .
Bronke . . . sweetheart . . . don't cry. I'll ask the
Parness for my back pay . . . I promise. I'll make him
give it to me. . . . [BRONKE *sobs louder.*] Don't cry . . .

little pigeon . . . please . . . I'll make him pay me the whole year's back pay!

[*Suddenly* BRONKE *swings her ladle arm around,* HERSHEL *ducking under it by instinct. The sobs are turned off like a faucet.*]

BRONKE: Now!

HERSHEL [*Suddenly tentative.*]: I just left him. Tomorrow? Next week?

BRONKE: Now!

[*Shrugging,* HERSHEL *turns, looks back, sees her pointing inflexibly with the ladle.*]

NARRATOR [*As the* PARNESS *laughs hugely.*]: Hershel . . . truly you are the King of Fools.

HERSHEL: Yes, Master . . . and I can prove it. What would you call a man who works in another man's field for nothing and neglects his own?

NARRATOR: Why . . . a fool!

HERSHEL: So—I have labored for you for a whole year . . . with not a copper to show for it. Surely I must be the King of Fools.

NARRATOR [*Coughing to change the subject.*]: Hershel . . . times are much better. Admit it—haven't you found it easier to prepare for Passover this year than last?

HERSHEL: Oh yes, Master . . . much easier. Last year I had to carry my table to the pawnshop. This year I'll only have to carry my chair.

NARRATOR: Hershel . . . I've decided to pay you the money. . . . [HERSHEL *lights up.*] If . . . I'm convinced you deserve it. [HERSHEL's *light is turned out.*] I shall test you. You must take a journey to the city of Leitishev and perform a good deed. If the good deed shows a good heart, you'll have your back pay and a hundred guldens beside. That's fair enough, isn't it?

HERSHEL: But, Master, the road to Leitishev is swarming with bandits!

NARRATOR: But, Hershel, what can harm you? Don't you know that Heaven protects a man on his way to do a good deed?

HERSHEL: Ah yes, Master, I know it, *you* know it, and *Heaven* knows it! But do the *bandits* know it?
[*Black out.*]

NARRATOR: But the Leitishev road was long and dusty, and Hershel's shoes were thinner than a pauper's soup. So thin he used to say he could stand on a book and read it with his toes. But finally—inspiration struck! [HERSHEL *leaps off his perch into the air in a caper of sly triumph, then he whirls.* HERSHEL *in another angle. He holds an imaginary whip in his hand and snaps it. The sound of the snapping whip is heard.*]

HERSHEL [*Shouts.*]: Hear ye, good people. Pay attention to Hershel the Coachman. I'm taking passengers to Leitishev for half-fare. Half-fare to Leitishev!
[*Now* JOSEPH *the merchant, dressed in the basic black costume, with an enormous fur hat, a gold chain around his neck, and a broad ornate sash. He is prosperous and pompous.*]

JOSEPH: What's that—half-fare?

HERSHEL [*Cracks his "whip" again.*]: Half-fare—I'm taking people to Leitishev—

JOSEPH: Well, that's a bargain. I'll take one ticket.

HERSHEL: Cash . . . in advance!

JOSEPH: But . . . but . . . you can trust me. I'm the biggest merchant in Leitishev!

HERSHEL: In advance . . . after all, it's half-fare.

JOSEPH: Well, yes . . . yes . . . I understand. [*He hands him money from a heavy purse at his belt.*] There . . . now . . . where are the coach and the horses?

HERSHEL: Don't worry, Master . . . just follow me. [*He cracks his whip. The music marches with them.*]

[HERSHEL *and* JOSEPH *walking "in place."*]

JOSEPH: Here now, Coachman . . . we've come to the edge of town. Where are the coach and horses?

HERSHEL: Master, trust me . . . a little farther. [*They walk on. The music marching along as* HERSHEL *cracks the whip.*]

[HERSHEL *and* JOSEPH *walking. The music and* JOSEPH *are rather tired.*]

JOSEPH: Here now, Coachman—enough! We've come miles already! Where are the horses? I'm turning back, we're over halfway to Leitishev!

HERSHEL [*Cheerfully.*]: Then there's no point in turning

back, is there? Don't worry, Master. [*He cracks the whip.*] Just follow me. . . . [*They start up again.*]

[JOSEPH *and the music are pooped.* HERSHEL *stops, cracks his whip and shouts.*]

HERSHEL: Here we are—Leitishev. Last stop! Change for Berditchev, Byalystok, and points west!

JOSEPH [*Footsore and weary.*]: Swindler . . . thief . . . give me back my money.

HERSHEL [*Astounded.*]: But—why?

JOSEPH: You tricked me. Where were the horses and the coach?

HERSHEL [*The dawn breaks.*]: Oh . . . you mean . . . horses! But, Master, did I or didn't I promise to take you to Leitishev for half-fare? And what did you pay? Half-fare! Where are you now? Leitishev! Who said anything about a coach and horses?

[*The light blacks out on the outraged* JOSEPH. *As* HERSHEL *skips to one side, he flips the coin up in the air.*]

HERSHEL: Now I've got enough for a good dinner at the Inn . . . [*He stops as he hears a* GIRL *humming.*] Ahhh . . . a girl . . . a pretty young girl!

[*The light comes up on* JUDITH *sitting on a bench. She is sewing, and singing to herself.*]

JUDITH [*Sings.*]:
"Mama, Mama, I am dying,
Send for the doctor, send for the Rov,
Mama, Mama, I am dying.
I am going to the world above . . .
So where . . .

[HERSHEL *interrupts, picking up the verse singing as the* "*mother*" *in the song.*]

HERSHEL [*Sings.*]:
"So where does it hurt you,
My darling daughter,
Where does it hurt you,
Where is the pain?"

JUDITH [*Holding her heart.*]:
"Here, Mama, here is the pain."

HERSHEL:
"I won't call the doctor my daughter
I won't trouble the learned Rov.
The cure for you is a man, my daughter."
BOTH:

"The cure for $\left\{ \begin{array}{l} \text{you} \\ \text{me} \end{array} \right.$ is a man to love!"

[HERSHEL *ends the song with a happy caper, but suddenly, as he looks down, he sees that the* GIRL *is crying.*]

HERSHEL: What—crying after such a beautiful duet? Why, anyone as young and pretty as you should be laughing!

JUDITH: Laughing! [*Sobs.*] What have I got to laugh at?

HERSHEL: Why, there's always something to laugh at. Take me. I'm a jester—a clown on annual retainer. What could be funnier than a poor man who must be witty or his children go hungry? A learned man who must be a fool or his cupboard stays bare? That's a joke that improves with the years. It never fails to set me roaring with mirth. Now, sweetheart . . . why wet the dust of the road with tears? In my experience a woman cries for either money or love. Which is it?

JUDITH: Both.

HERSHEL: Then move, move over . . . you'll need help weeping. You're in love? With whom?

JUDITH: David, the son of Joseph the merchant. But, sir, I'm an orphan with no dowry. David's father says he forbids his son to marry a . . . a . . . pauper! [*She cries.*]

HERSHEL: Love and money. Now, suppose we discuss this over supper, and . . .

JUDITH: But I have no money. I haven't eaten all day.

HERSHEL: You should be ashamed of yourself. You'll injure your health. Here, take this. [*He presses the money on her.*] It's enough for a fine meal.

JUDITH: But, what will you do?

HERSHEL: Take it. Properly handled, my girl, gold is like strudel dough—it stretches. Now, stand by me and try to look frightened. [*He turns and pounds on a table which happens to be right there.*] Innkeeper. Innkeeper! [*The* INNKEEPER, *wearing the "basic black" with a white apron tied around, comes bustling into the light.*]

INNKEEPER: Who's howling out there?

HERSHEL: Please, sir. I'm hungry—give me something to eat.

INNKEEPER: Where's your money?

HERSHEL: I haven't any.

INNKEEPER: A beggar eh? Well, for you there isn't a bit of food in the house.

HERSHEL [*Loud*.]: What—no food?

INNKEEPER: No food.

HERSHEL [*Sinister and ominous*.]: In that case, I'm afraid I'll have to do just what my father did!

INNKEEPER: Huh? What . . . what's that? What did your father do?

HERSHEL [*Very ominously*.]: Never mind! My father . . . did what he did!

INNKEEPER: What . . . what . . . what could his father have done? [*He addresses* JUDITH *nervously*.] You know? I'm all alone in the inn. [*Back to* HERSHEL, *nervously now*.] You'll . . . do what your father did?

HERSHEL [*Leaning back on his bench*.]: Absolutely!

INNKEEPER: That . . . that's terrible.

[*Wringing his hands*.] His father might have been a . . . a murderer! Just w—w—wait right here, sir. I'm sure I can . . . find something for you to eat . . . don't . . . don't do anything! Ohhhhh . . . [*From a tight shot of the trembling* INNKEEPER *to* HERSHEL *at the table picking the last crumb out of his teeth. He wipes his mouth, leans back with satisfaction. The* INNKEEPER *is still wringing his hands*.] Everything satisfactory, sir?

HERSHEL [*Rising*.]: Excellent. Had enough, Judith?

JUDITH: Oh yes, sir.

INNKEEPER: You're feeling better now, sir?

HERSHEL: Much.

INNKEEPER: Then . . . if you don't mind my asking . . .

HERSHEL: By all means—ask!

INNKEEPER: I know it's presumptuous . . . but . . . would you mind telling me . . . what was it your father did?

HERSHEL: Oh . . . my father. [*He takes* JUDITH'S *hand, backing away just a little*.] Whenever my father didn't have any supper . . . he went to bed without it!

[*He turns and, pulling* JUDITH *with him, flies off into the darkness, leaving the* INNKEEPER *to go through a*

*traditional, you should excuse the expression, Edgar
Kennedy burn—while the music fiddles.*]

HERSHEL: And now, my dear girl, we must turn our attention to . . .

[*As he turns, he stops.* JUDITH *is deep in an embrace with
a* YOUNG MAN *who wears the black basic, with a little
white scholar's cap, a shawl around his neck with the
black stripes and fringes.*]

HERSHEL [*Shrugs.*]: 'Twas ever thus. A poor man feeds a
bird for someone else to consume. When a poor man
eats a chicken, either the man is sick . . . or the chicken
is. [*He coughs.* JUDITH *and* DAVID *relinquish their embrace, at least partially.*] For the sake of morality, I trust
this is the young man you love?

DAVID: I'm David, son of Joseph the merchant.

HERSHEL: Good . . . good. And do you love this girl?

DAVID: More than anything . . . except . . .

HERSHEL: Except? How can you love except?

DAVID [*Sadly.*]: My father has forbidden me to marry her.
I cannot disobey him. Judith would feel that she came
between a father and his son, and we should never be
happy.

HERSHEL: But you would marry her if he gave his consent?

DAVID: Tomorrow . . . no . . . today. This minute!

[JUDITH *rewards him with a renewal of the embrace.*]

HERSHEL: Well . . . that settles that.

DAVID: But my father will never consent. He insists on a
rich dowry for my bride, and Judith is an orphan without a copper.

JUDITH: It's hopeless.

HERSHEL: It was. But now, you have Hershel on your side.
You've solved my problem—I've found a good deed.
Now it's only fair that I solve yours. . . .

[*He waves goodbye and swirls into the black, leaving*
JUDITH *and* DAVID.]

[HERSHEL *steps boldly up to a "door" and knocks . . .
knocks again. . . .* JOSEPH *comes to the other side of the
"door."*]

JOSEPH: Who's there?

HERSHEL: The famous Shadchan, the marriage interventionist from the city. Open up!

JOSEPH: A marriage interventionist? [*He opens the "door" . . . then takes.* HERSHEL *is equally surprised. They both shout "You!" simultaneously.*]

JOSEPH: The Coachman . . . the thief . . . out of my house . . . swindler! [*He grabs him by the back of his collar.*]

HERSHEL: Hold on . . . Master. . . . I can do you a great service.

JOSEPH: Liar, good-for-nothing. . . . [*Take.*] What service?

HERSHEL: I have a bride for your son. A beautiful girl, fine cook, a good heart and a loving nature.

JOSEPH: Hmm. Who is the girl?

HERSHEL: Lovely, charming, gracious, a lyric soprano. . . .

JOSEPH: Enough, enough. What's her name?

HERSHEL: Judith.

JOSEPH: Judith? The orphan girl?

HERSHEL: I suppose you could put it that way. Her parents are . . . just a little dead.

JOSEPH: How dare you propose a pauper for my son? Out . . . [*He heaves* HERSHEL *clear out of the light, dusts his hands.*]

[HERSHEL *comes flying, rolling, sprawling, ending up at the feet of* JUDITH *and* DAVID.]

JUDITH: Are you all right?

HERSHEL: Everything is fine . . . fine . . . We have won the first battle!

JUDITH: Did David's father give his consent?

HERSHEL: No . . . he threw me out!

DAVID: What good does that do us?

HERSHEL: We'll see . . . we'll see. . . . [*He springs up lightly.*] Remember—we have him trapped.

DAVID *and* JUDITH: Trapped?

HERSHEL: Before he can throw me out again . . . why, he has to let me in! [HERSHEL *marches off into the dark triumphantly.*]

[*We see* JOSEPH *choleric with rage.*]

JOSEPH: You here again? I told you to stay out or I'll call the town watch! Swindler . . . liar . . . cheat . . . no-good!

HERSHEL: But, Master . . . I have a bride for your son . . . a queen, an empress.

JOSEPH: A marriage broker can exaggerate a sneeze into the day of judgment. Who is it this time?

HERSHEL: The youngest daughter of his Magnificence the Grand Parness of Miedziboz!

JOSEPH: Oh? He's the . . . the richest man in the province. What a match . . . but . . . [*Suspicious*.] . . . you really know the Parness?

HERSHEL: Of course. I see him every day.

JOSEPH: And you spoke to him about a marriage with my son?

HERSHEL: Would you doubt me?

JOSEPH: What did he say?

HERSHEL: To think that you called me names—swindler, cheat, no-good.

JOSEPH: I apologize, sir. What did the Parness say?

HERSHEL: When I suggested a match with your son?

JOSEPH: Yes, yes. What did he say?

HERSHEL: What did he say?

JOSEPH: For the love of Heaven, man—what did he say?

HERSHEL: Just what you said. "How dare you propose such a match for my child. Swindler . . . liar . . . cheat . . . no-good." And he threw me out of the house.

[*We see* DAVID *and* JUDITH *standing waiting as* HERSHEL *comes barreling out of the darkness head over heels as before.* JUDITH *and* DAVID *kneel beside him.*]

HERSHEL: The second battle is ours!

DAVID: But my father threw you out again.

HERSHEL: Exactly. You see—if the seat of my britches holds out, we'll have him worn down till he can't raise his arm.

DAVID: But what's the use of just going back this way? He won't change his mind and let me marry Judith.

HERSHEL [*Getting up*.]: Ah . . . but each time I go back he turns redder and sputters louder. An angry mind is not the best counselor . . . and besides, it's getting easier each time. I know each cobblestone like an old friend.

[*We see* JOSEPH *on a bench, presumably in bed asleep.* HERSHEL *climbs in a "window."*]

HERSHEL: Master Joseph. . . . Master Joseph. . . .

JOSEPH [*Waking.*]: Huh . . . what . . . who is it?

HERSHEL: Master Joseph. . . .

JOSEPH: How did you get here? Go away! I've had a hard day. Stop haunting me. . . .

HERSHEL: I've got another match for your son, a lovely girl. . . .

[JOSEPH *keeps trying to lie down,* HERSHEL *keeps pulling him up.*]

JOSEPH: Walking all the way from Miedziboz . . . let me alone. . . .

HERSHEL: You want your son married, don't you?

JOSEPH: No . . . I mean yes. . . . I'm asleep. Come back tomorrow. I'm all confused.

HERSHEL: You are?

JOSEPH: I'm what?

HERSHEL: Confused.

JOSEPH: Of course not. I know what I'm saying. Why should I marry your son? . . . I mean, why should you marry my daughter? Ohhh . . . go away . . . let me sleep!

HERSHEL: First we've got to get your son married off. . . .

JOSEPH: Go away.

HERSHEL: You want a dowry for your son, don't you?

JOSEPH: No. . . . *YES!*

HERSHEL: Would you marry him to a girl with, say, three thousand guldens?

JOSEPH: Yes . . . yes . . . anything . . . only let me sleep!

HERSHEL: Will you swear it? On your sacred honor?

JOSEPH: Yes . . . yes . . . I swear it . . . now let me . . .

HERSHEL: Good . . . then it's settled. . . .

JOSEPH [*Sinking back.*]: Now let me . . . sleeeeeeeep!

[*We see* JUDITH *and* DAVID *waiting as before. The chaser music which accompanied* HERSHEL'S *being thrown out is played. They wait, looking down at their feet, for him to skid into view. Suddenly he speaks behind them and they whirl.*]

HERSHEL: Well, congratulations.

DAVID: What do you mean?

HERSHEL: It was easy.

JUDITH: You mean David's father gave his consent?

HERSHEL: Of course. All we have to do is give him the dowry—three thousand guldens.

JUDITH: But . . . but . . . I . . . I don't have any money. I've never even seen three thousand guldens. [*She starts crying.*]

HERSHEL: Neither do I, but am I crying? Now, leave everything to me . . . both of you. Be ready tomorrow in your finest clothes and we'll sign the wedding contract.

JUDITH: Oh, David. . . .

DAVID: Sweetheart. [*They embrace.*] Hershel . . . I don't understand, but it's a miracle. Only the patriarchs in Heaven know how you're going to do it.

HERSHEL: They do? Well, I wish they'd let me in on it before morning. I'm completely in the dark!

[*We see* JOSEPH, *tight, grisly dismay written all over his face.*]

JOSEPH: What's going on here. Isn't it bad enough that some mad man keeps me up all night? What's this? David—what are you doing?

DAVID: I'm going to be married, Father.

JOSEPH: You're *what!* To whom?

JUDITH: To me, may it please you, sir.

JOSEPH [*Exploding.*]: The orphan girl—never! I forbid it! David, get into the house!

HERSHEL [*Bounding forward.*]: One moment, Master. You forgot your oath.

JOSEPH: What oath?

HERSHEL: You swore you'd marry your son to any girl with a dowry of three thousand guldens.

JOSEPH: I just said that to get rid of *you.* Besides, this pauper girl hasn't got a copper.

HERSHEL: You're right, Master. She has no copper—but gold . . . [*He dumps out a bag of coins on the table.*] Three thousand guldens. . . .

JOSEPH: Three . . . thousand . . . ?

HERSHEL: And here is the marriage contract. Sign it . . . and the celebration can begin.

[JUDITH *and* DAVID *fly into their favorite embrace.*]

[HERSHEL *starts slowly clapping and snapping his fingers. Singing "la la la . . ." of a wedding dance, gathering speed, until he is dancing. He pulls* JUDITH *into the dance with him, then* DAVID, *and then* JOSEPH, *until all are going round in a wild circle dance, singing and stamping gaily, going round one way, then back the other, until it works into a mad climax. And then cuts out suddenly.*]

[*We see the imposing figure of* BRONKE, *standing arms akimbo, the ladle at the ready.*]

BRONKE: Well, Hershel? You're back from Leitishev. Have you been to the Parness for your back pay?

HERSHEL: I've just come from his house.

BRONKE: He said if you did a good deed, you'd get your money. Did your good deed satisfy him?

HERSHEL: He said a saint himself couldn't have been nobler.

BRONKE: Then the back pay? He'll give us the money to buy wine and clothes and matzos for Passover?

HERSHEL: Well . . . there is a complication. . . .

BRONKE: A complication?

HERSHEL: You see, in order to give the orphan girl a dowry, I had to have three thousand guldens, so I borrowed it from the Parness in advance and gave it to her.

BRONKE: You gave her . . . three thousand guldens?

HERSHEL: It was the only way I could do my good deed.

BRONKE: Oh no—a whole year's pay. You didn't.

HERSHEL: Naturally. It's logic. Without the good deed, I couldn't get the money, but without the money, I couldn't do the good deed.

BRONKE [*A big sigh.*]: Well, it *is* a blessing to give a dowry to a poor girl. Hershel . . . Hershel . . . Hershel . . . we'll have a hungry Passover and a shabby one, but we'll have laughter in the house, won't we?

HERSHEL [*Putting his arms around her.*]: So we will, wife, so we will. . . .

BRONKE: But . . . wait . . . the Parness promised an *extra* hundred guldens over your back pay if you did the good deed—that will be plenty for matzos and wine. . . .

HERSHEL: Well . . . to . . . to tell the truth . . . I gave the hundred guldens to David and Judith.

BRONKE [*Springing up.*]: What! Our last copper! Why did you do such a thing?

HERSHEL [*Brightly.*]: Well, I was the best man at the wedding. The least I could do was give the newlyweds a fine wedding present!

[BRONKE *stares at him for a moment, then brings her arm back with the ladle.* HERSHEL *leaps to the bench. She swings at him back and forth as he gracefully skips over the ladle, snapping his fingers and starting the "la la la" of the wedding dance.* BRONKE *stops, looks at him.* HERSHEL *leaps off the bench and swings her into the dance with him.*]

LEE AT GETTYSBURG

by Alvin Sapinsley

PROLOGUE

[*Fade in:* GENERAL HOOD, *standing before a portion of the setting.*]

GEN. HOOD: This place is Gettysburg: We've built it here
    Of wood and canvas, squeezed its mile or so
    Of rolling, fertile fields within this square
    Of bricks and mortar, brought its streams and hills
    Beneath this roof, arranged them as they were
    In 1863, when fifty times
    A thousand fighting men laid down their lives.
    To actors, waiting now beyond our view,
    Great names, like Lee and Longstreet, we've assigned,
    And lesser names to those who will portray
    The lesser figures in this evening's play.
    And so, with players, sets, and cameras, we
    Request a hearing for our tragedy.
    [*Fade out.*]

ACT ONE

[*Fade in: Brandy Station, Virginia; June 9, 1863.* TWO CONFEDERATE CAVALRYMEN, *unshaven, weary, and wearing torn, dusty uniforms, come out of the small, rural railroad station onto the wooden platform surrounding it. One of the men carries his arm in a sling, the other sports a bandaged head. It is the start of a warm summer's day.*]

1ST CAV. [*In disgusted tones.*]: "Return to your brigade,"
    the sawbones says.
2ND CAV.: That's easy said. The last I seen of them
    They're heading south for Kelly's Ford with half
    The Union Army snapping at their heels.
    If they'd been riding north at half the speed
    I seen them riding south, by now they'd be
    In Washington, and we'd have won the war.
1ST CAV.: We reined in, though, and drove the Yankees back,
    But not before five hundred of us fell.
    You know, at first I thought I must be drunk.
2ND CAV.: I *was* drunk. I thought I'd gone off my head.
    I hadn't seen a pint of honest stuff
    Since Fredericksburg; so when the dancing stopped
    I picked this Richmond kitten off the porch,
    And found an unattended quart of hooch,
    And off we went to talk philosophy
    Behind the courthouse. Everything was fine:
    We drank, and talked, and when the night got cool
    She snuggled up, and purred, and I was just
    About to show her what the fighting man
    Required to finish off this war in half
    The time expected, when I heard a noise
    That sounded like a million horses' hooves.

"Well, now," I said. "I've lost my head for hooch!"
She started yelling, "Yankees!" "Honey child,"
I said, "you're loopier than me. There ain't
No Yankees within fifty miles of here!"
Well, man, those horses' hooves are louder now,
And heading right to where I'm all sprawled out,
And I don't even have the time to roll,
When every Yank who ever owned a horse,
It seems like, charges round that clump of trees,
A-hooting, yelling, screaming, waving swords
And shooting off their pistols. "Well," says I,
"I reckon I was wrong, and you was right.
I ain't no general, but it looks to me
Like Brandy's been invaded, and I guess
I ought to go and lend the boys a hand."
So off I went—and, man, that was a fight!

1ST CAV. [*Shaking his head in chagrin.*]: We looked like
     farmers, sure enough, last night.
     [*They move off along the railroad platform.*]

[*Dissolve to: Robert E. Lee's headquarters in the vicinity
of Brandy Station is a small, square, whitewashed room,
containing little more than the necessary table and chairs,
a cot, a large military map on the wall. Enter* GENERAL
LEE, GENERAL LONGSTREET, *and* GENERAL STUART.]

LEE: How many did we lose?

STUART [*Avoiding their eyes.*]: Five hundred, sir.

LEE [*Distressed.*]: Five hundred. We're hard put to spare
     these men.

LONGSTREET [*With elaborate irony.*]: I wouldn't say it's
     been our blackest day.
     At Fredericksburg five thousand of us fell;
     Another ten or so at Chancellorsville.
     Of course, we called those battles! [*With a venomous
        glance at* STUART.]
     Don't you think
     Five hundred might be looked upon as high
     For losses at a *dress-parade?*—

STUART [*Smarting.*]: Have I
     Been called here to be lectured? If that's so—

LEE [*Quietly.*]: You'll not be lectured, General Stuart; yet
     It's fair to tell you how you may have harmed
     A most important, crucial strategy.

STUART: I held a dress-parade! [*To* LEE; *almost pleading.*]
  You knew of it!
LEE: I knew of the parade, sir, that's quite true.
STUART: You authorized it!
LEE: Not what followed it:
  Carloads of women brought here for a ball;
  Your men intoxicated, off their guard—
  An open invitation which the North
  Could hardly be expected to decline. [*To* STUART.]
  Those Northern horsemen who attacked your troops
  Returned with more than Southern scalps to boast
  Of to their comrades in the ranks. They saw
  My infantry, encamped, prepared to march;
  For all we know, our strategy's revealed.
STUART [*Insisting doggedly.*]: You gave me leave! I came
    to you and said
  A dress-parade would bolster troops' morale!
  I said I planned a ball; I asked your view!
LEE: And I replied, sir: "Do you think it wise?"
  Is that approval?
STUART: Yes! I thought it wise!
LONGSTREET: You thought it wise?
STUART: I did.
LONGSTREET: Well, by the book!
  They're thinking, now, this jockey corps: What next?
  Here's Hannibal, come down from icy Alps
  To give us seminars in strategy!
  By God, we'll hear the answer now, at long last
  To what's been plaguing us for centuries:
  How did you get the elephants up there?
STUART: I warn you, Longstreet, that's enough!
LONGSTREET: Agreed!
  Enough and more! Is this a war we fight?
  Are we an army, or a ragged group
  Of schoolboys on an outing in the woods?
  The men who died for your conceit stay dead;
  They don't just lie there till a whistle blows,
  And then get up and brush their trousers off!
  They're dead forever!
LEE: Gentlemen: we mourn
  The death of these brave men; but how much less
  We'd be than those who fight us were we now
  To make our war a thing of hate and rage,

To snarl and bicker, catch each other up
At every faulty judgment, every snag
That seems to make our way more difficult.
We fight the North; let's fight as Southerners;
Let's fight compassionately, fight as men
Who stand upon a field of honor; not
As dogs, as wolves, as naked savages,
Who fight because they fear the whip, and not
Because a common purpose moves them.

LONGSTREET: Sir,
If soldiers aren't made to answer for
Their blunders, then they'll blunder on, and soon
A day will come when we'll have lost this war!
And on that day, the blame will rest with those
Who countenance these blunders. . . . Well, I see
I'll only end up making myself hoarse.
I'll say no more about it.

LEE: Thank you.

LONGSTREET: But . . . [*Stuart reenters and joins them.*]
The beans are spilled, that's clear enough; we'll have
To hold our forces here, call off our thrust.

LEE: We cannot, sir. Virginia's barren ground.
Her soil no longer feeds my troops. I must
Look elsewhere for supplies, and only one
Direction lies ahead of us—the north.
The Union made this war, and I intend
To leave these devastated Southern fields
And *end* their war back where they fashioned it.

LONGSTREET: I never liked this plan, and if it's known,
I like it even less. If we stay here—

LEE: We starve, I'm very much afraid. Few wars
Were ever won by starving men.

LONGSTREET: Nor by
An army on the move. The way to fight
A war's to get behind a good stout wall,
Protect your rear and drive the Yankees off.

LEE [*Smiling slightly as he goes to the map.*]: I'm sure, sir,
that you'll find these Northern walls
And fences ample for your purposes.
[*Tracing the route on the map.*]
The Shenandoah Valley is our field.
We'll journey northward till we reach these grounds,
And then, if it seems proper at the time,

We'll stand and fight them on their own terrain.

LONGSTREET [*Pointing to the map; skeptical.*]: And what
    of Hooker with his Yankee troops,
  Camped here at Stafford Heights? He'll learn we've left
  And follow.

LEE: Three days' start is all we'll need.
  [*Indicating a spot on the map.*]
  We should be here when Hooker learns; he's not
  A crafty man, he fights by rote. When he
  Receives the news we're moving north he'll force
  His soldiers to give chase at breakneck speed.
  His army will arrive strung out and weak
  From hunger and hard marching, hardly fit
  To fight a battle. When they reach this point,
  Before there's time to coil and concentrate,
  I'll throw an overwhelming force against
  His leading corps, and crush it back upon
  The one behind, and that upon the next,
  Until they hardly know their friends from foes;
  In this way will his army be destroyed.

LONGSTREET: And what if Hooker doesn't play the role
  Assigned to him

LEE: I'm confident he will.
  [*To* STUART.]
  I ask you, sir, to screen our northward thrust,
  And be my eyes. Keep Hooker well in sight.
  The instant he gives chase come north at once,
  So we may know exactly where he is.
  To such an end remain *unhindered*, sir—

STUART: I won't be hindered!
  [*Eagerly.*]
  What if there's a chance
  To harry him, disrupt his lines, and sow
  Confusion in his column from the rear?

LEE: I only ask that you do not commit
  Yourself and cavalry to anything
  That might prevent your bringing us the news
  The moment the Potomac's crossed by him.

STUART: You'll have the news, I guarantee!

LONGSTREET [*Doggedly; still at the map.*]: As soon
  As we reach Pennsylvania, then, we'll hold,
  And make them come and fight us? Get behind

Those fences that you spoke of, dig in deep,
And hold them off?
LEE: If it be wise we will.
And let us, gentlemen, remember this:
We seek not vengeance, only victory.
Our men are brave, our cause contains no flaw;
Success will end for once and all this war
That even soldiers recognize to be
A danger to our land, our liberty.
If we but seize our chance, urge on our men,
With God's assent we'll soon have peace again!
Today's the ninth: you'll move out on the twelfth.
[STUART *and* LONGSTREET *acknowledge the orders, salute
and leave the room. Alone,* LEE *sits at his table and
commences to write out orders. After a moment, he rises,
returns to the map, and stands, his hands behind his
back, contemplating it.*]

[*Dissolve to:* GENERAL LONGSTREET *moving stumpily
across the station platform. Out of the station house steps*
GENERAL HOOD, *meeting him.*]
HOOD: Good morning, General Longstreet.
LONGSTREET [*Stopping.*]: General Hood.
I want to see brigade commanders in
My hut as soon as possible. I've come
From Lee. We've got our marching orders.
HOOD: Then,
In spite of Stuart's blunder—
LONGSTREET: You know Lee.
Virginians can't do wrong, and Stuart's of
The chosen few: they're all Lee's favorites.
It makes him sad each time he thinks that men
From Georgia or from Tennessee, or from,
God help us, Carolina, like I am,
Are fighting in this war, and winning it,
Beside his proud Virginia men. That's why
Jeb Stuart goes scot-free, and why we still
March north, although by now the enemy
Knows all about it. Never mind: I got
This much concession: when we've gone a mile
Or two—enough to comfort Lee—we'll take
A stand and fight the way an army should.

Defensively. You see, Lee's not a fool.
He knows I'm right. He can't admit it, though,
Because I'm not *Virginia,* that's the truth.
[GENERAL STUART *enters and starts across the platform.*
LONGSTREET *fixes him with a heavily ironic eye.*]
Well, here's our master of the revels, now.
What circus have you planned for us today?
A little bareback riding, or perhaps
The flaming hoops this time—which will it be?

STUART: We'll see who fights the best!

LONGSTREET: *Fights,* did you say?
You're not to fight—you heard the orders, sir!
Your job's to scamper here and there, that's all;
You're ordered to keep out from underfoot,
And do your dancing where it won't get in
The way. Behave yourself, you wouldn't want
To bring disgrace on *proud Virginia,* sir!
[*To* HOOD *briskly.*]
I'll see brigade commanders in my hut
As soon as you can round them up.

HOOD: Yes, sir.
[*He salutes and goes off.* LONGSTREET, *after a satirical
look at* STUART, *follows.* STUART, *his eyes flashing,
watches him leave. Furiously, he whips at his booted leg
with his crop.*]

STUART [*Solus.*]: I'm ordered not to fight? Who ordered
   that?
Not Lee: Lee never said I mustn't fight.
"Do not be *hindered*"—that was all he said.
I know what's in their minds—in Lee's mind, too.
I blundered here at Brandy—I could see
The look he gave me: disappointment, pain.
I failed him, failed Virginia, failed my men;
And of the three, to fail Lee—that's the worst.
I'll make it up to him, I swear I will!
I'm relegated to a minor role
In this campaign? All right! Before it's done,
I'll make that minor role a major one!
[STUART *strides off. The station platform is empty. Fade
out.*]

[*Fade In: With the Confederate Army in the field, July 1,
1863.* GENERAL LEE'S *tent on the outskirts of Gettysburg*

is the usual temporary command post of an army on the move, roughly furnished, lacking in most of the comforts. Through the raised flaps some of Pennsylvania's rolling countryside can be seen. GENERAL A. P. HILL, *Commander of the Army of Northern Virginia's III Corps, is bending over the rude table, studying a map. He seems unwell, and from time to time closes his eyes and passes his hand across his forehead. Some sporadic firing is heard from somewhere in the distance.* HILL *looks up, frowning at the sound. Picking up the map, he goes out of the tent. Upon the ridge outside the tent* LEE *stands, viewing the terrain through his field glasses. He lowers them as* HILL *approaches. Off to one side stand a* SENTRY *and a* STAFF MESSENGER.]

LEE: You heard that firing, General Hill?

HILL: I did.

LEE: It's to the north, I think. I'd like to have
An officer dispatched to bring back word
Of its significance.

HILL: You, Messenger!
[*The* MESSENGER *steps forward quickly.*]
Find Major Thompson of my staff. Tell him
I want that hubbub scrutinized, and word
Brought back at once. You hear?

MESSENGER: Yes, sir. At once!
[*He hurries off.* HILL *looks off in the direction of the firing, and consults the map he is holding.*]

HILL: Where do you estimate it?

LEE [*Using his glasses again.*]: I believe
You'll find it on the map as Gettysburg.

HILL: It could be locals, sir, or farmers, for
That matter. General Heth's Division has
Been foraging in those precincts today.
They're in there on the trail of shoes and hats.
It's possible they didn't feel inclined
To pay full value for their purchases.

LEE: I think my orders were specific, sir:
Supplies are to be paid for! Either with
A formal requisition, or in cash.
I will not tolerate a single act
Of looting or destruction by my men.
I will not have it, sir; I cannot be
Too definite upon this point: it strikes

The very root and heart of all our aims.
We must remain austere, aloof, removed
From any actions reminiscent of
The way our enemy behaved when he
Marched southward through *our* towns and villages.
This war's a holy war: it must be fought
On principle alone. To steal one loaf
Of mouldy bread, to touch one finger to
An innocent civilian is to give
The lie to all we hope for, all we pray
May be established when this war is done.

HILL [*Helplessly*.]: My brigadiers are well-instructed, sir;
I'm not a mother hen, to cluck about
The barnyard, making sure each haversack
Contains receipts for every item there.

LEE: Of course not, General Hill, my ire was not
Directed at you personally, but
I greatly fear misunderstanding of
Our aims by those who dwell upon the rim
Of this crusade. I read the papers, sir;
It frequently appears as though we fight
Two different wars: the editors' and ours.
Can it be possible one million men
Have risked their health and safety, courted pain
And death for no more gallant purpose than
To barter, buy and sell their fellowmen?

HILL: You don't approve of slavery.

LEE: I don't!
I keep no slaves. Of all the practices
Devised by man to gainsay God's commands,
The two most vile are slavery and war.

HILL: And yet with all your will you prosecute
The second practice to insure the first.

LEE: No, sir, I do not look upon this war
As being fought to keep one single slave
In bondage. I have drawn my sword to save
The independence of Virginia, and
Of any state who feels her sovereign laws
Remain superior to Federal ones.
My fight is simply this.

HILL: For my part, sir [*With a wry grin and another indi-
cation of his ill-health*], I leave these weighty thoughts
to weighty minds.

My job's to see how many Northerners—
Whatever their persuasion—I can kill;
So if you'll give me orders to that end,
I'll get about the job of doing it,
And leave the journalists and you to fight
The philosophic battles of this war.

LEE: You're not well, sir.

HILL [*A shrug.*]: The soldier's ailment, sir.

LEE: I'm sorry.

HILL: Thank you.

LEE: Now—

[*He takes the map from* HILL *and spreads it on a flat,
raised rock.*]

The move is this:
Tomorrow you shall break your camp and march
In this wise, northeast. We'll group at this spot.
Dick Ewell's corps, recalled from Harrisburg,
I estimate should almost be here now.
My wish for you is—

HILL: I'm reluctant, sir,
To move so freely without cavalry.
It's been a week and Stuart's sent no word
Of Union movements. All we know is that
They've thrown out Hooker, put Meade in his place;
But as to where he is, we're in the dark.

LEE: It's true we should have heard from Stuart long
Before today, but lacking any word,
We must assume that General Meade has failed
To gain on us; for were he near these parts,
We'd know of it from Stuart. [*Bending over the map.*]
Therefore, sir—

[*A detonation of much greater strength than the earlier,
sporadic rifle fire is heard. Both* LEE *and* HILL *look up
quickly.*]

HILL: That's cannon!

LEE: Cannon!

[*Seizing his glasses and focusing them in the direction
of the sound.*]

North of here. That's odd.
You said this neighborhood was free of all
But local squads, militiamen: they don't
Have cannon in their armaments.

[*The* MESSENGER *hurries in and salutes.*]

MESSENGER [*Breathless.*]: Sir—

HILL: Well?

MESSENGER: From Major Thompson: Heth's Division, sir,
Is fighting a pitched battle on the edge
Of Gettysburg.

HILL: Impossible!

LEE: With whom?

MESSENGER: The Union Army, sir, the major says.

HILL [*To* LEE, *alarmed.*]: Meade's up? Why didn't Stuart
bring us word?

LEE: The fact remains he didn't, General Hill;
And we must improvise to meet the threat.

HILL: We're in detail, sir: Ewell's miles away,
And Longstreet still a day's march from these fields.
How can we fight?

LEE: As yet, sir, we don't know
Meade's strength, or if, in fact, it's really Meade.

HILL: We don't know anything! With Stuart off—

LEE: We're forced to do our best without his help.

MESSENGER: Excuse me, sir, the major also says
A Union courier's been flushed and caught.
They're questioning him now.

LEE: Good; General Hill,
Go down there, if you will; perhaps from him
We'll find out who these people are, and what
Brigades and corps they represent.

HILL: Yes, sir.

[HILL *hurries out. The* MESSENGER *falls back to await
further orders.* LEE *strides to the crest of the hill and
raises his glasses. The cannonading is fuller now, inter-
spersed with rifle shots. Out of sight of* HILL, LEE *allows himself to assume a more worried expression.*]

LEE [*As he scans the terrain.*]: If these indeed be Meade's
brigades I've lost
A valuable initiative, and placed
Myself and men in dreadful jeopardy.
Why isn't Stuart here to scout this ground?

[*The cannonading increases.* LEE *lowers his glasses in
frustration.*]

What good are glasses? Stuart is my eyes.
Without him I remain as ignorant
As any drummer-boy within the corps.
An army that's deprived of cavalry

In strange and hostile land is as a man
Who's been deprived of eyesight, and beset
By enemies. The man may never be
So brave or strong, and yet he cannot know
The way to deal one single, telling blow.
[HILL *hurries in, followed, at a slightly slower pace, by*
GENERAL HETH. LEE *turns from his contemplation of the*
ridge as HILL *comes to him.*]
Well, sir?

HILL [*Grimly.*]: It's Meade, no doubt of it: he's here
In strength. We got it from the courier.
The action's indecisive; we still hold
The ground we started with.

LEE [*With a wry smile, as* HETH *arrives.*]: Well, General
Heth;
It seems your foraging has brought to light
A little more than shoes and hats.

HETH: Our guns
Have had the better of it, nonetheless.
We're holding them in check. Just now my men
Are resting in the line of battle. We're
Prepared to open up a new assault
As soon as Pender can bring up support.

LEE: No, sir, we'll fight no major battle here
Until my army concentrates; that's Meade
Down there; I know him well—the man is sly.
He's managed to creep past us; now he'd like
To turn our plan against us, make us fight
In straggling lines, and fall back on ourselves.
I won't oblige him, though he used to be
A friend. We'll hold these lines as best we can
Until Longstreet's and Ewell's corps are up,
And then we'll form and fight him.

HILL [*Who has been studying the terrain through his*
glasses.]: General Lee!
[LEE *and* HETH *turn quickly.*]
The enemy is shifting to the north.
Somebody's moving in on his right flank!
[*He points.* LEE *and* HETH *use their glasses.*]

LEE [*Suddenly exuberant.*]: It's one of our divisions!
Ewell's corps!
Ahead of schedule!

HILL: If we sent for him,
　　He couldn't have arrived more happily!
　　This changes everything!
LEE: No, let's not fall
　　Into a trap; we're still below Meade's strength.
　　That man's no Hooker; he won't make mistakes.
　　We must be cautious.
HETH [*Pointing excitedly.*]: Sir, look over there!
　　Beyond those trees—more troops are coming up!
　　They're falling on the Federals' rear!
LEE: It's more
　　Of Ewell's corps, arriving just in time!
　　You're right, sir! *Now* this changes things, indeed!
　　We must not lose this opportunity!
　　Take your men in there, General Heth!
HETH: Yes, sir! [*He rushes out.*]
LEE: And, General Hill, bring Pender up at once!
HILL: I will, sir! Messenger!
　　[*He scribbles a note hastily. The* MESSENGER *leaps forward.*]
MESSENGER: Yes, sir!
HILL: Take this!
　　[*He hands him the note. The* MESSENGER *dashes off.*
　　HILL *studies the terrain intently through his binoculars.*
　　LEE *paces the ridge in subdued excitement, alternately
　　raising and lowering his glasses as he follows the off-
　　screen action.*]
LEE [*Solus.*]: They fight like men possessed, these North-
　　　erners;
　　They sense finality in this advance,
　　We brave them in their very gardens, now;
　　Their war's come home to them, they feel its breath
　　Upon their doorsteps . . .
HILL [*Excited; pointing.*]: We've achieved a break!
　　Look, sir!
LEE [*Focusing his glasses.*]: They're falling back on yon-
　　　der hill,
　　I'd like some guns to bother them up there.
HILL: I'll bring a battery around!
LEE: Please do. If we
　　Could seize that hill and drive them off again,
　　We'd have control of this whole area!
HILL: I'll see about our prospects.

LEE: Thank you, sir.

[HILL *hurries off*. LEE *looks once again through his glasses, then lowers them. Solus.*]

A general plans a battle, fits each piece
Beside its brother, weighs its worth, its risk,
In flesh and fodder, cannon, cart and cost,
Selects his ground, inspects each rock and tree,
Each blade of grass, each stream, each hill, each
     fence . . .

[*With a slight smile.*]

Then fights it somewhere else, some score of miles
From where he planned it, sends his men across
Terrain as little like his chosen ground
As these excited charges and retreats
Are like the orderly advance he spent
So many days and nights in plotting out.

[*He pauses, and looks out over the field again, then lowers his glasses.*]

At West Point, I remember, we'd complain
Of how the maps we studied never showed
The holes and boulders, walls and orchards, pits,
That soldiers could fall into and destroy
The carefully formed lines and triangles
We'd draw so studiously upon those maps.
We should have added, neither did they show
The enemy, for sometimes we must fight
Our battles on *his* maps and not our own.
And so, from this point on we improvise,
Observe our chances, seize initiative,
And show these people that we're not impressed
By their plans any more than they by ours.
This place, they say, is Gettysburg; well then,
Let Gettysburg be where I place my men.
As soon as Longstreet's up we'll mount a thrust
To turn George Meade's divisions into dust.
I'll not be bound by blueprints any more;
At Gettysburg we'll terminate this war!

[*He raises his glasses again and stares out across the ridge. Fade out.*]

ACT TWO

[*Fade in: It is early evening, and around a small camp-fire a group of men are lounging, some eating, some smoking, others making repairs to their arms, equipment and uniforms. Lee's* MESSENGER *is holding forth to the group on the afternoon's accomplishments.*]

MESSENGER: Well, sir, says Lee, we've took the town, and
    now
    The thing I want to do is take that hill!
    We've pushed them onto it; I'm sure if we
    Could push them off again we'd own this ground!
    I've never seen him act like that before;
    He looked as though, if nobody was there,
    He might have even danced a step or two.
    The only thing that bothered him, he said,
    Was what was taking Longstreet such a time
    In coming up. With Longstreet there, he said,
    We'd make a double-pronged attack from left
  -And right together, bringing to a close
    The whole damn war right here in Gettysburg.
    But Longstreet wasn't there, so Lee wrote out
    A note to General Ewell, asking him
    To take the heights and push the Yankees off.
A SECOND SOLDIER: I heard they *shot* old Bald Head?
MESSENGER: Ewell? Yes.
    They shot him in the leg—the *wooden* one.
    When I got down there he was hopping mad—
    And I mean hopping—cursing out the Yanks
    And swearing he'd get back at them for it.
1ST SOLDIER: He had his chance then.
MESSENGER: Yes, but Lee's note said
    To take it only if it wouldn't start
    A general engagement, on account

Of Longstreet and his corps not being up.
Well, Ewell takes a gander at the hill,
And says they're digging in too deep for him.
Go back to General Lee, he says, and say
I'll take his hill for him, if someone else
Can occupy the high ground on the right.
If that's not done, he says, they'll be too strong,
And we can't push them off without a fight.
So back I go to Lee to tell him that,
And all the pleasure went right out of him.

2ND SOLDIER: What did he say to you?

MESSENGER: To me? He thanked
Me most politely for my trouble, and
He asked me if I'd "dined"; when I said no,
He sent me off to get my grub.

1ST SOLDIER [*After a moment.*]: That Lee's
A gentleman.

2ND SOLDIER: There's no one else I'd live
Like this for; no, sir!

MESSENGER: All the rest of them
I wouldn't give a Yankee dollar for.

1ST SOLDIER [*Suddenly furious.*]: Let's get that hill for
Lee! He wants us to!
Old Bald Head tells him, "Not without a fight."
It's what we're here for—fighting: isn't it?
[*A* THIRD SOLDIER *comes into the scene. He locates the*
MESSENGER, *and goes to him.*]

3RD SOLDIER: You're wanted, Messenger.

MESSENGER: By whom?

3RD SOLDIER: By Lee.
Longstreet is up: I think we're going to move.

MESSENGER [*Scrambling to his feet.*]: I'm on my way!
[*He runs out.*]

1ST SOLDIER: So Longstreet's here at last.
That means we'll take that hill, and take it fast!
Well, I'm glad Longstreet got here—it saves me
The job of taking it alone for Lee.
[*The soldiers begin to put away their mess gear and
arrange their equipment.*]

[*Dissolve to: The ridge outside Lee's tent. Enter* LEE *and*
LONGSTREET.]

LEE: As you can see, we hold advantage here.

The day's been ours; we whipped them handily. [*Pointing.*]
We forced them to positions on that hill;
One solid push before they've caught their wind,
And Meade's destroyed: his army and his war!

LONGSTREET [*After a moment of observation; lowering his glasses.*]: I think, however, we're much better off
In following the plan agreed upon.

LEE: What plan is that?

LONGSTREET [*A bit impatient.*]: What plan, sir? Why the plan
We formulated thirty days ago.

LEE: The plan was to march north.

LONGSTREET: That part's complete.
This ground is good: we only need to form
A strong position to receive attack,
And when we do, we'll whip them roundly and
Be left in full possession of the field.

LEE [*Trying to keep the excitement and impatience out of his voice.*]: We're placed right now to strike a stinging blow!
They lie exhausted on that hill; we've won
A sizeable encounter. If we press
Them warmly now, and drive them from that hill,
We cannot fail to profit from the move!

LONGSTREET: We'll profit more by keeping to our plan!
Dig in behind a wall—remember, sir?
Defensive war in Pennsylvania?
Agreements are agreements!

LEE: Facts are facts.
Your plan would simply place us in the same
Position we broke out of to march north.
Why should they fight us? They can sit for months
Upon that hill, while boxcars bring them food
And arms and reinforcements! All we have
Is what we carry with us; you know that.

LONGSTREET [*Hedging.*]: At least we ought to wait a day or two
Then, *if* they don't attack us . . . well, we'll see.

LEE: You know as well as I Meade faces us.
He'll not be idle, he'll employ each hour
In strengthening his works; the longer we
Avoid engaging him, the harder will

Become our task when once embarked on it.
I know your views, sir; I respect them too.
However, I request you move your corps
Into position on my right, so that
I may employ these last few daylight hours
In capturing that hill.

LONGSTREET [*Flatly; playing his trump card.*]: My corps's
not up.

LEE [*Taken aback.*]: Not up?

LONGSTREET: I came ahead.

[*For a moment* LEE *stares at him expressionlessly.* LONG-
STREET *returns the glance, then lowers his eyes.*]

LEE [*On a smothered sigh.*]: And when, sir, may they be
expected here?

LONGSTREET [*Matter-of-fact; his eyes everywhere but on
the evidence of* LEE'S *disappointment.*]: McLaws' Di-
vision's six miles off, I think;
And Hood's behind him, maybe—maybe not.
George Pickett was left back at Chambersburg
To guard the trains.

LEE: I see.

[LEE *turns and goes back into his tent.* LONGSTREET *follows. Inside the tent,* LEE *unrolls a map without looking
at* LONGSTREET. *Almost to himself, sadly musing.*]

George Pickett . . . he
Should be here now; he'd plant Virginia's flag
Upon the summit of that hill before
The moon could rise tonight.

LONGSTREET: Will that be all?

[LEE *looks at him briefly, then looks away again.* LONG-
STREET *hesitates.* GENERAL HILL *pushes through the flaps
into the tent.*]

HILL: Good evening . . .

[*Seeing* LONGSTREET.]

Longstreet: well, you've caught us up. [*To* LEE.]
Look here, I've just seen Ewell, and he says
He'll take that hill if I can occupy
The high ground to the right.

LEE: And can you, sir?

HILL: With Longstreet in support I think I could.

LEE: Unfortunately, General Longstreet's men
Are still upon the road—they won't be here
For several hours yet, and by then I fear

It will be much too dark. We must delay
Our plans till morning.

HILL: That gives Meade the night
To fortify his works.

LONGSTREET [*Almost jubilant, but concealing it.*]: Then it's
too late,
And we had better dig in, after all.
[*For a moment* LEE *is silent. Then he turns to* LONG-
STREET, *looking steadily at him.*]

LEE: At dawn tomorrow, sir, I think we must
Attempt to take that hill. If your corps's up
By then, you'll strike the major blow. I'll send
To Ewell with the word he'll not attack
Until he hears your guns. And, General Hill,
You'll do the same: your movements will be timed
To Longstreet's. Although Meade will spend the night
In strengthening his works upon that hill,
And reinforcing those who hold his lines,
The darkness will impede him just as much
As it does us. If then, when daylight comes,
We seize our opportunity, and strike
Before his works are ready, we will crush
These people and secure the ground. But we
Must not delay beyond first light.

LONGSTREET [*Grumpily.*]: My men
Will still be weary from their march.

LEE: Hill's men,
And Ewell's, too, are doubly tired, for they
Have fought today, while yours have only walked.
[*A pause.*]
If I seem arbitrary, gentlemen,
I hope you'll both forgive me, but I can't
Remember when I've felt so positive
About the wisdom of a planned assault.
Elated by today's success, our men
Are eager to renew the battle; when
An army *wants* to fight, a battle's won
Almost before it starts; the men who do
The fighting are the best barometers
Of when to make a thrust or a retreat,
And never have these splendid men of ours
Been more prepared, more eager to engage
The enemy. [*To* LONGSTREET.]

Sir, though we disagree
On tactics, methods, schemes and strategy,
I'm sure we're one in saying that these are
No ordinary soldiers. This proud band
Of men that we've the honor to command
Is capable of deeds beyond the dry
And hackneyed problems that we studied at
West Point. Let's use them, therefore, worthily.
[*Another pause.*]
I'll not delay you longer, gentlemen;
You've many preparations still to make.

HILL: I'll say good night then. [*Pausing at the tent flaps.*]
Coming?

LONGSTREET [*After a moment; to* LEE, *gruffly.*]: Yes. Good
night.

[HILL *and* LONGSTREET *go out.* LEE *remains.*]

LEE [*Solus.*]: And so at dawn we fight a battle which
We should be fighting now. When daylight comes,
I wonder what the cost of this delay will be?
[*The tent flaps undulate.* LEE *hunches his shoulders.*]
I feel a chill . . . the night's still warm.
[*He buttons his jacket.*]
The mechanism rusts, the wheels slow down;
You're fifty-six . . . not old, and yet an age
When many of your fellows seek the hearth,
The pipe, the armchair by the fire, to live
The twilight of their lives in tranquilness.
The columned portico, the tree-lined drive,
The morning coffee from the silvered pot,
The rumpled whites, the flowing tie, the soft
And liquid syllables of neighbors who
Arrive on pointless errands, bide awhile,
And leave refreshed, no wiser than before.
[*He goes to the tent flaps, raises one, and looks out.*]
But where am I at fifty-six? I'm here,
Alone upon a hostile bank of earth,
Opposing one who used to be my friend,
Intending to commit my followers
To what, at best, can only mean the gain
Of one square mile of dirt—at worst might be
The loss of precious lives. . . .
[*Disturbed at his own reflections, he lets the tent flap fall
back, and turns away.*]

Why do I think
These thoughts tonight? Am I in error? Have
I blundered, is my strategy at fault?
That hill's the pivot—surely it must fall!
It lies between my men and victory.
Remove that keystone and the northern wall
Will crumble, I've no single doubt of that!
Am I at fault, then, waiting until day?
Should we be, even now at this dark hour,
Assailing them with cannon, making move
To press across this plain and force them from
Their stronghold? *Now,* before they're reinforced?
But Longstreet's corps's not up yet, Hill's is spent,
And Ewell took the brunt today with his.
These men are not machines, they need their rest;
Again, I cannot doubt my wisdom here.
What is it, then? What questions stir the breeze
To chill me on this sultry summer's night?
The cause for which we fight's an honest one;
No army ever moved on nobler ground. . . .
[*He stops, a look of distress crossing his face.*]
Do I misread the cause? Why *do* we fight?
Can it in truth be simply to maintain
This wretched institution . . . slavery?
If so, my errand here's a dirty one,
And dirty will the blood be on my hands
Of those who die tomorrow. If it's that,
And only that, I'll have small heart to send
My men against George Meade. It can't be true!
For that would make Meade's fight the worthy one,
Instead of mine. I'd be a tyrant then:
About to sacrifice these many lives
For doubtful purposes, unworthy ends.
But in life's long run, evil cannot win!
And if that's true, why did we win today?
We turned confusion into victory;
We won the round, when all events conspired
To halt us in our tracks. If we were meant
To lose this war we would have lost today
When losing would have been so easy . . . but
We won instead.
[*From somewhere outside a round of hearty laughter is
heard, followed by a raucous, off-key song.* LEE *listens.*]

They sing around their fires.
Are villains carefree at their task? Do men
Whose mission is a dark one laugh and sing?
These boys are scarcely bearded; men so young
Are still unlearned in malice, where would they
Be taught unworthy motives?
[*He steps out of the tent. In the darkness of the ridge
outside the tent, the* SENTRY, *standing easy, snaps to
attention as* LEE *comes out. The* MESSENGER, *also taking
his ease nearby, gets to his feet. Farther away, around a
campfire, a group of soldiers is singing softly.* LEE *con-
templates the scene. To the* SENTRY.] Stand at ease.
[*The* SENTRY *relaxes.* LEE *moves to the* MESSENGER.]
Good evening!

MESSENGER: 'Evening, sir.

LEE [*Pointing to the ground around the fire.*]: What men
are these?

MESSENGER: The Forty-first Virginians, sir.

LEE: They laugh
And sing as though they'd just been freed from school.

MESSENGER [*Grinning.*]: We heard the Yankees singing on
that hill,
And thought we'd better give them back a tune
To show we're not downhearted.

LEE: Are you, then?

MESSENGER [*Surprised.*]: Downhearted? No, why should
we be, sir? We've
Just met the Yanks right in their own backyard
And made them yell for uncle, and retreat.
We only stopped because we're gentlemen,
And gentlemen, as everybody knows,
Don't fight when dinner's over; it's not done.
We figured we'd give them the evening off;
Tomorrow, when they've had a little sleep,
We'll go and take their hill away from them.

LEE [*Smiling slightly.*]: Then you've no doubt about the
outcome?

MESSENGER: I've
No doubt we'll win.

LEE: Nor any other doubts?
Our cause, our motives? Are we right in what
We do? When, for the moment, everything
Is quiet, and the battle's far away,

And night obscures the blood, the severed limbs,
The mutilated bodies on the field,
When fires die down, and soldiers lie asleep,
And nothing but the sentry's step is heard,
Do you, or any of you, lie awake,
And in the darkness ponder?

MESSENGER: If we did,
We wouldn't get much fighting done, I think.
A soldier leads a very busy life;
He shouldn't think too much: it slows him up.

LEE: But free men fight for cause, and we're all free;
We must have reasons, otherwise we fight
Like Roman slaves, because we're ordered to.

MESSENGER: Why, we've the perfect reason, sir: we fight
Because you've kindly asked us to, and we're
All gentlemen.

LEE: Just that, and nothing more?

MESSENGER: That's quite a bit, sir, if you'll pardon me;
It means we trust you, think you're right, accept
Your reasons, sight unseen, and say if Lee
Thinks this is right, that's good enough for me.
We know you're wise, sir; know you'd never send
Us into battle for an evil end;
When things get cloudy, like they do in war,
We know that Lee knows what we're fighting for,
And we're content; it means our minds are free
Of any doubts . . . because we don't doubt Lee.

[*Looking from the* MESSENGER *to the group at the fire,*
LEE *is silent awhile.*]

LEE [*Finally.*]: Good night. It's late; tomorrow we have
work
That can't be carried on by sleepy heads.

MESSENGER: Good night to you, sir.

[LEE *turns back toward his tent.*]

LEE [*With a nod to the* SENTRY.]: Sentry.

SENTRY: Good night, sir.

[LEE *goes into his tent. Inside, he stands for a moment
over his table, looking down at his maps and papers.*]

LEE [*Solus.*]: They don't doubt Lee—what right have I to
doubt?

[*With a tired, wry, ironic smile.*]

Win first . . . *then* find out what you fought about.

[*A distant snare drum beats out taps.* LEE *leaves the table and sits down on his cot. For a moment he sits without moving. On the table a candle flickers. Fade out.*]

[*Fade in: It is early morning, the campfire has burned out, and the* THREE SOLDIERS *and the* MESSENGER *lie curled up in their blankets. Daylight grows slowly. From some distant point, the rat-tat-tat of the snare drum beating reveille is heard. . . . The* FIRST SOLDIER *stirs in his blanket, opens an eye, listens to the drum roll and sits up. He shakes the* SECOND SOLDIER.]

1ST SOLDIER: Wake up!

[*The* SECOND SOLDIER *opens a bleary eye.*]

2ND SOLDIER: What for?

1ST SOLDIER: You deaf, man? Can't you hear?
It's reveille.

2ND SOLDIER [*Listening a moment.*]: You're right, but it's
not ours.
It's theirs.

1ST SOLDIER: It is?

2ND SOLDIER: Sure. Over on the hill.

1ST SOLDIER [*Listening.*]: By god, you're right. It limps.
These Yankees got
No sense of rhythm; it's no wonder they're
So evil-tempered.

MESSENGER [*Waking.*]: Time to get up?

1ST SOLDIER: No.
We'll let the Federals use the backhouse first.

MESSENGER: They're up ahead of us?

2ND SOLDIER: Of course they are.
They're playing host today, so naturally,
They want to make sure we'll be comfortable.

[*A closer drum beats out the order.*]

3RD SOLDIER [*Waking.*]: That's reveille.

1ST SOLDIER: You heard it brother, sharp
And true. That's Southern drumming that you hear;
It's crisp and crackling; hear that rat-tat-tat!

3RD SOLDIER [*Peering sleepily off.*]: Those Yankees up
yet?

MESSENGER: If you listen close,
You'll hear them cursing while they lace
Their shoes.

[*From the unseen Northern camp, the drum is heard again. The* FIRST SOLDIER *listens critically.*]

1ST SOLDIER: They're falling in. What time do we begin
This battle?

MESSENGER: Longstreet's corps goes first. Lee said
To move as close to daybreak as he could.

3RD SOLDIER: It's after daybreak—guess it's nearly time.
We'd better eat our breakfast; I've a hunch
We might not get the chance to stop for lunch.

[*The nearby drum beats out "First Call." The soldiers start to gather together their equipment, mess kits, weapons.*]

[*Dissolve to: Seminary Ridge.* LEE *paces the ground in quiet impatience, occasionally raising his glasses to peer out across the field that is slowly becoming lighter as daylight advances. He is followed closely by his* AIDE, *and watched by a small group of* STAFF OFFICERS *who stand nearby.*]

LEE [*To his* AIDE.]: What hour, sir, do you make it?

AIDE [*Consulting his watch.*]: Half-past four.

LEE [*Looking.*]: This Cemetery Hill's well-peopled, I
Observe, but not so strongly manned as to
Make inadvisable our planned assault.
[*With growing enthusiasm.*]
I also see that southern ridge is bare!
If we could—[*Turning and shouting.*]
Messenger!
[*The* MESSENGER, *always hovering nearby, leaps forward and salutes.*]
My compliments
To General Longstreet: if he's ready now,
And can attack *at once*, that ridge is *his*.
And he can use it as a ramp to seize
The hill!

MESSENGER [*Saluting.*]: Yes, sir!
[*He hurries out.* LEE *looks up into the sky.*]

LEE: The daylight grows; I pray
His lines are formed and ready to move out! [*He raises his glasses again, and sweeps the field with them.*]

[*Dissolve to:* GENERAL LONGSTREET *sitting on a log in front of his tent, pulling on one of his boots. His hat lies on the log beside him. The* MESSENGER *is standing before him, has just delivered Lee's message.* Longstreet's AIDE *is nearby.*]

LONGSTREET: Tell General Lee I'm in detail; McLaws' and Hood's divisions aren't up yet; besides,

It's only five: I don't see what's the rush. [*He rises from the log and stamps his foot once or twice to ease the boot.*]

As soon as those two get here I'll attack.

Tell General Lee that.

MESSENGER [*Saluting.*]: Yes, sir.

LONGSTREET [*Dismissing him with a wave of the hand.*] Run along.

[*The* MESSENGER *goes out.* LONGSTREET *turns his attention to the distant, unseen hill, and inspects it through his glasses, grumbling half to his* AIDE *and half to himself as he observes the hill.*]

This all-important hill, now that I see

It clearly in the morning light, appears

Less monumental even than it did

In last night's darkness. Can you tell me, please,

What use we'll make of it when once it's ours?

The ground we hold right now is just as good.

Perhaps we've studied war from different books;

Destroy the enemy: that's what I took

To be a war's objective; if your aim

Is merely to acquire small bits of land

From time to time, then let's resign our ranks,

And take up real estate; we'd soon get rich.

[*Turning to his* AIDE.]

I'll see McLaws and Hood as soon as they

Arrive.

AIDE: Yes, sir.

LONGSTREET: It seems we've got to take that hill—

Unless there's some way to get out of it.

[*Dissolve to:* GENERAL HETH, *his head bandaged, sitting on a mound of grass, a square of canvas tucked under his chin for a napkin, eating out of a mess kit. Behind him, pale and drawn,* GENERAL A. P. HILL *is pacing.*]

HILL: What time's it now?

HETH: Eight.

HILL: *Eight!* It can't be! [*Looking at his watch.*]
  What
  The Devil's holding up the damn parade?
  Longstreet's a heavy sleeper but, by God,
  Don't tell me they forgot to wake him up?

HETH: Pete Longstreet never rushes into things.

HILL [*Looking up at the sky.*]: That sun's a red-hot cannon
    ball up there.
  If we don't start this push a-pushing soon,
  We'll bake our brains out on that open field.

HETH: I've heard a whisper of a rift between
  The two of them.

HILL: Who? Lee and Longstreet?

HETH: Yes.

HILL: A whisper, man? That Longstreet's got a voice
  That makes my sergeant wince and close his eyes.
  He's told the army what he thinks of Lee;
  The wonder is he hasn't yet told *Meade,*
  But if he runs across him here today,
  I don't doubt that he'll mention it to him.
  He's fought with Lee more than he's fought the North,
  But, still, he wouldn't disobey *commands.*

HETH [*Thoughtfully.*]: That's true, sir . . . but he might
    refuse *requests.*
  [*They look at one another.*]

[*Dissolve to: The Confederate Encampment. Its lines
are in a state of lethargy as the day advances. Soldiers
loll about, their muskets and equipment ready. Officers
stand here and there, making last-minute preparations,
but over everything is an aura of indecision, puzzlement.
There is much consulting of watches, frowning glances
at one another, peering off through binoculars. Business
is at a standstill.*]

[*Dissolve to: Seminary Ridge; the day is growing warm
and the officers of General Lee's staff are beginning to
sweat in their heavy uniforms as they stand, first on one
foot then on the other, waiting for some sort of action
to commence.* LEE *is pacing impatiently, pausing now
and again to kick at a loose rock along the ridge. His
AIDE follows doggedly in his footsteps.*]

LEE [*Pausing in his walk.*]: The time *now*, sir?

AIDE [*Looking at his watch.*]: Ten-five.

  [LEE *moves away from the others.*]

LEE [*Solus.*]: Six hours, almost,
  Since this attack was scheduled to begin.
  We stand, like Grecian statuary, poised;
  Forever frozen into attitudes
  Of violent action: yet we do not move.

  [*The* MESSENGER *hurries into the scene and up to* LEE.
  He salutes.]

  Well, Messenger?

MESSENGER: McLaws and Hood arrived
  Two hours ago.

LEE: Two hours? [*For a moment he is silent; finally.*]:
  Find General Longstreet, please,
  And tell him that I'd like to see him here.

  [*The* MESSENGER *exits.*]

  Two hours, and not a move. Have I been wrong
  In treating him as I'd be treated if
  My place were his, and his position mine?
  Would Longstreet, were he Lee, forbear so long,
  Or would his orders be peremptory?
  Must I, then, be a sergeant, rant and roar,
  Flush red, and curse my fellow officers?
  Must I break Longstreet's sword, reduce his rank,
  Convene a court and charge him with his acts?
  Shall I play king, then? Make this ridge my throne?
  Bark out commands, be deaf to arguments?
  Am I to fight my army *and* my foe?
  I'm not equipped for such a task, if so.

  [*He pauses. His* AIDE *comes up to him.*]

AIDE: Here's General Longstreet, sir.

  [LEE *turns, as* LONGSTREET *saunters in casually.*]

LONGSTREET: Good morning.

LEE [*Coming to him, keeping his voice quite calm.*]: Sir,
  I understand your corps is now complete.

LONGSTREET [*Quickly.*]: Not Pickett: Pickett's still in
  Chambersburg.

LEE: I know of Pickett's absence; last night, we
  Did not include him in today's assault.

LONGSTREET [*Hesitating.*]: He leads a strong division . . .

LEE: No one knows
  Of Pickett's value, General, more than I;

But he's not *here*, and time is vital to
Our plan.

LONGSTREET: Of course. I only mention it.
I thought the situation might have changed.

LEE: It has changed, sir; like perfect gentlemen,
We've given General Meade six extra hours
To reinforce and fortify his works.
Our job is harder now.

LONGSTREET: Well, then, perhaps,
We *ought* to wait for Pickett.

LEE: Pickett, by
Your own report, is still at Chambersburg.

LONGSTREET: Did I say "still"?

LEE: You did.

LONGSTREET: Excuse me, sir.
McLaws reports he left there yesterday.
With Pickett here, my corps is up to strength,
And I can take that hill of yours with ease.

LEE: If Pickett moved out yesterday, he's still
A half-day's march from here; to wait that long
Would be disastrous; Meade would have the hill
And ridge so fortified we'd surely fail.
You've two divisions; I must ask that you
Employ them now.

LONGSTREET: Of course, sir: as you wish.
I'll ask McLaws and Hood to form their lines.

LEE: They're not yet formed?

LONGSTREET: The men were tired. I had
To give them time to catch their breath.

LEE [*Dryly*.]: And have
They caught their breath?

LONGSTREET: I think so, sir.

LEE: Then please
Move out at once.

LONGSTREET: Yes, sir.

[*He exits.* LEE *watches him go, then turns his attention
once more to the distant hill, looking at it through his
glasses.*]

LEE [*Solus*.]: We cut it thin,
But if we act with speed we still can win.

[*He continues to study the distant arena.*]

[*Dissolve to: The Confederate Encampment, still in a*

state of suspended animation as afternoon approaches. Soldiers continue to stand, sit and lie about, waiting for the word to advance, the word that has thus far still not been given.]

[*Dissolve to:* GENERAL HILL *still striding to and fro, as* GENERAL HETH *hurries in to him.*]

HETH: Do you know Hood's been here since eight?
HILL: Since *eight?*
   McLaws too?
HETH: Both of them! Since eight!
HILL [*Growing angry.*]: I want
   A message sent to Lee. A soldier likes
   Some order to his day! I want to know
   What's happening around here, where we stand,
   And do we take that hill, or do we not?
   And if we do, let's not sit here and rot!
[HETH *goes off* HILL *continues to stare off through his glasses.*]

[*Dissolve to: Seminary Ridge.* LEE *paces in the company of his* AIDE *and staff. The* MESSENGER *holds himself in readiness a short distance away.*]

LEE [*His patience obviously all but exhausted.*]: What time
   is it?
AIDE [*Looking at his watch.*]: It's half-past three.
LEE: Do you
   Know General Longstreet's whereabouts?
MESSENGER: Yes, sir!
   Have you a message—? [LEE *pauses for a moment.*]
LEE [*With quiet decision.*]: No ... I'd be obliged
   If you would take me to him.
MESSENGER: This way, sir.
   [*They start off.*]

[*Dissolve to:* LONGSTREET, *who is pacing his command post in company with his* AIDE. *He pauses to wave angrily at the unseen objectives across the field.*]

LONGSTREET: If we had Pickett with us, I'd not wait
   An instant, but we're one division short,
   And I'm the sort of man who doesn't like
   To start a battle with one boot still off!
AIDE [*Looking off.*]: Here's General Lee!

[LONGSTREET *swings around, as* LEE *enters with* MESSEN-
GER.]

LEE: It's nearly four, sir; still
   You haven't moved!

LONGSTREET: I'm ready now, sir.

LEE: Then, what holds you back?

LONGSTREET: Sir, General Hood is out
   Inspecting the terrain. I'm holding off
   Until I have his findings.

LEE: The terrain's
   Been thoroughly inspected; all reports
   Are in your hands, the situation's clear.
   There is no further need for you to wait.

LONGSTREET: An hour, or two . . .

LEE: No hour, no half-hour, sir!
   This war hangs in the balance, and that hill
   Grows stronger every minute that we wait.
   We take it now—or in the histories,
   When Gettysburg is mentioned, they will write
   Of how the Southern armies foundered here,
   And lost their war, because they would not fight.
   I want that hill attacked at once, sir! Is
   The order clear?
   [*He looks fully at* LONGSTREET. LONGSTREET *meets his
   eye for a moment, then looks away*.]

LONGSTREET: It is.

LEE [*More gently*.]: Then, let me wish
   You Godspeed and success. [*To* MESSENGER.]
   Where's General Hill?

MESSENGER [*Pointing off*.]: He's in this sector, sir.

LEE [*Going off*.]: I'll see him now.
   [LEE *and* MESSENGER *exit.* LONGSTREET *turns to his
   AIDE.*]

LONGSTREET: And now you've heard what I've been lis-
   tening to
   Since yesterday! March here! March there! Do this
   And that, and everything except the thing
   A reasonable general would prescribe
   In such a place as this! But this is Lee!
   The idol of the troops! The gentleman!
   They hang on every syllable he breathes,
   And march into the cannon's mouth because
   The son of Light-Horse Harry asks them to!

While I was fighting, he was teaching school!
And now this bookish man is in command,
And I'm ticked off to decimate my corps
To make his name immortal! Very well!
Professor Lee has ordered an assault;
We've got to do it or we'll be bad boys;
He'll slap our wrists and keep us after school!
Therefore, we'll do it.
[GENERAL HOOD *hurries in.*]

HOOD: General Longstreet . . .

LONGSTREET: Well?
What is it, Hood?

HOOD: I have my scout's report.
The heights and ridge are strongly fortified;
Meade's men are there in strength; their works extend
Completely to the south, along the line
Of our proposed attack. However, he
Reports the southern bluff is free of troops.
If we strike *there* instead, we're better off.
Shall I send this report to General Lee?
[LONGSTREET *is silent for a moment; then his expression hardens.*]

LONGSTREET: Return to your command: we're moving in.
We have our orders: Lee was here just now.

HOOD [*Surprised.*]: But he's not heard this news yet:
shouldn't we
Hold back until . . .

LONGSTREET [*Interrupting brusquely.*]: He's ordered an assault,
And I'm about to give him what he wants.
No matter what's in front, we march at four!
I'm tired of playing villain in this war!
[*He strides out angrily, his* AIDE *following.* HOOD *looks after him, worried, puzzled, then follows.*]

[*Dissolve to: Seminary Ridge overlooking the battlefield.* GENERAL LEE *stands, glasses to his eyes, his* AIDE, *staff and* MESSENGER *in attendance.*]

LEE: The time, sir?

AIDE: Four.
[*A single cannon booms.*]
That's Longstreet's cannon, sir!
[*The artillery barrage commences.*]

LEE [*Solus.*]: Once more we're soldiers, doing soldiers'
   work.
   At last we end twelve hours of bickering;
   We call a halt to half a day of hate.
   [*The barrage increases.*]
   I ordered this attack at dawn; it's now
   Midafternoon . . . and I'm about to pay
   The price of letting Longstreet have his way.
   I only pray that we may meet the cost;
   We'll only know that when we've won . . . or lost.
   [*He raises his glasses again to survey the field. Fade
   out.*]

ACT THREE

[*Fade in: It is evening, and a glum group is gathered in General Lee's tent, consisting of* GENERALS LONGSTREET, HILL, *and* HETH.]

LONGSTREET: Well, gentlemen, I hope you're satisfied.
　Hood's lost an arm, we've all lost troops; and still
　We haven't gained an inch of ground.
HILL [*Angrily.*]: By rights,
　The way we fought, they should have thrown us back
　To Chambersburg, at least! I've never seen
　Such absence of accord, such random moves,
　Such utter failure to coordinate! [*Glaring at* LONG-
　　STREET.]
　Why didn't you hold back a minute when
　You learned the ridge was fortified?
LONGSTREET [*Hotly.*]: I was
　Instructed to attack!
HILL: Against a force
　Superior to yours by two to one?
LONGSTREET [*Almost exploding.*]: Am I supposed to guess
　　opposing strength?
　It's Stuart's job to tell us what's in front,
　And where was Stuart? Where's he now, in fact?
　We're playing games of blindman's buff because
　Our cavalry's out fox-hunting somewhere!
HILL: I understand you got a clear report—
LONGSTREET [*Cutting him off abruptly.*]: What difference
　does it make now? The result
　Is that we've failed!
　[*Enter* LEE.]
LEE: Good evening, gentlemen.
HETH: Good evening, sir.
HILL: Good evening, General.

LONGSTREET: Sir.

LEE: Well, gentlemen, it now appears that we
Must spend another night at Gettysburg. [*To* LONG-
STREET.]
Your men fought splendidly . . . [*To* HILL.]
Yours too . . . [*To* HETH.]
And yours. [*To all of them.*]
We did *not* fail this afternoon! We gained
Some useful ground, we held, we reached the ridge,
And got a look at victory—although
The glimpse was but a brief one. We fought well.
Tomorrow we'll renew the battle, and
Achieve the prize we should have had today.

HETH: We waited too long, sir: we should have hit
That hill at dawn; we gave them too much time
To fortify.

LEE: We erred at many points.

LONGSTREET [*Smouldering.*]: The error was in trying it at
all! [*To* LEE.]
All right! We've tried it, and they've thrown us back;
We've lost sufficient troops to make it look
As though we've fought a glorious campaign!
We'll all get laurels for our work today,
So let's forget about it, and return
To what we should have done before: dig in,
And let them try to take the ground from us!

LEE: Which they won't do, sir, rest assured of that!
If we dug in we'd simply dig our graves.
Believe me, sir, they *need not fight*, and we
Must either fight or give up what we've won.
[GENERAL STUART, *frayed, dusty, enthusiastic, strides into
the tent.*]

STUART [*Beaming.*]: Good evening, gentlemen! I hear
there's been
Some fighting in these precincts recently!
[LEE, *after one flashing glance at him, turns sharply
away.*]

HILL [*Ironically.*]: Too bad you missed it, Stuart.
Where've you been?

STUART [*Debonair; preening.*]: Oh, I've been active, have
no doubts of that;
You're not the only ones who've been at war.
I've been behind the Federal lines for days,

Disrupting their communications, and
Detaching wagons from their supply trains.
I've brought about two hundred of them back
With me. They're full of oats!

LONGSTREET: They're full of oats!

HILL: It's possible we might have used you here.
Perhaps to more advantage.

STUART: I'm here now!
My men are ready for whatever comes;
They're ordered not to dismount, but remain
In saddle through the night, prepared to ride!

LONGSTREET [*Suddenly roaring at* STUART.]: Did you know
Meade was moving north, that he
Had learned our plans?

STUART: I did, but—

LONGSTREET: Did you know
He'd got to Gettysburg ahead of us?

STUART: How could I?

LONGSTREET: How? How could you? Am I wrong,
Or wasn't that the work we sent you on?
Intelligence! That's what the job is called!
That's why you've got those fancy trousers on,
Those braids and trinkets hanging on your chest!
What good are *wagons,* for God's sake, when we
Are fighting with our thumbs in both our eyes?
Go out and count the dead upon that field!
They're there because you didn't do your job!

STUART [*Hotly*.]: My orders were—

LONGSTREET: Your orders were to tell
The men who do the work what sort of work
Was lying up ahead in store for them!
Two hundred loads of oats! I'd make you start
Tonight, and eat your way through all of them!
[STUART, *speechless with rage, makes a move toward*
LONGSTREET. *He is checked by* HILL.]

HILL [*Sarcastically*.]: Let's fight among ourselves: it's
easier
Than fighting Meade!

LEE [*Turning back*.]: We've done some things today
That hardly justify our pointing out
Another's errors.
[LONGSTREET *stares blackly at* LEE, *then lowers his eyes*

as LEE *returns the gaze steadily for a moment.* LEE *turns to* STUART.]
General Stuart, it
Will not be necessary for your men
To sit their saddles until morning. Let
Them get their sleep and save their strength. I've word
That General Pickett has arrived. I count
On his fine men to tip the scale and turn
The tide to our advantage. He will lead
The day's assault. Good evening, gentlemen.
[*The* GENERALS *rise to leave.* LEE *stands in their midst, his expression firm and resolute. Fade out.*]

[*Fade in:* GENERAL LONGSTREET'S *command post. It is daylight.* GENERAL PICKETT *is sitting on the log. He rises as* LONGSTREET *comes out of his tent.*]
PICKETT [*Heartily.*]: Good morning, General.
LONGSTREET [*Acknowledging the greeting gloomily.*]:
    Pickett.
PICKETT: My command
    Is up and waiting for a job!
LONGSTREET [*Contemplating him sourly.*]: It's got
    One that it won't forget so fast. Come here.
    [*Taking* PICKETT *to a point from which the field can be observed.*]:
    You see that grove of trees across the field?
    They say it's fourteen hundred yards from here;
    I don't know what arithmetician made
    The calculation, but they say it's that.
    The ridge *above* those trees is what Lee wants.
    It's fortified and reinforced, and there . . . [*Pointing elsewhere.*]
    On Cemetery Hill Meade's got more guns,
    So anyone who's mad enough to try
    To cross that field will get his head blown off
    By frontal firing, and by enfilade.
    In fact, I'd say that anyone who tried
    To get across that field deserves to have
    His head blown off, and wouldn't miss it, since
    He's obviously brainless if he tried.
PICKETT: When do I start?
LONGSTREET [*Staring at him, then shaking his head in wonderment.*]: You, too? You want to be

A hero like the rest of them? Like Lee?
[*In the distance, cannon begins firing steadily.*]
That's Alexander opening his fire.
He'll blast away until he thinks he's knocked
The Yankee guns out. When the firing's stopped,
Lee's ordered—I'm against it, mind!—that you
Advance your infantry across the field
To where those trees are.
PICKETT: Very simple, sir.
LONGSTREET [*Grimly.*]: You think so, do you?
PICKETT: If their guns are out,
  How can they hinder me?
LONGSTREET: You think they're fools?
  Suppose they hold their fire? How can we know
  Their guns are really out?
  [*The cannonading is loud and furious now.*]
PICKETT [*Listening.*]: More guns. I'll form
  My lines. Where do I look to get the word
  To move?
LONGSTREET: From Colonel Alexander, he's
  In charge of my bombardment; when he feels
  The enemy barrage has slackened off,
  And estimates their guns have been knocked out,
  He'll signal you to move your infantry.
PICKETT: That's splendid, sir; I must thank General Lee
  For handing me this plum! Excuse me, now;
  I'll rally up my men!
  [*He hurries out.* LONGSTREET *looks after him gloomily.
  The artillery duel is reaching immense proportions.*]
LONGSTREET [*Solus.*]: Another fool!
  Another fool who wants to risk his head
  For States' Rights, smilax, mockingbirds and Lee!
  [*Suddenly, the truculence is gone from his face, and is
  replaced by a sober sadness never before seen in him.*]
  I've shouted wolf too often; this strange hate
  That makes me rail at Lee, both to his face,
  And to his friends behind his back, that makes
  Me try to prove him wrong despite the fact
  Events have proved him right, as they have done
  These last two days at Gettysburg, this grudge
  I have against the man, it's now come home
  To roost, and no one heeds me. I'm the man
  Who drags his feet, holds back, makes alibis

To keep from fighting. Now, when, in all truth,
I think, I *really* think this time we're wrong,
And shouldn't try to take this hill, they say,
"That's only Longstreet making noise again."
They say I'm jealous, that I want Lee's job,
Because I think an army's something more
Than fifty million Southern gentlemen,
Let loose to teach the heathen of the world
That when God made mint juleps life had reached
Its highest point! The way they nod and bow,
And tumble over one another to
Obey the orders Lee "requests" of them!
I'm forced to rage and rant and stomp my feet
In order to persuade my orderly
To bring my dinner; Lee says, "I'd be much
Obliged if you could see your way clear to
Go out and die," and twenty thousand men
Stampede each other for the privilege
Of dying first, because Lee asked them to!
My orders are obeyed because it's known
I'll shoot them dead if they refuse, but Lee
Need only say, "Can you?"—they roar, "We can!"
Because it's Lee who asks: they love the man.
I hate Virginians, hate the way they talk,
The way they smile, the way they dress and walk;
I hate the way they always think they're right;
I hate them! [*With a rueful smile.*]
But, by God, how they can fight!
[*The* MESSENGER *hurries in.*]

MESSENGER: From General Lee, sir: he detects a pause
In Union gunfire, and requests that you
Stand ready to send Pickett in.

LONGSTREET [*Suddenly his old self again; angry, truculent.*]:
I will
As soon as I'm convinced their guns are still!
Tell Lee that!

MESSENGER: Yes, sir!
[*He runs out again.*]

LONGSTREET [*Solus.*]: In an hour we'll see
Which one of us was right.
[*With unusual compassion.*]
I hope it's Lee!
[*He starts off.*]

[*Dissolve to: Seminary Ridge, where* LEE *paces impatiently and eagerly, occasionally pausing to search the terrain with his glasses. He is attended by his* AIDE, *and by* GENERAL HILL, *as well as other members of his staff. The cannonade continues.*]

HILL [*Cocking an ear; nodding.*]: Their fire is slackening,
  no doubt of it;
I give them five more minutes at the most.

LEE: I've ordered our artillery to cease
  The moment theirs does; Longstreet's been informed;
  As soon as both are still, then we'll commence
  This final charge: I've two divisions, plus
  Another two brigades of Pender's men;
  That's fifteen thousand, set to cross this mile
  Of open field, to rush the Yankee heights,
  And end our work at Gettysburg.

HILL [*Listening to the diminishing fire.*]: We stopped
  Their batteries.

[*The last cannon fires, and silence pervades the scene.*]

LEE: That part's done. Pickett should
  Be ready to march out; where is he?

[*He searches the field with his glasses. The silence is eerie, unreal.*]

Strange:
This sudden stillness that pervades the air
Before a battle; not a sound, a breath;
As though, throughout the world, all work has ceased,
And mankind waits, attending our next move.

[*Another pause. Then the silence is broken by a sustained drum roll.*]

The moment's passed; the world's at work again!

[*The drum roll rises to a crescendo, then takes up a staccato marching beat.* LEE *watches eagerly.*]

They leave the shadows, march out into light.
A column almost two miles wide, its lines
Dressed handsomely; a string stretched flank to flank
Would touch the rifle butt of every man
That's marching there! There's Pickett out in front,
His sword above his head, his horse reined in.
Let anyone who claims wars must be fought
By dull-eyed snipers hiding behind walls
Watch my Virginians cross a hostile field,

Cross ditches, fences, walls, without a break
In their formation, as they're doing now.
There's Kemper down there . . . Garnett . . . Armistead.
I know these men! Virginians all. There's more
To this than just an infantry advance.
Our answer to the North's down there; our pride,
Tradition, love of home, our way of life.
We claim the right to live the way we choose,
And prove the claim by fighting as we live:
Erect and proud, disdainful of a foe
Who crouches behind barricades, and puts
His faith in trenches. . . . One more yard or two,
And we'll reach out and touch the Union guns!
There go the horses, breaking into stride!
[*The beat of the snare drum increases.*]
The line moves faster: they're about to charge!
The slope's ahead of them, they're almost there!
Meade holds his fire; he's waited too long; now,
My men are almost on him; let him do
The worst he can, I know the hill will fall!
Because my soldiers are invincible!
[*The snare drum is beating a rapid note. . . . Suddenly,
a tremendous barrage of cannon drowns out the drum.
. . .* LEE, *his glasses to his eyes, staggers back, himself,
from the impact. . . . There is an expression of utter
dismay, almost disbelief, on his face. . . . There is another loud detonation.* HILL, *Lee's* AIDE, *the* MESSENGER,
*and the staff are staring in the direction of the bom-
bardment.*]

HILL [*Shouting at* LEE.]: They've caught our center, sir!
[LEE *looks at him blankly.*]

AIDE [*To* HILL.]: I thought their guns
Were out.

HILL [*Grimly.*]: They're in again.
[*Another explosion.* LEE *turns away.*]
They've hit the left now.

MESSENGER [*Pointing; excited.*]: Sir, we've reached that
    clump
Of trees! We broke their lines!

HILL: For every man
Who still advances, two lie on the field.

AIDE: We're pressing forward still! We're holding! If—
[*A third cannonade explodes.*]

HILL [*Wincing as he regards the unseen carnage.*]: They've
   struck our right. We scatter now, like ants!
   We still move forward, to be blown to bits.

MESSENGER: We haven't given up! We're fighting them!
   It's hand to hand now!

HILL: But we're falling back.

[GENERAL STUART *enters, disheveled, and goes straight
   to* LEE.]

STUART: Sir, I've been behind Meade's lines; I thought
   That I could break his flank. He cut me off!
   I never saw such opposition, sir!
   They stopped me in my tracks—I couldn't move!

LEE: You're not alone in that, sir, I'm afraid;
   We've also found the opposition strong.

HILL [*Watching through his glasses; dully.*]: They're break-
   ing now; retreating; falling back.
   They're scrambling over comrades' bodies; some
   Are crawling; others have no knees to crawl.
   [*The firing continues.*]
   We reached their lines! We reached them . . . then they
   threw
   Us back.
   [GENERAL LONGSTREET *rushes in.*]

LONGSTREET: We're routed, sir! In full retreat!

LEE: I see that, General Longstreet. I presume
   That Meade will now attempt to wipe us out.
   We must arrange to meet a countercharge,
   And hold against him when he makes his move.

LONGSTREET [*Starting to go again.*]: I'll pull Hood's men
   around . . .
   [*He stops suddenly, turns back to* LEE.]
   And by the way . . .

LEE [*Quietly, gently.*]: Yes, sir? You'd like to say that if
   we'd fought
   Defensively, as you suggested, we'd . . .

LONGSTREET: That part of it goes without saying, sir!
   The thing I want to tell you now is that
   You'd better put the blame for this on me.
   [*As* LEE *stares at him.*]
   I'm thinking of the army: you're the man
   They love, their hero! Heroes can't be wrong.
   If we expect these men to rally, and
   To fight again some day, perhaps to win,

I think you'd better say, I blundered here.

LEE [*After a moment; gently but firmly*.]: I thank you, sir;
   once more, it seems I'm forced
   To counter your desires; this blame is mine,
   And I shall bear the weight of it alone.
   [PICKETT, *dirty, disheveled, defeated, enters.* GENERAL
   LEE *goes to him immediately*.]

PICKETT: We're beaten, sir!

LEE [*Gently*.]: Our plans have gone awry,
   But never have I seen troops act like yours!
   Before Meade's fire they held, and held, until
   They had to fall! Today, Virginia's name
   Is written higher than it's ever been
   Before!

PICKETT: But we were there! We'd crossed the field!
   The heights were at our fingertips! If we
   Had been supported properly—

LEE: We've failed
   In many tasks today; we must not fail
   In stemming Meade's advance. Return to your
   Division, please, and place them in the rear
   Of this hill, so if Meade should try a thrust . . .

PICKETT [*Almost weeping*.]: Division, sir? I've no division
   now!
   They're dead!
   [*A shudder passes through* LEE's *body. He turns quickly
   to* LONGSTREET *and* HILL.]

LEE: We must restore some order here,
   And try to save what remnants we have left.
   Please place your men in readiness to make
   An orderly retreat from Gettysburg.
   Our business in these parts is done, and we
   Must move back south to bind our wounds and plan
   How best we can repair the damage we've
   Sustained, and regain the advantage that
   We've lost. Return to your commands; inform
   Yourselves of your requirements, calm your troops,
   And wait for my instructions, if you will.

HILL: Yes, sir.

LONGSTREET [*Gruffly*.]: We'll see what we can do.

LEE: Thank you.
   Your help will be appreciated; this
   Defeat has been my fault, and mine alone;

But I believe, in spite of this, we'll win;
We can't expect a victory each time
We fight a battle.

HILL: That part's true enough.
Well, Longstreet?

[HILL *goes.* LONGSTREET *hesitates a moment looking straight into* LEE'S *eyes.*]

LEE [*Quietly.*]: Well, sir?

LONGSTREET [*After a moment; dropping his eyes.*]: I'll be with my troops.

[*He goes. The others, with the exception of* PICKETT, *have drifted away by now.* PICKETT *comes to* LEE.]

PICKETT: If they had killed me, I'd be happy now!

[*He goes out.* LEE *walks to the ridge and looks off across the field.*]

LEE [*Solus.*]: I, too, could wish some sympathetic shell
Had found this ridge and closed these burning eyes,
Now dripping tears of blood upon this blood.
I'd be deaf now, that I may never hear
The sound of guns again; and blind, that I
May never look again upon the sights
I've seen today. But far beyond the sight
Of my Virginians, marching in their pride,
And faltering before Meade's angry guns,
I see a sadder vision still; I see
The end of this crusade, the end of all
Nobility in war; we'll never fight
As gentlemen again; we'll never stand
And meet our foe with heads and spirits high.
A cause, a war, a way of life are lost
Today at Gettysburg; the world I've loved
Is gone—it fell with Pickett's infantry,
And lies destroyed upon this Northern field,
To be replaced by . . . what? I cannot tell.
It may be good, or bad: I only know
It won't, it can't be, what it was before.

[*Off screen, he hears one or two shouted commands, a ruffle of drums.*]

They wait for my commands; they still have hopes.
That makes my task a sad and bitter chore;
To fight as though we still could win this war;
To lead my men, pretending there's still chance
To rally from this blow, again advance;

From now until the final battle's through,
I must conceal what I know to be true;
Present a smiling face for all to see,
And mouth the hollow hopes of victory.
And that's the saddest task a man could choose:
To fight to win while knowing he must lose.

[*He stands for a moment or two, alone on the ridge, a proud, solitary, dignified, although defeated, man— Then, with slow, tired, but steady steps, he turns away and moves to where his* AIDE, *his staff, and his* MESSENGER *stand in a group, watching him and awaiting his instructions. Fade out.*]

THE BIG DEAL

by Paddy Chayefsky

ACT I

[*Fade in: Interior restaurant—not too posh, but the tables
have linen tablecloths. Camera wends its way between
two tables at which various chatting people are eating
their luncheon. A waiter and a couple crowd their way
past camera. General effect of crowded café.*
[*We narrow our attention to a little man of fifty-odd
years, seated at a table, studying a cup of coffee in front
of him. He has on a blue pencil-stripe suit, single-
breasted, and which somehow gives the feeling of the
1930s. His tie is tied into a narrow, elegant knot; but
it is slightly askew. His shirt collar turns up at the edges.
His fedora rests on the table at his elbow. This is Joe
Manx. He looks up, and his face perks up a bit as he
recognizes someone approaching his table. A moment
later a pretty girl of twenty-six comes to his table . . .
bends over him, gives him a quick kiss.*]

DAUGHTER: Hello, Pa.

JOE: Sit down, Marilyn, sit down. You want something to
eat? Eggs, a sandwich, anything like that?

DAUGHTER [*Sitting.*]: No, Pa, I'm meeting George for
lunch in about fifteen minutes.

JOE: Sure. Give him my regards when you see him. I
won't hold you. I happen to need about ten, fifteen dollars if you happen to have it on you.

DAUGHTER [*Promptly opening her purse.*]: Sure, Pa.

JOE: I ran across a very interesting proposition today, and
I'd like to take the man out for a couple of drinks. I
have an appointment with him at four o'clock.

DAUGHTER [*Extracting some bills from her purse.*]: Are
you sure fifteen bucks will be enough?

JOE: Oh, plenty, plenty. I'm just going to take him for a
couple of drinks. [*Takes the bills.*] I might be able to

pay you this back on Thursday, because I'm playing a little pinochle over at Harry Gerber's tomorrow night, and I usually come out a couple of bucks ahead. Listen, Marilyn, don't let me hold you. I know you're anxious to get to see George.

DAUGHTER: All right, Pa. I'll see you later.

JOE: Just let me say that this is a very interesting proposition that I ran across today. I don't want to sound premature, but I have a feeling that this might be the deal I've been looking for. I won't bore you with the details. I only want to say this proposition involves Louie Miles, if the name is at all familiar to you. He happens to be one of the biggest contractors in the business. Eighteen years ago, he was a lousy little plasterer. I gave him his first work. Well, I was down the Municipal Building today. It happened that I . . . Well, look, I don't want to hold you. I can see you're anxious to see your boy friend. Go ahead, go ahead. Give him my regards. Don't tell your mother you gave me some money.

DAUGHTER [Who has been smiling fondly at her father throughout his speech.]: Okay, Pa, I'll see you.

JOE: I'll see you. I'll see you. Have a good lunch. [The DAUGHTER exits off. JOE sits a moment, fingering the two bills his DAUGHTER has just given him. Then he suddenly lifts a hand imperiously and calls sharply out.] Waiter! Check!

[Dissolve to: A section of one of those little restaurants you always find around hospitals. We see two booths. . . . Camera dollies past first booth, which contains two young doctors, one middle-aged doctor, and a young nurse—all in traditional white hospital uniforms.

[We move in on second booth, which contains the DAUGHTER and a young resident doctor named GEORGE. He is wearing the conventional white-jacketed uniform, with innumerable pencils and pens clipped into his outer breast pocket. They have their pie and coffee in front of them—also the dishes of the meal they have just eaten, which have not been taken away yet. The DAUGHTER is eating her pie, but GEORGE is just fiddling with his fork. They are both obviously caught in deep discussion.]

DAUGHTER: I know these aren't ideal circumstances to get married in, but who gets married in ideal circumstances? Do you know what I mean?

GEORGE: I know, I know.

DAUGHTER: I mean, everybody has problems when they get married. They got parents to support, and finding a place to live, and they don't have enough money. These are just things everybody has to face when they get married. Look at Alex and Ann Macy. Neither of them had a job when they got married. We're lucky compared to them, for heaven's sakes.

GEORGE: Well, what do you want to do? You want to get married then?

DAUGHTER: Yeah.

GEORGE: Well, let's get married then. Let's get it over with.

DAUGHTER: Let's get it over with. You make it sound like I was going to electrocute you.

GEORGE: Look, Marilyn, marriage is a responsible business. I've got two more years of residency. You're going to have to support me for two years. That's the trouble with being a doctor. The first half of his life he has to be supported by somebody. It's a terrible thing to feel that somebody is sacrificing for you all the time. My mother and father, they went through torture to make me a doctor. Every time my old man sends me a check, I get a little sick in my stomach. And they don't understand, you know what I mean. They don't understand why I just don't rent myself an office on Halsey Street and open up a practice. I finished my year of interning. I'm an M.D. They don't understand why I'm taking all these years of residency at a salary of twenty-two dollars a month. . . . Well, I want to be an internist, that's why. I like internal medicine. I don't want to be a G.P. There's a thousand G.P.'s on Halsey Street now. Every ground-floor window you walk by, there's another G.P. . . .

DAUGHTER: George . . .

GEORGE: Well, the point is, Marilyn, I've got two more years of residency ahead of me, and you're going to have to support me for two years.

DAUGHTER: I'm making a good salary, George.

GEORGE: You're already supporting your mother and father.

DAUGHTER: I've got the five thousand dollars my Aunt Eva left me.

GEORGE: Look, Marilyn, you want to get married, it's all right with me. Let's get married. [*The* DAUGHTER *frowns down at her plate.*] I mean it. I'm not on call tomorrow. We'll go down to City Hall and get married. What do we need, blood tests? All right, I'll take you up the blood lab right now—finish your coffee—we'll go up the blood lab and we'll get our specimens taken. What do we have to wait, three days? What's today, Tuesday? All right, we'll get married on Friday. [*They both look down at their plates. A moment of uncomfortable silence.*] My mother is dead set against this marriage, you know that, don't you? Even my old man, who likes you a lot, says I can't afford to take on a wife at this moment.

DAUGHTER: Take on a wife! What am I, some kind of a bundle you're going to carry on your back?

GEORGE: I didn't mean it that way.

DAUGHTER: You're a boy, you know that? You're a seventeen-year-old boy. What do you think marriage is? Death in a gas chamber? Marriage is making somebody happy. You get better from marriage, not worse. Maybe you might find the next two years a little easier if you had somebody near you who wants you to be happy with all her heart and soul. [*The* DAUGHTER'S *eyes are wet with tears now.*] I want you to be an internist! I want you to finish your residency! I don't care if I have to support half of Toledo, Ohio! It's no sacrifice to me if it makes you happy! And I expect the same from you! [*She hides her eyes in her hand and tries to master herself.* GEORGE *sits in the sudden vacuum left by the* DAUGHTER'S *outburst, looking down at his hands folded in his lap. Then he looks up and across at his girl friend and smiles gently.*]

GEORGE [*Rises—crosses around table—sits beside her.*]: Marilyn, honestly, I don't know why I'm making such a crisis out of this. I'm a little scared, that's all. You just forget how much you love the girl. I would like to officially set our wedding for this coming Friday, if you'll have me, and I promise to make you happy. So what do you say?

DAUGHTER: I finally collared you, eh?

GEORGE [*Beaming.*]: Yeah.

[*Dissolve to: The front hallway of a four-and-a-half room apartment. We are looking at the front door, which now opens and admits* JOE MANX. *He closes the door behind him, takes off his hat, puts it on the mail table. Then, carrying himself with a sort of bantam erectness, he passes into the living room. The camera ambles along after him.*

[*The living room is furnished with what had been good, solid, expensive middle-class furniture two decades ago. The dominating piece in the living room is a large dark mahogany table with thick, intricately carved legs. At the head of the table is a massive chair with thick armrests, obviously the chair of the master of the house. It is to this chair that* JOE *marches. He takes off his jacket, drapes it around the back of the chair, rolls up his shirt sleeves two turns, loosens his tie, unbuttons his collar, and then sits down in the chair, placing his arms on the armrests. For a moment he just sits there, enjoying a small feeling of majesty. Then he lifts his head and calls out.*]

JOE: I'm home!

[*The* WIFE *appears in the kitchen doorway. She is a strong woman of about fifty. She is dressed in a house dress and is carrying a dish towel. On her face there is the anticipatory smile of someone who is about to impart a secret. Her secret becomes immediately apparent when the daughter appears behind her in the kitchen doorway.*]

WIFE [*Surveying her husband with that smile.*]: Joe, I got something in the nature of a pleasant shock to tell you, so get a good hold on your chair. I don't want you to fall off and hit your head on the floor. [*She comes into the living room, takes a chair at the far end of the table.*]

JOE: I ran across a very interesting proposition today.

DAUGHTER [*Also sidling into the room, wearing a smile.*]: Hello, Pa.

JOE: I was down the Municipal Building. I was with Martin Kingsley. Martin was having a little permit trouble, so he says to me: "Joe, come on down with me to the Housing Department." After all, Commissioner Gerber is a very good friend of mine. He figured I might put in a couple of good words for him.

WIFE: Did you talk to Harry Gerber about that other matter?

JOE: Doris, I'm telling a story, don't interrupt. Well, all right, I went down to the Municipal Building. I'm standing in the hallway by the water fountain. I went over to get a drink . . . so . . .

WIFE: Joe . . .

JOE: A man comes over to me. A big fat bald-headed man. He looks at me, he says: "Aren't you Joe Manx?" So I look at him, I say: "You'll have to excuse me. Your face is familiar, but I can't quite place you." So he looks at me, he says: "I'm Louie Miles!" Doris, you remember Louie Miles? Seventeen, eighteen years ago. He was a plasterer.

WIFE: Joe . . .

JOE: It seems he's a big construction man now in Cleveland. Well, that's neither here nor there. So anyway, we got to talking about this and that and it seems that he's bought himself a piece of land, about fifteen acres, out near Willaston, with the intention of putting up sixty or eighty houses, small ranch houses, fifteen thousand, maybe sixteen-fifty tops. Well, he starts to dig a little, and Boom! He runs into water. I said to him: "Louie, for heaven's sakes, if you would have asked me, I would have told you. The whole Willaston area is nothing but marshland." Well, the upshot of it is, he wants to sell the land. We made a date for four o'clock at the Statler Hotel. [*Rises, crosses to his* DAUGHTER.] Sweetheart, I wonder if you would do me a very big favor.

DAUGHTER: Sure, Pa.

JOE: I wonder if you could get me a small glass of cold water. I'm very thirsty.

DAUGHTER: Sure. [*She promptly exits into the kitchen.*]

JOE: Well, I began to do a little quick thinking. If I had one hundred and fifty acres of that land, that's six million square feet . . . with a fifty-foot frontage, I could put up a thousand houses. With a thousand houses, it's worth the trouble and expense of draining. Now, my dear lady, we are talking in terms of a million-dollar proposition. One thousand small houses, nothing big, low-income houses, like that Levittown in New York. . . .

Have you any idea how much money that man Levitt made? Countless millions! Countless! [*The* DAUGHTER *returns with the glass of water, which she sets at her father's place.*] Thank you, sweetheart, thank you.

WIFE: Joe, Marilyn also ran across a very interesting proposition today.

JOE: The upshot of it all was, at four o'clock, I went to the Statler. . . . I said: "Louie, what do you think of this idea? Louie," I said, "why don't we buy up another hundred and fifty, hundred and sixty more acres, and instead of setting up a lousy sixty houses, we'll set up a thousand!" Well, I'll tell you something. If you ever saw a man get shocked, you should have seen Louie Miles's face when I said that. He looked at me like I was crazy.

WIFE: He was right, too.

JOE: That's very funny. When I built those houses on Chestnut Street and Halsey Street and King Boulevard, everybody also looked at me like I was crazy.

WIFE: That was in 1934.

JOE: That whole Chestnut Street district was nothing but swamps. Snakes and frogs. The grass was so high you could get lost in it.

WIFE: All right, Joe, what was the upshot of it all with Louie Miles?

JOE: The upshot of it all was that he couldn't see it. He wants to sell that fifteen acres. He wants to get out of the whole deal. So I said to him: "Louie, what do you want for that fifteen acres?" So he says: "Four thousand dollars." So I said: "Louie, I may take that land right off your hands." And that's the way it stands at this moment.

WIFE: As long as you were down the Housing Department today, did you go in and see Harry Gerber? [JOE *suddenly scowls.*]

JOE: Doris, I want to get one thing straight right now. I don't want to hear anything more about Harry Gerber. I don't need your advice and counsel. It seems to be your pleasure to make fun of me. . . .

WIFE: I don't make fun of you, Joe.

JOE: As far as you're concerned, I'm a big talker without a nickel to his name, who thinks he's a big shot. All right, I'm broke. I'm strapped. But I was once the biggest builder in this city, and I'm still a respected name in the trade. Go to Frank Daugherty and Sons. Mention the name of Joe Manx, see what he says. Deputy Housing Commissioner Harry Gerber still calls me up once or twice a week for a little advice. State Senator Howard Schram came halfway across a restaurant to ask my opinion about a bill he's pushing through up in Columbus. So when I tell you this is a million-dollar proposition don't be so clever. Don't be so smart. When I die, there will be a million dollars in my will, don't worry. [*Returns to his master chair, sits down, disgruntled and scowling. An uncomfortable silence falls over the family. At last,* DAUGHTER *leans to her* FATHER.]

DAUGHTER [*Smiling.*]: Pa, I'm getting married Friday. [JOE *turns his head slowly and regards the* DAUGHTER *with open-mouthed shock.*]

JOE: When did this happen?

DAUGHTER: Just at lunch, just after I saw you.

WIFE: I told you we had a shock for you.

JOE: Well, for heaven's sakes! Which one is this, the doctor? George? [*The* DAUGHTER *nods her head happily.*] Well, where is he, for heaven's sakes? This calls for some kind of a celebration. Seems to me we should have some wine, a little festivity. For heaven's sakes! A man comes walking home, and his daughter casually remarks, she's getting married! Listen, call him up on the phone, tell him to come over tonight. . . .

DAUGHTER [*Smiling.*]: He's on duty tonight, Pa.

JOE: I'm taking the whole bunch of us out for a real celebration.

DAUGHTER: He's coming over tomorrow night, Pa. [JOE *is staring at his* WIFE, *who is beaming.*]

JOE: What are you sitting there in a house dress for? Your daughter's getting married. Go put some lipstick on, for heaven's sakes!

WIFE: I just found out myself fifteen minutes ago.

DAUGHTER: Pa . . .

JOE: What's the fanciest restaurant in town?

WIFE: I got chicken in the stove now.

JOE: We'll eat it cold tomorrow. [*He is herding his* WIFE *out of her chair.*] Come on. Into the bedroom. Put on a dress with feathers on it. Joe Manx's daughter gets married, this town is going to hear about it.

DAUGHTER [*Laughing . . . to the* WIFE, *who is being crowded to the door.*]: All right, Ma. I feel like celebrating myself.

WIFE [*Over her* HUSBAND'S *shoulder to her* DAUGHTER.]: Marilyn, do me a favor. Go in the kitchen, turn off all the fires.

DAUGHTER: Sure, Ma.

[*The* WIFE *exits. The* DAUGHTER *goes into the kitchen.* JOE *stands by the kitchen doorway.*]

JOE [*More or less to* MARILYN *in the kitchen.*]: Well, this is certainly an occasion. A nice young fellow. He's going to make a success out of himself. In a couple of years, mark my words, he'll be making twenty, thirty thousand bucks a year . . . [*Crosses to the kitchen doorway and stands on the threshold watching his* DAUGHTER.] Under a little different circumstances, I would have given you two kids a wedding, the whole city of Toledo would talk about it for weeks. I'd have a thousand dollars' worth of cold cuts alone. You'd have some big shots at your wedding, believe me! State Senator Howard Schram would be there, I can tell you that. They'd pour the whisky out of barrels. The ballroom would be littered with drunks. Very important drunks. Men worth in the millions. [*The* DAUGHTER *joins him at the kitchen doorway and stands listening to him with a smile of deep fondness and understanding. For a moment* JOE *returns her gaze, obviously very fond of his daughter. Then his eyes drop. His voice lowered.*] Marilyn, I'll need a couple of bucks to cover the evening. It might come as much as twenty, twenty-five dollars.

DAUGHTER [*Smiling.*]: Sure, Pa. [*She reached out with her hand and lightly touches his face. Then she turns and moves to the dining-room table, where her purse lies. Camera stays on* JOE *for close-up. His eyes are closed. He has to control himself, or else he would cry.*]

[*Dissolve to:* JOE *and* DORIS MANX'S *bedroom late that night. Actually, we open up on the* WIFE, *dressed now in an old batiste nightgown. She is standing by the window applying lotion to her hands and looking down, watching the operation. Then she turns and looks over to her* HUSBAND *and then back again to her hands.*

[*The camera pans slowly to* JOE, *who is unbuttoning his shirt—also wrapped in his thoughts. The push and ag-*

gressiveness have gone from JOE. *He seems tired and a little slumped.*

The WIFE *now shuffles down the aisle between the twin beds and perches on hers. She rubs the lotion into her hands, but it is clear that she is fishing for the best way to open the conversation.*]

WIFE [*Still looking down as she creams her hands.*]: Joe, she's going to have to support her husband for a couple of years. She isn't going to be able to pay the rent on this house no more. Maybe, we're going to have to move. I don't know. But we're not taking another penny from that girl. Even with Eva's five thousand dollars, it's going to be hard enough on her as it is. [JOE *sits on the far end of his bed, his back to his* WIFE, *a little slumped.*] Harry Gerber says he has a job for you with the city. Why don't you at least go down and talk to him about it?

JOE [*Mumbling.*]: I'll see Harry tomorrow. We're playing pinochle tomorrow night at his house.

WIFE [*Who didn't quite hear him.*]: I'm sorry, Joe. I didn't hear what you said.

JOE [*A little louder.*]: I said, I'll see Harry tomorrow night. We're playing pinochle at his house tomorrow night.

WIFE: All right, you'll see him tomorrow night. [*Having finished rubbing her hands, she brings her feet onto the bed and picks up a newspaper from the bed table between the beds and starts to read.*]

JOE [*Muttering.*]: If you want to know, I went to see Harry Gerber last week.

WIFE [*Reading.*]: What did you say, Joe? [JOE *rises.*]

JOE: I said, I went to see Harry Gerber last week, if you want to know the truth. [*The* WIFE *looks up from her paper.*]

WIFE: When was this?

JOE: Last week some time. I don't know. Tuesday, Wednesday. What do you think, I don't want a decent job? You think I like being supported by my daughter? You don't think it hurts?

WIFE: So what happened with Harry Gerber?

JOE: It was some job he had for me. A building inspector. Thirty-six hundred dollars a year. Thirty-six hundred dollars. Newspaper money. I put Harry Gerber into business. He was a seventy-five-dollar-a-week accountant. I took him in and made him a partner. He offers me a thirty-six-hundred-dollar-a-year job. Now, he's a big shot. Deputy Housing Commissioner. I told him what he could do with his job. [*The* WIFE, *unable to think of anything appropriate to say, looks back at her newspaper. Crying out.*]: I'm not a thirty-six-hundred-dollar-a-year man!

WIFE: All right, don't yell so loud. She'll hear you. [*She puts the newspaper down, sits up.* JOE *moves around to the inside of his bed, sits down on his bed, faces his* WIFE.]

JOE: Doris, I was a big operator at one time.

WIFE: That was fifteen years ago, Joe. . . .

JOE: All right, the bottom fell out of the real-estate market. I went broke. All right. I still got it up here . . . [*Indicates his head.*]: I can't think in terms of thirty-six hundred dollars a year. I'm not a candy-store owner, keeping an eye on the kids so they won't steal the pennies off the newsstand. I'm a business man. . . .

WIFE: Joe, how many businesses have you tried? You tried the trucking business. You tried the . . .

JOE: I was out of my element. I'm a builder. This is my racket.

WIFE: I won't let you take any more money off that girl.

JOE: What do you want me to do? You want me to take this job as a lousy building inspector?

WIFE: Joe, don't talk so loud.

JOE: You want me to walk around with my hand out, waiting for a five-dollar pay-off? I won't do it. Some of the biggest men in the business are my friends.

WIFE: All right, Joe, sit down. Don't be so excited. [JOE, *who has risen from his bed, now sinks back, his breath coming heavily.*]

JOE [*Looking down at his knees.*]: Don't worry about me, Doris. We're not going to take another penny off that girl. If you don't think it sticks me in my heart to ask her for ten dollars here, fifteen dollars there, so I can play a little pinochle. Don't you think I have a little contempt for myself? I don't have to be reminded. I love that girl. What have I ever given her? I couldn't even afford to send her to a decent college. I haven't even got a life-insurance policy so that she could at least benefit from my death.

WIFE: Oh, for heaven's sakes, Joe, don't be so dramatic.

We had money once, we don't have it any more. You've had a long time to get used to that fact.

JOE [*Pounding the bed table.*]: I'm going to leave that girl a million dollars in my will!

WIFE: Joe, what are you yelling about? Go wash yourself and let's go to bed. You're in one of your moods, and I don't want to argue with you.

JOE: Listen, Joe Manx may be broke. He may be strapped. But he still got it up here.

WIFE: Thirty-six hundred dollars a year would suit us fine. What do we need more? We're getting on in years.

JOE: There's a million-dollar proposition in that Willaston land. A little manipulation, a little maneuvering, and a man who hasn't got a nickel rides around in a Cadillac. Right now all I need is four thousand dollars. I want to pick up Louie Miles's land. You gotta have a piece of land to start with. You can't build without land. . . . [JOE *has forgotten his wife as he gets involved in his manipulations. He begins to pace slow, measured strides up and down beside his bed, his hands behind his back.*] All right, four thousand dollars. That's not so hard. I'll walk into Frank Daugherty's office, I'll say: "I want four thousand dollars," and that's all there is to that. . . . [*The* WIFE, *long familiar with these mutterings of her husband, turns her bed lamp off, turns over on her side, and tries to go to sleep. The only light in the room now is the bed lamp over* JOE's *bed.*] But now comes the manipulation. One hundred and fifty acres, draining and construction costs the way they are today, it's going to run at least two hundred, two hundred and fifty thousand dollars. . . . [*He lies back on the bed now, his hands folded over his paunch, his eyes wide and glowing.*] I'll have to have the land and at least fifty thousand dollars before I can go to the banks. I'll call Sam Harvard first thing in the morning. This is something that might interest him. . . . [*Camera begins to move up slowly onto his face as he lies there dreaming aloud.*] I could possibly realize two hundred thousand dollars out of this. A very interesting proposition. A very interesting proposition. . . . [*The camera moves right into his eyes. Fade out.*]

ACT II

[*Fade in: Film—Construction work going on in a city. A high wooden fence has been erected around the large corner area of the construction. Towering above fence are the skeletal girders of the proposed building. Noise and sounds of construction.*

[*The camera pans slowly across this view and up and onto a huge wooden sign on which is written:*

A NEW 12-STORY OFFICE BUILDING
WILL BE ERECTED ON THIS SITE—
TO BE COMPLETED SEPTEMBER 1953
FRANK DAUGHERTY AND SONS,
GENERAL CONTRACTORS.

[*Close in on name of Daugherty.*

[*Cut to: Interior, construction shack, crudely furnished. A wooden table, piled with papers and blueprints, a portable typewriter. A telephone. Coveralls hang from wall nails. On the wall an artist's conception of the proposed office building with Daugherty's name in bold printed letters at the bottom.*

[*Two men are in the shop, both in their forties. Both are rough-hewn types. Both wear baggy suits and hats, despite the fact that it is a July day. They are leaning over a large blueprint spread out on the table, muttering indistinctly to each other. Suddenly one bursts out.*]

FIRST MAN: So what are we gonna do with all those guys sittin' out there?

SECOND MAN: Nothin'. The reinforcement rods aren't here yet. [*The two men return to the blueprint. There is a knock at the door.*]

SECOND MAN [*Without looking up, barks out.*]: Come in!
[*The door opens and JOE MANX comes in, dressed as he*

was in Act I. He closes the door behind him. Neither man looks at him.]

SECOND MAN: I knew that Andy Constantino would never come up with those five-eighths rods. So he said he would. So I said, drop dead. Well, who's right now, you tell me. [*Turns to* JOE] Wadda you want, mister?

JOE: I'm waiting for Frank Daugherty.

SECOND MAN: Waddaya wanna see him about?

JOE: I have a personal matter I want to see him about.

SECOND MAN: You can't wait in here. Wait outside.

FIRST MAN [*Looking out the little window.*]: Here comes Frank.

SECOND MAN: Oh, he's gonna blow the roof off about those rods, boy. I told him yesterday, they ain't gonna be here, and he said . . . [*The door opens and a tall, angular Irishman of about fifty comes in.*] Listen, Frank, the rods didn't come in yet. I gotta whole crew outside waiting to get started. You told me yesterday, get them ready for the morning . . .

DAUGHERTY: Where's Andy?

SECOND MAN: I don't know. He ain't here yet either.

DAUGHERTY [*To the first man.*]: Get Andy on the phone for me. [*To Joe.*]: Hello, Manx. Wadda you want?

JOE: I'd like to have a couple of minutes alone with you.

DAUGHERTY: I ain't got time now, Manx. [JOE *looks at* DAUGHERTY, *then at the scowling faces of the other two men.*]

JOE: I need four thousand dollars, Daugherty. I got a very interesting proposition.

DAUGHERTY: What is it?

JOE: I can get ahold of a piece of land . . .

DAUGHERTY: What land?

JOE: Fifteen acres out in the Willaston area.

DAUGHERTY: Not interested.

FIRST MAN [*On phone.*]: Is Andy Constantino there? . . . Well, where is he? Get ahold of him, tell him Frank Daugherty wants to talk to him right away—[*To* DAUGHERTY, *as he hangs up.*] He ain't there, Frank.

SECOND MAN: He's probably out trying to round up some rods now.

JOE: Daugherty, I know it's marshland. But if you think in terms of a thousand houses . . .

DAUGHERTY: That land won't hold houses. Louie Miles was around here yesterday, trying to sell me that piece-a-land. I tell you what I told Louie. I tried to build in Willaston five years ago. I was knee-deep in water. I don't want no part of it. I'm not interested. [*He crosses to door.*] Are we gonna have to pay those men-a-yours while we're waiting for those rods?

SECOND MAN: Yeah.

DAUGHERTY: Call the union. . . . Manx, that land won't hold any kind of foundation. I told Louie Miles to try and sell it to the city. They're looking for some land to put up a community playground.

SECOND MAN [*On phone.*]: Is Herbie Swanson there? Daugherty wants him.

DAUGHERTY: That land might hold some tennis courts. That's about all it's good for.

JOE: I think you're making a mistake, Daugherty.

DAUGHERTY: It won't be the first time. [*Takes the phone from the* SECOND MAN.]: Have you got them yet? [*Into the receiver.*]: Hello? Hello? This is Frank Daugherty. Who'm I talking to? [*The camera moves onto* JOE MANX. *His face shows a mixture of envy for the activity going on around him and embarrassment at his futility in front of the other men. Over him comes* DAUGHERTY'S *voice.*] Listen, Herbie, I got a crew of lathers here, but I can't use them for at least a couple of hours. Do I have to pay them? . . . Ah, come on, Herbie, for Pete's sakes. I can't afford to throw seven hundred dollars down the sewer. I'm doing this job close to the skin as it is . . . [JOE *turns and starts out of the shack.*] Well, maybe, you can help me out this way. You know where I can get ahold of fourteen hundred rods right away? . . . I already tried Constantino. He was supposed to have them here this morning. . . . [JOE *exits, closing the door behind him.*]

[*Dissolve to: The restaurant of Act I, Scene 1. Actually, we fade in on a short, stout little man of about fifty, named* SAM HARVARD. *He is hunched over his coffee, which he sips slowly and methodically in between small pieces of Danish pastry. Once he looks quickly across the table to* JOE *and then back to the pastry in his hand. He chews.*]

HARVARD [*Without looking up.*]: Joe, why do you always hit me for these interesting propositions of yours? Why don't you hit someone else for a change?

JOE: I came to you, Sam, because . . .

HARVARD: You came to me four, five years ago with some lunatic proposition about going into the trucking line, and I gave you two thousand dollars then, which I knew was money out the window when I gave it to you. And wasn't there something once about a tool-and-die plant you wanted to invest in, another of your interesting propositions that cost me a thousand, I think. Joe, why don't you hit somebody else for a change?

JOE: Sam, I'm going to tell you the truth. I went to Daugherty. I went to Irving Stone. I went to J. C. Shirmer Incorporated. They're getting old. They only want sure-fire propositions. Office buildings. Government jobs. I didn't want to come to you, Sam. I'm very conscious of the money that I owe you.

HARVARD: Don't be so conscious. You don't have to pay me. I don't need the money. But Joe, don't ask me for another four thousand dollars for such a lunatic proposition as this thousand ranch houses in Willaston.

JOE: I just want to remind you, I built houses before. I'm not a baby in this game. Go walk in the Chestnut Street area. Before I poured a footing there, the whole area was snakes and frogs. The grass was so high you could get lost. . . . [HARVARD *breaks off another piece of Danish, looks up from under his heavy brows.*]

HARVARD: Joe, the answer is no. [*He sips his coffee and chews slowly and methodically. We fade out.*]

[*Dissolve to: A clock sitting on the buffet chest in the* MANX'S *dining alcove. A telephone is ringing. The* WIFE *comes out of the kitchen to answer it. She wears what might be her best dress, but her sleeves are rolled up.*]

WIFE: Hello? . . . Hello, Joe, how are you? Where have you been all day? . . . Oh, plenty of things have been happening here. You missed all the fun. The groom's father called up about four-thirty and invited us over to their house this afternoon. . . . Yeah, we just came back about ten minutes ago. Quite a pair of in-laws we've inherited. . . . The father is all right, but the mother is a real cold potato. . . . [*The* DAUGHTER *enters the room. The* WIFE *interrupts her phone conversation to speak to the* DAUGHTER.] Marilyn, do me a favor. I started some water boiling for the vegetables. Put some salt in it. Then take the chicken out of the refrigerator. . . . [*The* DAUGHTER *nods and passes on into the kitchen.*] Well, Joe, when are you coming home? . . . Why not? . . . Don't talk so fast. I can't understand you. . . . Joe, did something happen today to upset you? You sound very depressed. Are you depressed? . . . How do you feel, Joe? You don't sound good to me. Maybe you better give up the card game tonight and come on home and get some rest. . . . All right, don't get angry . . . all right, Joe, give me a call when you get to Harry Gerber's . . . good-by, Joe. . . . [*Hangs up. She turns from the phone, frowning. The* DAUGHTER *comes out of the kitchen and sets a bowl of salad on the table.*] He's not coming home for dinner . . . so let's just have the chicken from yesterday, and the vegetables, is that all right with you?

DAUGHTER: That's fine with me. [*The* DAUGHTER *goes back into the kitchen. The* WIFE, *still frowning, goes to the buffet chest, opens a drawer, and extracts some silverware. She starts setting two places, but her thoughts are elsewhere. She sits, brows knit in thought. The* DAUGHTER *comes back from the kitchen with a large plate on which sits a cold roast chicken, two other large plates, and some paper napkins, sets up places for her mother and herself.*]

WIFE: I'm worried about him. I'm worried about him because he's beginning to talk like a fool. Four, five years ago, you listen to his big propositions, and you say: "Well, maybe. Maybe, some of his old friends will help him out." But now, it seems to me, he's beginning to sound like a comic character. What do you think, Marilyn?

DAUGHTER: Oh, he'll be all right, Ma.

WIFE: Do you think so? I don't think so. I think something terrible is going to happen to him. He doesn't talk like a completely sensible person any more. I look at him sometimes; it seems to me he's in another world, dreaming. [*The* DAUGHTER *sits across from her* MOTHER, *studies the dish before her.*]

DAUGHTER: He was a big shot once. He had a taste of what it was like. It's hard for a man of his age to adjust to new situations.

WIFE: It's not a new situation. It's fifteen years old. He's got to understand that it's not important to be the Governor's best friend. He was like that as long as I've known him, even as a boy. He was always the big spender. Before we were married, he used to take me to the Hippodrome in New York City. At that time, the Hippodrome was the big date of all dates. They used to have big spectacles there, like circuses. It used to cost a dollar. In those days, a dollar was a dollar. He used to take me every week. I never knew where he got the money. He never had a job in his life. He was always in this business or that business. He was always what we used to call a sport. He was the first one in our whole crowd to have a car. I'll never forget. He came driving down the street, wobbling from one sidewalk to the other. He was a kind, generous man, your father. He had an open hand to everybody. You were too young then. You don't remember. The parties we used to give when we lived in the big house on Rogers Boulevard! Every Sunday, I tell you that house used to be filled till two, three o'clock in the morning. Well, we don't give big parties any more. He'll have to change. Eat some cold chicken!

DAUGHTER: He's not going to change, Ma. Not at his age.

WIFE: He's got to go out and earn a living, Marilyn.

DAUGHTER: Ma, why talk foolish? He isn't going to go out and get a job. In the first place where's he going to get a job? Who's going to give it to him?

WIFE: Harry Gerber offered him a job.

DAUGHTER [Surprised.]: Oh, yeah? When was this?

WIFE: A couple of weeks ago. It's a small job, a building inspector. It would be fine for us. He don't want to take it.

DAUGHTER: Ma, don't push him. It isn't in him. He likes big things. It would kill him to be a little man. I know that you're probably nagging him to take this job. You're thinking what a burden you and Pop are on me, especially now I'm getting married. It's no burden. Believe me. I don't resent it.

WIFE: Marilyn, you're not going to support Joe and me any more.

DAUGHTER: Ma, I talked this all out with George long ago. I'm going to take a couple of thousand out of Aunt Eva's money, and we're going to put it down on a little house somewheres, probably out in Kingston, and you and Pop are going to live with us. George says it's perfectly okay with him. . . .

WIFE: You're twenty-six years old. It's time to have babies.

DAUGHTER: Sure, it's time to have babies. When a baby comes, we'll worry about it. Listen, Ma, you don't think George and I haven't discussed this a thousand times between us? But life doesn't dovetail so nicely. . . . Don't worry about us. We'll have plenty of babies. [*The doorbell rings.*] How much you want to bet that's George? [*She plucks a piece of chicken loose, rises, and goes to the door munching away. The* WIFE *suddenly starts from her seat.*]

WIFE: Oh, for heaven's sakes, I forgot the vegetables. The water's probably all boiled out already. [*She hurries into the kitchen. The* DAUGHTER *opens the door of the apartment. It is, indeed,* GEORGE *standing there.*]

DAUGHTER: I knew it was you.

GEORGE: I haven't seen you in an hour. I missed you. Well, what are you going to do?

DAUGHTER: Come on in. You want some cold chicken? [GEORGE *comes in. The* DAUGHTER *closes the door behind him.*]

GEORGE: Tell you the truth, I figured we might go to a restaurant tonight, have a celebration. Because you know what?

DAUGHTER: What?

GEORGE: My mother likes your mother.

DAUGHTER: Hallelujah. Come on in, sit down for a minute. [*She leads him back to the dining table, where they take seats. The* DAUGHTER *calls to her* MOTHER *in the kitchen.*] It's him again, Ma.

GEORGE [*Calling.*]: Hello, Mrs. Manx.

WIFE [*Off in kitchen.*]: Hello, George. Give him some chicken, Marilyn.

DAUGHTER [*Calling to the* WIFE.]: We're going to go out and eat, Ma, if you'll excuse us.

WIFE [*In kitchen.*]: Sure. Go ahead, go ahead. [*She appears in the kitchen doorway, holding a saucepan.*] I burned the vegetables anyway. Go on out. Have a good time. [*Disappears back into the kitchen. The* DAUGHTER *and* GEORGE *sit for a minute.*]

DAUGHTER: My father was offered a job. [GEORGE *looks up vaguely.*]

GEORGE: Yeah?

DAUGHTER: Yeah. It would be nice, eh?

GEORGE: Sure. Is he going to take it? [*The* DAUGHTER *thinks awhile, then shakes her head.*]

DAUGHTER: I don't think so, George. But it would be nice. I could even quit my job after a year.

GEORGE [*Smiles.*]: Yeah. Well, what do you say? You want to go?

DAUGHTER: Is this dress okay?

GEORGE: Sure. [*They both stand. The* DAUGHTER *moves slowly to* GEORGE, *and for a moment they stand, hazily warm and comfortable in their communication. She looks softly at him.*]

DAUGHTER: But it would be so nice. [GEORGE *smiles at her.*]

GEORGE: Sure. [*The* DAUGHTER *turns her head to call good-by to her* MOTHER, *is shocked to see her standing in the kitchen doorway, holding the saucepan, watching them with troubled eyes.*]

DAUGHTER: Good-by, Ma.

WIFE: Good-by, Marilyn, Good-by, George. Have a nice time.

GEORGE: Good-by, Mrs. Manx. [*The young couple move into the foyer, open the door, and pass out into the outside hallway—closing the door after them. The* WIFE *stands unmoving, watching them, even for a long moment after the door has closed behind them. Then she moves slowly to the telephone table, sets the saucepan down, dials a number, and waits expressionlessly for an answer.*]

WIFE: Harry? Is this Harry Gerber? . . . Harry, this is Doris Manx. Listen, did I take you away from your dinner? . . . Harry, I'll tell you why I called. Joe says he's coming over to your house for cards tonight. . . . Yeah, well I'm a little worried about him, Harry. He called up from downtown, he sounded very depressed. . . .

Harry, make him take the job. . . . I know, Harry, but please make him take the job. . . .

[*Dissolve to:* JOE MANX *leaning forward over a table, reaching for some cards in front of another player. The camera dollies back to show the pinochle game taking place in Harry Gerber's living room. Four men sit around the table. On* JOE'S *right sits the* COMPLAINER, *and directly across the table from* JOE *sits the* WELL-DRESSED MAN, *so named for reasons that will soon be obvious. On* JOE'S *left sits* HARRY GERBER, *a heavy-set sympathetic man of fifty. The living room is comfortably furnished: in particular, an easy chair.* JOE *has apparently just won the last hand and is to deal the next.*]

COMPLAINER [*Leaning across to Gerber.*]: Why did you play the king? You knew he was sitting there with a singleton ace? If you led the ace, I woulda put the king on. . . .

WELL-DRESSED MAN: All right, all right, how much did this hand cost me?

GERBER: Half a dollar. [GERBER *and the* WELL-DRESSED MAN *send half a dollar to* JOE'S *little pile of money.* JOE *is riffling the cards. The* COMPLAINER *is still complaining to* GERBER.]

COMPLAINER: If you run the government, Harry, like you play pinochle, no wonder we're in the condition we're in. [*To* JOE.] How much do I owe you, Joe?

JOE: Half a dollar.

COMPLAINER [*Pushing two quarters over to* JOE.]: I haven't won a hand all night, you know that? I get nothing but nines and jacks.

WELL-DRESSED MAN: So I was telling you, Harry, I went into this store, and I told the salesman: "Look, money is no object. I want a suit that will hold its shape in hot weather." So he takes out this bolt of cloth . . . [*Camera moves in on* JOE *as he riffles the cards. His eyes are down. He is obviously thinking of other things than the card game. Over close-up, we hear the others' voices.*]

COMPLAINER: Right now, all I want out of life is to see one flush, preferably in spades.

WELL-DRESSED MAN: Harry, feel this cloth, will you? Have you any idea how much this suit cost me? A hundred and eighty-nine dollars. . . . [JOE *begins to deal out the cards, three at a time first round, then four at a time until the deck runs out.*]

COMPLAINER: Joe, are we or are we not old friends?

JOE: Sure.

COMPLAINER: Then, deal me a decent hand, will you?

WELL-DRESSED MAN: Joe, take a guess. How much do you think I paid for this suit? A hundred and eighty-nine dollars. It's a special cloth, imported from Egypt. They wear this kind of material on the desert.

COMPLAINER [*Picking up his cards as they come in.*]: Joe, what are you dealing me here? What are you trying to do, bankrupt me?

WELL-DRESSED MAN: This material is as light as paper, but it wears like iron. . . .

COMPLAINER [*Leaning over and showing his cards to* JOE, *who, as dealer, does not play in the hand.*]: Look what you gave me, will you? Do you see fifty points meld in this whole hand? [*To the others.*] All right, all right, who bids?

WELL-DRESSED MAN: So, Joe, let me tell you about this suit . . .

COMPLAINER: Harry, what do you say?

GERBER: Three hundred. . . .

WELL-DRESSED MAN: So, Joe, this suit, rain or shine, it holds its crease. It doesn't wrinkle. I could jump in the river and swim in it, it won't wrinkle. The only trouble is, it makes me sweat so much. I'll be honest with you. I don't know how they manage in Egypt with it.

COMPLAINER: Hey, Lewisohn, what do you say?

WELL-DRESSED MAN: What?

COMPLAINER: Pick up your cards, will you? Gerber says three hundred. It's up to you.

WELL-DRESSED MAN [*Painfully picking up one card at a time.*]: I was telling Joe about the suit.

COMPLAINER: Lewisohn, do me a favor. The next time you come for a pinochle game, come naked, will you? . . .

WELL-DRESSED MAN [*Screwing up his face as he examines each card and puts it into place in his hand.*]: Let's see, what have I got here? [*Silence descends over the card-players as they wait for the* WELL-DRESSED MAN *to figure out his hand. In the silence,* JOE *leans forward, folds his hands on the table before him, and speaks quietly.*]

JOE: Listen. I need four thousand dollars. Can you give it to me, you fellows?

COMPLAINER [*Turning to him.*]: What?

JOE [*To the* COMPLAINER.]: What do you say, Davis? We've been playing pinochle together twenty years almost. Will you lend me four thousand dollars?

COMPLAINER [*A little nervously.*]: Lend it! Another couple of hands, and you'll win it from me.

WELL-DRESSED MAN [*Laying his cards down and turning to* JOE.]: What do you need the money for, Joe? Are you in trouble?

JOE: I need it for a business proposition. I want to buy a piece of land.

WELL-DRESSED MAN [*Picking up his cards again.*]: Oh, land. Land I don't know anything about. If you were in some kind of trouble—if you needed an operation or if you wanted to pay off a mortgage, something like that, I might be able to dig up a couple of thousand for you. But land I'm not interested in. . . . [*Studies his cards again.*] Let's see. What's the bid to me?

COMPLAINER [*With nervous embarrassment.*]: Come on, come on. Let's play cards. Gerber said three hundred. What do you say, Lewisohn?

WELL-DRESSED MAN: Three hundred is good with me.

COMPLAINER: It's good with me too. You want it, Harry, or not? [GERBER *is regarding* JOE MANX *with concern.*]

GERBER: Joe, what is this proposition you want the four thousand for? [JOE, *in a sudden burst of irascibility, slams the table with his hand.*]

JOE [*Almost snarling.*]: Come on! Come on, Harry! Let's play cards! It's three hundred up to you! Do you want it or not?

GERBER [*Without even looking at his hand.*]: I don't want it.

JOE: All right, throw in the hand. Here, deal. [*He pushes the discards, as they are thrown down, toward* GERBER.] Look. Are we going to play cards, or are we going to talk! If we're going to play, let's play! If we're going to talk, let's talk! [*He suddenly stands, growing more frenzied.*] My friends! My friends! My good friends! Four lousy thousand bucks! You can't lend me four

lousy thousand bucks! What am I, some kind of a bum
or something? I built plenty of houses in my time! Good
double-brick houses, three coats of plaster! [*He seizes
the few bills and silver in front of him and scatters the
money on the table.*] Here! A couple more bucks for
you! [*He turns and walks out.* GERBER *rises quickly from
his seat.*]

GERBER [*Calling.*]:   Joe! [*He moves quickly after his friend.*]

[*Slow dissolve to:* JOE MANX, *sitting in the easy chair in
Gerber's living room. Some time has passed—about an
hour. The overhead lights of the previous scene have
been turned off, and now the only illumination comes
from the standing lamp behind the easy chair. There is
enough light to see, however, as we pull back, that the
cards still lie scattered on the table—except for a few
that* HARRY GERBER *is shuffling and reshuffling as he sits
at the table. There is a cup of coffee in front of Harry
Gerber, and* JOE *is holding his cup, sipping occasionally.
He appears to have calmed down a great deal, even to
the point of depression.*]

JOE: I went to them all, Harry. I went to Daugherty, to
Shirmer. I went to Sam Harvard, Marty Kingsley, Irving
Stone. Some of these men used to mix cement for me. I
couldn't raise four thousand dollars. I couldn't raise four
thousand dollars! Daugherty brushed me off him like I
was mud on his pants. I tell you, Harry, if somebody
told me yesterday that Joe Manx couldn't raise four
thousand dollars, I would have laughed in his face.
What does it mean, will you tell me? What does it mean?

GERBER: Joe . . .

JOE: Tell me the truth, Harry, do they laugh at me when
I'm not around?

GERBER: All right, I'll tell you the truth. You haven't got
a name in this trade any more, Joe, and you're kidding
yourself if you think you have. You can go on like
this the rest of your life, or you can act like a *mensch*
and face a couple of facts. I got a job for you. Come
and take it. It's the best job I can get for you. I tried to
get you a desk job where you could feel like an execu-
tive, but the flat truth is they wouldn't have you. I'm
leveling with you, Joe. Take it or leave it. It's thirty-six
hundred dollars a year. It'll pay your rent, and it'll give

you a little self-respect. [*Turns his attention back to the few cards he is shuffling.*] Joe, I'm your friend. Any time you need me, you know you can come to me. If I had four thousand dollars, I'd give it to you. But I want you to know I'd give it to you out of charity, and I'd never expect to see it again.

JOE [*Studying his coffee.*]: Well, that's straight talk. I respect you for it. But I don't want your job. [*He sets the coffee down on an end table.*]

GERBER: What is it, a question of pride? Are you ashamed to work for me?

JOE [*Stands.*]: Harry, I've been a bankrupt for fifteen years. When you're a bankrupt as long as I am, thirty-six hundred dollars a year ain't gonna turn the trick. It isn't going to make up for all the failures.

GERBER: What failures?

JOE: You talk about facing facts! All right, let's face some facts! I failed as a man! I failed as a father! What did I ever give those two women?! What did I ever give them?! My wife wears the same cloth coat for four years, do you know that?!

GERBER: You haven't failed anybody, Joe.

JOE: From the age of ten I never bought my daughter even a birthday present! She's getting married Friday. What will my wedding gift be? A house for the newly-weds? A ten-thousand-dollar bond? Do you know how it haunts me that I can't buy that girl something? What contempt she must have for me!

GERBER: Joe, you're talking like a fool. You're a wonderful father. Your girl is crazy about you. Stop torturing yourself.

JOE: Look, Harry, don't worry about me. I'm having a little rough time right now, but I'll come out of it. I'm fifty-two years old. Maybe, I can't run around the block any more, but I'm still operating where it counts.

GERBER: Joe, sit down a minute.

JOE: Apparently, nobody has any faith in me, not even my best friend. Well, Harry, I'll dig up four thousand dollars somewheres, one way or another, and I'll buy fifteen lousy acres of swamp. . . . [*His voice is beginning to rise.*] And I'll show you what Joe Manx can do with it! I'll put the Empire State Building on that swamp! I'm a man of respect! Bricklayers like Frank Daugherty will come on their knees to kiss my hand! [*He suddenly smiles, but there is something almost wild about him.*] And, Harry, when I die, I'll leave thirty-six hundred dollars a year for you in my will. [*He nods his head once or twice—then turns and stumps out of the room. Fade out.*]

ACT III

[*Fade in: The bedroom of* JOE *and* DORIS MANX, *later that night. The room is dark. We fade in on the* WIFE, *lying on her back on her bed, asleep. Suddenly her eyes open. Then her head slowly turns in the direction of her husband's bed. The camera slowly pans over to Joe's bed. It is empty. The blankets have been pushed aside, and the sheets are mussed—indicating that Joe has recently been sleeping there.*

[*The* WIFE *slowly sits up in bed, tense and apprehensive, but outwardly expressionless. She moves quickly around the beds to the door of the bedroom, opens it, passes into the dark hallway. She goes through the kitchen, opens that door, and steps into the living room.*

[JOE MANX *is seated in his large master chair, his arms resting regally on the armrests. He wears his trousers and bedroom slippers, but he has no shirt on. His hair is uncombed, and there is a distraught quality about him.*]

WIFE: What's the matter, Joe? You can't sleep? [*Joe regards his* WIFE *with wide eyes.*]

JOE: Doris, I'll tell you what I've been thinking. I think I'm going to go away for a couple of days. I just called the station. I can get a train to Saint Louis at four-forty-nine A.M. Then I catch a flyer for Las Vegas. [*Stands, begins to pace around, hands behind his back.*] . . . the convention last year in Atlantic City—a feller there from Las Vegas. He told me, Las Vegas is just booming. He says, houses are springing up overnight. A city jumping up out of the desert. Like Florida in the 1920s. Well, I think I'll take a look at this Las Vegas. Listen, a clever man can make himself a bundle. [*He's patting his pants pockets for cigarettes now.*] Then too, I might have a look in California, see what the situation on the Coast is.

Listen, I've heard wonderful things about the Coast. Los Angeles, San Diego. I've got some friends in San Diego. They told me: "Manx, any time you feel like switching your area of activity, there's plenty of room for you here."

WIFE: Joe, come to bed. [JOE *comes to the table, leans intently across to his* WIFE.]

JOE: Lady, I have a feeling Las Vegas is going to turn the trick. I was lying in bed thinking, and then, suddenly—like the burning bush—it came to me. It was like somebody spoke the thought aloud. "Go to Las Vegas." What am I pushing pennies in Toledo? Well, let's pack up a couple of things for me and a toothbrush. [*He starts briskly past his* WIFE *for the kitchen door, but his* WIFE *puts out a gentle hand on his forearm.*]

WIFE: Joe . . . [*Her touch seems to crumble him. He turns to her suddenly gaunt and broken.*]

JOE [*Crying out in sheer anguish.*]: Doris! I gotta get outta this town!

WIFE: I know, Joe, I know . . .

JOE: They're squeezing me here! You understand?! They're squeezing me!

WIFE: I understand, Joe.

JOE: Look at me, for heaven's sakes. They all make a living but me. What's the matter with me?

WIFE: There's nothing the matter with you, Joe. [*He crosses to sofa, sits, slack and empty.*]

JOE: I would just like to close my eyes and wake up with another name, because I'm sick in my heart of being Joe Manx.

WIFE: Joe, we don't want a million dollars from you. We love you, Joe, we love you if you build houses or if you don't build houses. We just want to have you around the house. We like to eat dinner with you. We like to see your face. [JOE *rises heavily from his seat and moves a few paces away. As he moves from the* WIFE, *he lets his hand rest lightly against her face in mute appreciation of her sympathy. The* WIFE *sits there, deeply weary herself.*]

JOE [*Muttering.*]: I don't know, maybe there's something in this Las Vegas.

WIFE [*More sharply than she intended.*]: There's nothing in Las Vegas, Joe! [*She sits, trying to hold the edge of impatience inside of her, fishing desperately in her mind for something to say to her husband.*] Joe, I'm tired myself. I'd like to have a little peace. I'd like to know we live in a certain place and that a certain amount of money is coming in every week, so at least we know where we stand. I don't want a lot of money. I just don't want to have to carry a sick feeling in my stomach all the time that you're going to come home depressed and miserable. I don't want to listen to you turning around in bed all night long. I want to be able to go to sleep peacefully, knowing that you're also having a good night's sleep. I don't have much strength left, Joe. This kind of living is eating us up. [*Deeply exhausted, she rests her face in the palm of one hand.* JOE *stands silently. She has reached home with him. Finally he comes to her and gently takes her arm.*]

JOE: It's all right, Doris, it's all right. Go to sleep.

WIFE [*Still hiding her face in her hand.*]: You owe this to me, Joe.

JOE [*Helps her from the chair.*]: Go to sleep. I want to do a little thinking.

WIFE: Joe, if I said anything that hurt you, it's because I'm all knocked out.

JOE [*Helping her to the door.*]: You didn't hurt me.

WIFE: Let's go to bed. We'll get some sleep.

JOE: Go to sleep, Doris. You're all knocked out. I'm going to work out something, don't worry. [*They stand now in the kitchen threshold, looking wearily at each other.*]

JOE: I don't deserve you, Doris.

WIFE: Come to bed, Joe.

JOE: In a couple of minutes. [*The* WIFE *turns and shuffles out of view.* JOE *watches her disappearing form for a few moments. Then he turns and begins again the slow, measured pacing up and down the dining room. We stay with him for four or five lengths of the room. Fade out slowly.*]

[*Dissolve to: Close-up of* DAUGHTER'S *face. She is sleeping. We are in her bedroom, which is just off the living room. It is dark. The* DAUGHTER *turns in her bed and then reverts back to her original position. Then—somehow aware that she is being looked at—she opens her eyes and awakens. She looks up.* JOE *is standing beside her bed, looking down at her. She is up on her elbow immediately.*]

DAUGHTER: Is something wrong, Pa?

JOE [*In a low voice.*]: I wonder if I could talk to you for a minute, Marilyn.

DAUGHTER: Sure.

JOE: Listen, Marilyn, I'm going to ask a terrific favor of you . . .

DAUGHTER: Sure, Pa . . .

JOE: First let me finish. I need your five thousand dollars. I want to buy Louie Miles's land. It's the only piece of land I can get my hands on, do you understand? It's a piece of swamp. It's marsh. But it's the best I can get. I have to have land before I can manipulate. I know what it means to you, Marilyn, the five thousand dollars. I know you need it for your marriage. But you have to have faith in me. I'll give it back to you a thousand times over. Marilyn, I wouldn't ask you this, but I need it.

DAUGHTER: Sure, Pa. I'll make you out a check now. You can cash it in the morning. [*She starts to sit up.* JOE *stares, at her, unbelieving. Then the accumulated tension breaks within him, and he begins to sob. He turns away from his* DAUGHTER *in shame and goes out into the living room, hiding his eyes in his hands, the sobs coming in hoarse, half-caught gasps. He walks aimlessly around the living room, hiding his eyes, crying uncontrollably. His* DAUGHTER *appears in the doorway of her room, watching him anxiously.*]

DAUGHTER: Pa . . . [*He turns to her, still hiding his eyes.*]

JOE [*Brokenly.*]: What did I ever give you? [*He sinks down onto a chair, cupping his face in both hands now. The* DAUGHTER *moves slowly to him.*]

DAUGHTER: Pa, look at me. Am I an unhappy girl? I'm happy. I love George. I love you. I love Mama. I got a responsible job. The boss is satisfied with me. That's what you gave me. I'll make you out the check. [JOE *has to shake his head a few times before he can answer.*]

JOE: I don't want it. [*He rises weakly and starts for the kitchen door.*]

DAUGHTER: Pa . . .

JOE: Go to sleep, go to sleep. . . . [*He goes into the kitchen, across it, and down the foyer to the door of his bedroom, opens it and goes in. His* WIFE *is lying on her bed and turns to watch his entrance. He doesn't look at her. He goes to his bed, sits down. He is over his tears now and is just breathing heavily.*]

JOE [*Mumbling.*]: All right, all right. I'll take the job with Harry Gerber.

WIFE: I didn't hear you, Joe.

JOE [*Louder.*]: I said, I'll take the job with Harry Gerber. At least, they'll have one honest building inspector. [*He lies back on the bed now, looking up at the ceiling.*] This was a crazy day, a crazy day . . . [*His eyes close and he dozes off. Fade out.*]

REQUIEM FOR A
HEAVYWEIGHT

by Rod Serling

ACT I

[*We open on a long angle shot looking down a bare cement corridor dimly lit by intermittent green shaded 25-watt bulbs. This is the underbelly of a fight arena and from off stage comes the occasional roar of the crowd. On one far wall are visible a couple of fight posters announcing the cards for that night and the weeks to come. Two men stand close to one of the posters and talk in low voice. From the far end of the corridor appear* "ARMY" *and a fighter named* HARLAN "MOUNTAIN" MC CLINTOCK, *walking slowly toward the camera, the fighter leaning heavily on the arm of* ARMY. *The two men pause under one of the lights, and we get our first definitive view of the fighter's face. He has a bathrobe thrown loosely over his shoulders, and his body is a mass of red welts and skin abrasions. The bridge of his nose has a red crack down the middle of it. One eye is shut, the other is swollen almost to the same point. On his cheek is a bleeding bruise, and his chest is covered with sweat.* ARMY *is an ex-fighter, a small man with long arms, in his late forties. He has thinning hair that reveals two thin scars which run down toward his cheeks on either side of his temples. Beyond that his face is open, fairly pleasant, rather intelligent.*]

ARMY: How about it, Mount, can yuh make it? Make it okay?
[*The fighter nods, wets his lips as if to say something, and then can't get it out. Over their shoulder we see* MAISH, *the manager, coming down the corridor. A man steps out from the wall and detains him.*]
MAISH [*Calls out to* ARMY.]: Army, stay there with him a minute will you? I'll be right there.

[*The camera moves over for a close shot of* MAISH *and the* MAN.]

MAN: Two words, Maish. Cough up.

MAISH [*Furtive look toward* ARMY *and the fighter.*]: Will you relax? I'll get it. I'll get it. Tell him I'll get it. Tell him to phone me.

MAN: Mr. Henson's no collection agency.

MAISH: I know. I know. Tell him he'll get it.

[*With this the camera moves away leaving them talking in low, unintelligible voices.* ARMY *and the fighter take a few more steps down the corridor until they stand very close to the two men who stand near one of the posters. They cast a few disinterested glances at the fighter, and then continue their conversation.*]

MAN #1: So I told him. And he said I gotta.

MAN #2: So what did he say?

MAN #1: He says I gotta.

MAN #2: Cut ice?

MAN #1 [*With a shrug.*]: Wid him? Ilokadisguy. Itellhimstraight. Djaeverseeany guywalkinaringwidabusted hand?

MAN #2: Whaddehsay? Cut ice?

MAN #1: Neh! I gottaputiminnextT'ursday.

[*At this point the camera pulls away from them so that we can no longer hear them, but see them in pantomime as they continue talking only an arm's length or so away from the fighter who stands bleeding in front of them, but totally oblivious to them.*]

[*Cut to: A shot of* MAISH *and* ARMY *appearing again at the far end of the corridor.* ARMY *now has his arms full with a bucket, some towels, and a pair of gloves. He starts to continue down the corridor when* MAISH *takes his arm, and with a nod toward the fighter still standing there.*]

MAISH: How is he?

ARMY [*Shrugs.*]: This wasn't the night, that's for sure.

MAISH: You are *so* right.

[*Then the two men continue down the corridor. They approach* MC CLINTOCK *from either side, each taking an arm, and help him move forward. They walk a few more feet and then stop by the door to the dressing room*

and usher him into it. A fighter and his manager are just coming by.]

MANAGER: What hit him?

MAISH: Don't get impatient, Jock, that's a fast track out there. [*Then he looks at the young fighter obviously ill at ease.*] You ought to see the other guy. [*The* MANAGER *hustles his fighter out, then* MAISH *closes the door.*] Not a mark on him.

[*Both he and* ARMY *help* MC CLINTOCK *onto a high rubbing table.* ARMY *pours some water into the bucket from a dirty sink, brings the bucket over to the table.* MAISH *takes a towel, dampens it, and starts to wipe away the sweat and blood.*]

MAISH: Mountain, can you hear me okay? [*The fighter nods.*]

MAISH: Give me some of that alum will yuh, Army? [ARMY *digs into his pockets and brings out a little jar.* MAISH *dabs his finger in it and starts to apply it to the fighter's face.*]

ARMY: I don't think alum'll do it, Maish. I think that's going to take stitches.

MAISH [*Peers into the fighter's face more intently.*]: Yeah. They get wider and wider.

ARMY: The doc's going to be coming in a minute anyway. He'll do it.

[MC CLINTOCK *wets his lips and now he speaks for the first time. His voice is heavy and belabored and still short of breath.*]

MC CLINTOCK: Maish? Hey, Maish—

MAISH: Go easy. Go easy, we've got a lot of time.

MC CLINTOCK: Maish—too—fast. Much too fast.

MAISH [*Nods.*]: Bum night, Kid. Just a bum night all the way around. There'll be others.

MC CLINTOCK: Sure. Others. [MC CLINTOCK *moves a bandaged hand awkwardly down to his side and feels.*] Check there will yuh, Maish? By the belt. [ARMY *hurriedly pulls the trousers down a quarter of an inch.*]

ARMY: You've got a little resin down there. It'll be okay. Rubbed a sore there. It'll be okay.

MC CLINTOCK: Hurts.

[*Then he breathes deeply again, and* MAISH *goes back to dabbing water on his face. The door opens and the*

DOCTOR *enters. This is a thin, vinegar-faced old man in his sixties with a single-breasted, old-fashioned suit with a vest, all the buttons buttoned. He carries a beaten-up black bag, which he tosses on the foot of the rubbing table.*]

DOCTOR: Mountain, haven't you had enough yet?

MAISH: It's his eye, Doc.

DOCTOR: I know. Just as well, Maish. If he hadn't folded I wouldn't have let him out for number nine.

[MAISH *nods but doesn't say anything. He pulls out the butt of a cigar from his pocket and lights it. The* DOCTOR *squints, pushes his arm away.*]

DOCTOR: Let me breathe, will you? [*He leans over the fighter and examines the eye, then pushes the face to the other side a little roughly and examines the other bruises and cuts. Then he snaps his fingers at* ARMY, *who picks up the bag and hands it to him.*]

DOCTOR: Where do you buy your cigars, Maish? I'll see that they condemn the store. [*Then he reaches in the bag and takes out some gauze, a stick with cotton on the end of it, and a bottle of medicine. He starts to administer to the fighter.*]

ARMY: How much longer you got, Doc? You're out this week, ain't you?

DOCTOR: Let's see. This is Wednesday—I leave Friday.

MAISH [*Staring down at the fighter and obviously making small talk.*]: Vacation?

DOCTOR: Vacation? Retirement. I'm the one man in the fight business who walks away without a wobble. Thirty-eight years, Maish. Retirement.

ARMY [*Clucks.*]: Thirty-eight years.

DOCTOR [*Administering to the fighter as he talks.*]: Thirty-eight years. Wife says I oughta write a book, but who'd buy it?

MAISH: You've seen some good ones.

DOCTOR: Good ones and bad ones. Live ones and a couple of dead ones. [*Then he straightens up, massages his back, and points down with the stick towards* MC CLINTOCK.] And almost dead ones. He's got no business in there, Maish. You hungry, is that it?

MAISH [*Picking up the fighter's hand and massaging it absently.*]: What do you mean hungry? In 1948 he was number five. You can check that in *Ring Magazine.* I could show it to you, number five, and that was in 1948.

DOCTOR [*Looks at him a little quizzically.*]: Only 1948? And this is 1956. And that means eight years ago. Too bad he isn't a machine, Maish. Too bad none of them are machines. [*Then he laughs softly.*] I've seen a lot of them. Thirty-eight years. When I first come in, they used to lay them out in front of me. They were human beings then. They were young men. Do you know what it's like now, Maish? Army? [*He leans back over* MC CLIN-TOCK *and starts to work again.*] Now it's like a guy who grades meat in a packing plant. They roll the carcasses down the line in front of him and he stamps them. Beef. Understand? [*He motions toward* MC CLINTOCK.] Just a hunk of something inanimate. That's what thirty-eight years has done. [*Then musingly.*] Thirty-eight years. And suddenly I don't have a single patient with a first and last name. A set of scars. A blood type and a record—that's all patients have. Look here, Maish, I want to show you something. [MAISH *leans over.*] Look at his pupil. See? Known as sclerotic damage. Look at the tissue there. Couple of good solid rights to that eye—and you can buy him a tin cup and some pencils. [*He straightens up again, puts his things back in the bag and says:*] Or maybe that won't have to happen. Maybe some night he'll bang his head on a bathroom door and bleed to death. Either way, Maish. It could happen either way. [*Then a long pause and a deep breath.*] No more. This was it. Mountain and I will both retire this week.

[MAISH *looks from the fighter to the* DOCTOR *and his voice is strained.*]

MAISH: What do you mean?

DOCTOR: No more.

MAISH: He could rest up. I've got nothing scheduled for him—

DOCTOR [*Interrupts.*]: He can rest up for the rest of his life.

MAISH: What're you talking about? He's fourteen years in this business. Suddenly he gets a cut, and we've got to put him out to pasture?

DOCTOR [*Turns to him.*]: Suddenly. It doesn't go fourteen years and then suddenly. And it's never one cut. It's four-teen years of cuts. [*He stretches, hoists up the bag.*] Yep, write me a book. All about my gladiator friends. You too can become pathological in thirty-eight years of relatively easy lessons.

MAISH [*Interrupts.*]: Joker. Big joker.

[DOCTOR *walks over to the door, turns the knob, then looks back at* MAISH.]

DOCTOR: Joker? [*He shakes his head, nods toward* MC-CLINTOCK.] Who's laughing?

[*He walks out of the room and shuts the door.* ARMY *and* MAISH *stare at one another, then both look toward* MC CLINTOCK. ARMY *goes over and starts to cut away the bandages on his hands.* MAISH *stands back a few feet smoking the cigar thoughtfully. Finally* MC CLINTOCK *sits up, closes his eyes, moves his mouth, and touches his jaw gingerly.*]

MC CLINTOCK: Doc here?

ARMY: He left.

MC CLINTOCK: It hurts, Maish.

MAISH [*Turns his back.*]: I don't doubt it.

[*The* MOUNTAIN *shakes his head, reacts with pain, touches the bandage on his eye.*]

MC CLINTOCK: Deep huh, Maish?

MAISH: Enough. You could hide your wallet in there. Go lie down. Rest up a minute, and *then* take your shower.

[MC CLINTOCK *pushes his feet around heavily so that they hang over the side. Then he balances himself with his hands. His head goes up and down, and he breathes deeply.*]

MC CLINTOCK: I'm coming around now. Oh Lordy, I caught it tonight, Maish. I really did. What did I do wrong?

MAISH: You aged. That was the big trouble. You aged.

[MC CLINTOCK *looks at him, frowns. He tries to get some thread of meaning out of the words, but none comes.*]

MC CLINTOCK: What do you mean, Maish? I aged. Don't everybody age?

MAISH [*Nods.*]: Yeah, everybody ages. Everybody grows old, Kid. Go ahead. I think a shower'll do you good. Try not to get that bandage wet.

[MC CLINTOCK *gets on his feet, a little wobbly. He holds the table for support, then walks out of the room toward*

the shower. ARMY *starts to pick up the dirty towels and put them in a big container alongside of the door.*]

ARMY [*Without looking up.*]: What're you going to do, Maish?

MAISH [*Shrugs.*]: I dunno. Maybe I'll cut my throat.

ARMY: Something's wrong, isn't there?

MAISH: Where were you when the lights went out? I just lost a boy! Get with it, Army.

ARMY: Besides that—

MAISH: Besides that, nothing. Forget it. [*Then with a desperate attempt at a kind of composure.*] I just gotta go huntin' and packin' around, that's all. Find somebody else. Maybe try a lightweight this trip.

ARMY: I was just wondering—

MAISH: You wanna pull out, huh, Army? A million offers, huh?

ARMY: I didn't mean—

MAISH [*Interrupts.*]: Don't gimme a whole megillah. I know you're good, Army. You're the best cut man in the city. I know that. You probably could take your pick. I don't know why you haven't before.

ARMY [*With his head down.*]: Never mind about me. What about the Mountain?

MAISH [*Reacts a little guiltily.*]: I dunno. He'll find something.

ARMY: It's been fourteen years.

MAISH: Fourteen years what?

ARMY: Fourteen years' fight. Then one night you get out of the ring—it's all over. And what've you got—

MAISH: You made a living, didn't you? You did all right. [*Then he chuckles.*] Remember how I used to tout you? "The Hero of the Argonne." I even gave you the na[me] "Army." So don't complain, Army. You came o[ut of] it with a name at least.

ARMY [*In a kind of wistful voice.*]: Still—a guy oug[ht to] have something to show for it besides the name. [*At [that] moment the sound of the shower water is heard [shut] off stage.* ARMY *looks up toward the shower.*] [He was] good, Maish.

MAISH [*Thoughtfully, turning toward [the shower.*]: [He was] the best. He had everything [once.] legs, brains. He could ta[lk] and you could fix him up with an aspirin. He was good all right. Oh brother—where am I ever gonna find one like him?

[*The camera pans over to the door leading to the shower. We get a shot of* MC CLINTOCK *from the waist up as he comes out. He dries himself off with a towel, then looks up.*]

MC CLINTOCK: Hey, Army. Bathrobe, huh? [*The bathrobe is thrown to him, and he puts it around him. We pull back for a cover shot as he walks back into the room toward the table. He stands there and does a little hop and jump routine on the floor, loosening up, throwing his shoulders and head back, breathing deeply, and moving his hands and feet.*] Feel better, Maish. Lot better. I kind of feels funny but—I'll be okay now. Got a lot of spring yet, huh? [*He moves his feet around, shuffling, ring-like. He shadow boxes a bit.*] How about it, Army? Still there, huh? [ARMY *nods, not able to say anything. He exchanges a look with* MAISH.]

MAISH [*Finally.*]: Mountain—sit down, huh?

[MC CLINTOCK *stops his dancing, looks from one to the other, goes over to the rubbing table, and sits down.*]

MC CLINTOCK: Sure, Maish. Sure. [*Then he waits expectantly.* MAISH *starts to say something, then he looks at* ARMY, *who turns away. Then he wets his lips.*]

MAISH: The doctor looked you over.

MC CLINTOCK [*Grins.*]: Yeah. I thought he was in here. I wasn't sure, though. [*He taps his head.*] A little groggy yet, you know?

MAISH [*Nods.*]: Yeah. Well, anyway he looked you over good this time.

CLINTOCK: Yeah?

H: He figures . . . he figures you've had it. [*Then turns away, coughs, takes out a cigar and lights it.* MC-LINTOCK *stares at him for a long moment.*]

CLINTOCK: What did you say, Maish?

H: The doctor says you've had it. No more. He says e got to leave now.

Leave? Leave where?

d and shouts.*]: Army! Lay it out for n, no more fights. You get it? You leave.

use. MC CLINTOCK *gets off*

the table, walks over to MAISH, *pokes at him with a
forefinger.*]

MC CLINTOCK: Leave? Maish, that's . . . that's crazy.

MAISH [*Shrugs, turns away.*]: So it's crazy. Maybe I think
it's crazy, but that's what the doctor says. Go fight the
commission. [*Deliberately turning his back on* MC-
CLINTOCK.] Have you got everything all cleared up here,
Army? [ARMY *nods.*]

MC CLINTOCK: Maish . . . ?

MAISH [*Without turning to him.*]: What do you want,
Mountain?

MC CLINTOCK: What'll I do?

MAISH: What'll you do? I dunno. You do whatever you
want to do. Anything you like. It's as easy as that.

MC CLINTOCK: I mean . . . I mean a guy's got to do something.

MAISH: So? A guy's got to do something. So you do something. Do anything you like.

MC CLINTOCK [*The words come out hard.*]: Maish, I don't
know anything but fighting. You know, fourteen years
pro. You know, Maish. I've been with you fourteen
years.

MAISH: And before that?

MC CLINTOCK [*Smiles and shrugs.*]: Before that what? Who
remembers?

ARMY: Why don't you go back home, Kid? You talk
about it enough. The green hills of Tennessee. Is that
what you call it? Go back home. Go gack to Tennessee.
The hills are probably still green.

MC CLINTOCK: What's back there? [*He takes a few steps
toward the other two men and looks from one to the
other as he talks.*] What's back there? I haven't been
back in all those years. I don't know anybody. Nobody'd
know me. [*And then suddenly as if struck by an after-
thought.*] Maish, we could try another state, maybe?

MAISH [*Shakes his head.*]: Now you're talking crazy. If
you don't pass muster in New York State, you don't pass
muster anyplace else. You know that.

MC CLINTOCK: Maybe some club fights. You know, un-
official.

MAISH: Where've you been? Those kind of club fights
went out with John L. Sullivan.

[ARMY *nods, follows* MAISH *to the door, then turns back toward* MC CLINTOCK.]

ARMY: Want me to help you dress, Mountain?

MC CLINTOCK [*Shakes his head.*]: No, no, I can dress myself. [*Then he looks across at* MAISH.] Maish?

MAISH: Yeah?

MC CLINTOCK: I'm . . . I'm sorry about tonight. I'm sorry I lost.

[*We cut to a very tight close-up of* MAISH *as his features work, and then he has to turn his eyes away*.]

MAISH: That's okay, Mountain. Don't give it another thought. [*He goes out and closes the door.* ARMY *sort of hangs back by the door.*]

ARMY [*Finally.*]: We can go over to the hotel later on and—and talk this out, make some plans.

[MC CLINTOCK *nods and doesn't say anything. Then* ARMY *goes out the door.* MC CLINTOCK *stands there numbly and motionless for a long moment.*]

[*We cut to: The corridor outside the dressing room.* MAISH *is walking very slowly down the corridor. He stops abruptly.*]

MAISH [*Waves and hollers.*]: Hey, Foxxy! Hey Fox!

[*A figure ahead of him pauses, turns, walks back toward him. This is a little mousy guy in a jacket, with a face like a weasel.*]

FOX: Whadda yuh say, Maish? I just seen Slaughter on Tenth Avenue. Was there enough left to sew together?

MAISH: Break your heart, does it?

FOX: I got my own troubles. [*And then very confidently.*] You want to see the kid now, Maish? I got him right out here. You said you might be interested—

MAISH: I said I *might* be.

FOX: Maish, he's a real sweetie. Middleweight. A good fast middleweight, but he's built like a tank and I can't get him matched on accounta the business.

MAISH: How is the business? Did you get that fixed up?

FOX: I was one year revoked. But you know that was a bum rap, Maish. To pinch a guy like me for fixing fights. It's a laugh. I swear, it's a laugh. I couldn't fix a parking ticket. But . . . an' . . . meanwhile, I got no contract with the kid because I got no license to manage,

so if he could just hook up with someone—you know—
a real solid guy to handle him for a bit—

MAISH: Foxxy, don't dress it up, will ya pal? If he's here,
put him on the block. Let's take a look at him. But
don't choke me with publicity.

FOX: Maish, you're a doll baby. You're an ever-loving
doll baby. [*He turns and shouts.*] Bobby! Bobby, Mr.
Loomis would like to look at ya.

[*At this moment a* FIGHTER *walks down the ramp from
out of the shadows and approaches them. He walks
with the stiff gait of an old rooster, and his face looks
like the battle of the Marne.*]

FOX: Here he is, Maish. Bobby Menzey.

MAISH [*Looks him over with the practiced eye of a
veteran.*]: So what's to tell, Foxxy? I'd like to see him
spar.

FOX: He'll spar—he'll spar. I'll get a boy lined up at the
gym tomorrow.

MAISH: Tell me about him. [*The* FIGHTER *starts to say
something.* MAISH *holds up his hand and points to* FOX.]
Let *him* talk.

FOX: Like I told you before, Maish, he's a sweetheart.
He's fought mostly out west.

MAISH: What's his record?

FOX [*Wets his lips.*]: Like I say, he's fought mostly out
west.

MAISH: Wins and losses. Lay them out. Is that hard?

FOX: Well . . . well, his record ain't so well known, Maish.
He was fighting out west.

MAISH [*Suddenly reaches out and grabs* FOX *by the vest,
pulling him toward him.*]: What are you trying to pull
off, Fox?

FOX [*With a worried look toward his fighter.*]: Go easy on
the kid, Maish—

MAISH: Kid? I'd hate to have my hands in boiling water
since he was a kid. [*Turns to the fighter.*] *What's* your
name?

FIGHTER: Menzey—Bobby Menzey. Maybe you heard of
me.

MAISH: I heard about you yesterday. But the last time I
saw you fight, your name wasn't Bobby Menzey. [*The*
FIGHTER *gulps and starts to stammer.*]

FOX [*Hurriedly*.]: You've got him mixed up, Maish? Menzey. Bobby Menzey. M-E-N-Z-E-Y.

MAISH: Stop it! Stop me if I'm wrong. La Plant, isn't it? In 1949 you were a lightweight—a real comer. Sixteen straight. Then you fought Red Johns in Syracuse. He knocked you out in the second round. Then you lost six or seven straight. After that I saw you in Detroit. That was three, four years ago. [*The* FIGHTER *looks at* FOX *helplessly*.]

FOX [*With a huge smile*.]: You got me, Maish. You really got me. I had him change his name—but that don't prove nothing about his fighting.

MAISH: It doesn't huh? It means you're trying to pass off a stumblebum on me as a comer [*He grabs* MENZEY'S *face and turns it to the light*.] Look at it. I know a bleeder when I see one. One punch and his face falls apart. And this is the sweetheart, huh? This guy will never live to see the day when he's anything else besides a poor, beat-up slob.

FIGHTER: What're you talkin' about? I'm as good as I ever was.

FOX: That's right. He's still got it, Maish. Would I try to put something over on you? [*He slaps him expansively on the arm*.] Would I? A wise one like you? Think I'm crazy or something? It's to laugh, Maish. I swear, it's to laugh. Go ahead Bobby. Box around a little for him. Go ahead. [*The* FIGHTER *starts to shadow-box in front of them*. MAISH *and* ARMY *exchange a look*.]

FOX: Who does he remind you of? Baer?

MAISH: Yeah, a big brown one with a ring in his nose.

FOX: Look, Maish—

MAISH: Knock it off. You'd better send him back to your factory. Right now.

FOX: Maish, give me a break, will ya?

MAISH: I've given you a break. I won't split your head. That's a break. I'll see you around, Fox. [*He turns and walks past him. The* FIGHTER, *suddenly seeing his shadow against a wall, begins to shadow-box*.]

FOX [*Pushes him*.]: Mud for brains! So stop already. No deal.

[*The camera picks up* MAISH *as he starts up the ramp. The* MAN *steps out from the wall once again and stops him*.]

MAN: Hey, Loomis . . .

MAISH: I'll get it! I'll get it! What does Henson need bail money? I told you I'd get it for you. Now lay off, willya?

MAN: Mr. Henson would like to know *where* you're going to get it.

MAISH: Mr. Henson'll have to guess.

MAN: Mr. Henson will take it out of your skin, Loomis. Just remember that.

[*He walks up the ramp and disappears.* MAISH *watches him go and the tight, set look on his face disintegrates, and suddenly he is very frightened. But he recomposes his face when he sees* ARMY *walking toward him.*]

MAISH [*With a forced smile.*]: Come on, I'll buy you a drink.

ARMY [*Looks toward the ramp.*]: Fox showing off his wares? You work fast, Maish.

MAISH: People have to eat—or are you different?

ARMY: I'm not the one drumming up trade five minutes after I get the word.

MAISH: I'm drumming it up for you, too, remember, Boy Scout! Fox has got a boy and he can't handle him. I've got no boy and I *can* handle him. That's simple stuff, Army. That's arithmetic. [*Then his shoulders sag.*] What difference? He was a clinker. The worst.

ARMY: What now?

MAISH: I think I'll go shadow-box off a cliff. Come on, I *need* a drink.

ARMY [*Nods toward the dressing room.*]: I'll wait for the kid.

MAISH: Sure. [*Then he looks up toward the ceiling and grins.*] The kid. That's what I call him, too. The kid. I think that's where we goofed. As long as they wear trunks and gloves, we think they're kids. They're old men. They're the oldest. I'll see you later on, Army.

[*He walks on up the ramp, pausing near the top to look at a poster which advertises the fight that night. On it is a picture of Mountain and his opponent, and the words "Main Bout" are prominent. He takes a few steps farther and looks at another poster. This one shows two big clowns in a plug for a wrestling match. He takes a few steps closer to the poster and stares at it, taps it thoughtfully with his finger.*]

[*We cut to: A brief tight close-up of* ARMY *noticing this.*]
[*Then we cut to: A long shot as* MAISH *disappears up the ramp.*]

[*Dissolve to: A shot of a little hotel and adjoining bar as seen through its front window.*]

[*Dissolve through: The interior, and get a cover shot of the entire place. This is about a twenty-foot-square dingy little bistro frequented by people in the fight business— mostly ex-fighters and ring hangers-on. On the wall are pictures of fighters going back to the 1800s. A championship belt is in a frame over the bar. Other than these, the place has no pretensions. It is simply there to serve drink and make up for what is probably a loss in the hotel business alongside. At the far end of the room there's a handful of fighters, obviously in nightly klatch. One fighter is holding sway with an excited blow by blow from some monumental battle of years before. As we pan around the room we pick up part of his speech.*]

FIGHTER #1: So he comes in at me. [*He holds both his hands up.*]

FIGHTER #2: Yeah. Yeah. Go ahead.

FIGHTER #1: He comes at me. I sized him up. He throws a left, I duck. He throws another left. I duck. Then he throws another left.

FIGHTER #2: You duck.

FIGHTER #1: No, I don't duck. I take it right smack dab on the jaw. I'm down. Oh man, am I down.

[*We pan past them at this moment for a shot of* MC CLIN-TOCK *and* ARMY *as they enter. The* BARTENDER *is a flat-nosed ex-pug who nods very briefly at them as they sit on the stools.*]

BARTENDER: How're you, Mountain? Army?

ARMY: Two beers, huh, Charlie?

BARTENDER: Two beers. [*He draws them and expertly shoots them down the bar, one at a time.* ARMY *takes out some money: three one-dollar bills. Separates them, lays one on the counter.*] How'd you do, Mountain?

MC CLINTOCK: Not so good, Charlie. Went the route, though. Doc says I'm over the hill now.

BARTENDER [*Clucks.*]: That's too bad. [*Then philosophi-*

cally.] So—now yuh can join the Wednesday evening coffee klatch. I'm getting tired of the same old stories. You can bring them up to date. [*He jerks with his thumb in the direction of the rear of the room, then with a long look at* MC CLINTOCK *he takes out a bottle and says:*] Have one on the house. This is the only one in the house that ain't watered. [*He pours healthy-sized glasses and shoves them in front of each of them, and walks back down the bar.*]

ARMY [*Turns to* MOUNTAIN, *holds up his glass.*]: To Mountain McClintock. A hundred and eleven fights.

MC CLINTOCK: He wasn't no good—but he never took a dive.
[ARMY *returns the laugh, starts to drink. He takes only the barest of sips, looking over the top of his glass at* MOUNTAIN, *a sad and knowing look on his face. At this moment* ARMY *sees the reflection of* MAISH *in the mirror. He turns around.*]

ARMY: Hey, Maish. Here we are. [MAISH *walks over to them.*]

MAISH: Let's get a booth.

MC CLINTOCK: How're you doing, Maish?

MAISH: I'll tell yuh when we get to the booth.
[*As they get away from the bar, a drunk tipsily bangs into* MAISH, *and* MC CLINTOCK *rather firmly places him out of the way.*]

MC CLINTOCK: Watch it. That's my manager. [*The three men go to the rear and sit in an empty booth.*]

MAISH [*Without any preliminaries. Obviously intent on getting this over.*]: What did you do with your dough, Mountain?

MC CLINTOCK: You mean—

MAISH [*Impatiently.*]: The dough for the fight. You got six hundred thirty-three bucks, didn't you? Where is it?

MC CLINTOCK: It's mostly gone. I owed the hotel half of it, Maish.

MAISH [*Wets his lips.*]: What about the other half?

MC CLINTOCK [*Very slowly.*]: Well, I suppose I've got some of it—

MAISH [*Excited, blurts it out.*]: Look, don't get cute with me. This is Maish. I asked you a question now. Have you got any money at all?
[MC CLINTOCK *reaches into his pants and pulls out a*

132   GREAT TELEVISION PLAYS

*crumpled roll of bills. He lays them out one at a time
on the table.*]

MC CLINTOCK: I've got some. Twenty, forty, fifty-five,
fifty-six, fifty-seven, fifty-eight bucks, Maish. [*He collects and shoves it over in a bunch to* MAISH.] Here.

MAISH: Fifty-eight bucks. [*He picks it up and looks at it.
He throws it back down on the table.*]

ARMY [*A little wisely.*]: What's the matter, Maish? You in
hock?

MAISH [*Nods.*]: Heavy.

ARMY: How much?

MAISH: Three thousand dollars.

ARMY [*Whistles.*]: Three thousand dollars.

MC CLINTOCK [*Very worried.*]: Gee, Maish, that's a lot of
money. How're we gonna get it?

MAISH: I don't know. But I haven't got much time.

ARMY: How did you get into that kind of a crack, Maish?

MAISH [*With a side look at* MC CLINTOCK, *his tone
changes.*]: You don't know, huh? Mountain, when you
were in the hospital last month with a bum hand, remember?

ARMY: That comes off the top. What're you givin' him?

MAISH: Sure. But I brought in a specialist, didn't I? And
that came out of here. [*He pats his pocket.*] And the
training camp. He wanted to go up to New Jersey, so he
went up to New Jersey. How much do you think that cost
me a month? A lot more than my cut, I'll tell ya.

MC CLINTOCK: Gee, Maish, I didn't know that—

MAISH: I'm not complaining. I'm not complaining. But
the money goes, you know. And one half of your take
hasn't been much lately. It doesn't cover expenses, so
I've been filling up the rest of it for you. Well, now we've
got to pay the fiddler, Kid. We're at the end of the line
now.

MC CLINTOCK [*His face very concerned.*]: I've been
thinkin', Maish, if I could get me a job—you know,
something to tide us over—

MAISH [*Barely listening to him.*]: Sure. Sure. [*Then to
ARMY:*] Jake Green's got a lightweight he's touting.
Maybe we could buy a piece. [*He looks up to the ceiling.*] Yeah, we could buy a piece. With what? We could
get his thumb. That I could afford.

MC CLINTOCK [*Very softly*.]: Get a new boy, Maish?

ARMY [*With a quick look at* MAISH.]: Not for a while yet, Mountain, just an idea.

MC CLINTOCK: Oh. Oh. I see. [*His eyes go around the room looking at the people, the tables, and the pictures. Very quietly.*] I remember the first night I come in here, Maish. I remember the guy's name even. Shipsky. Morty Shipsky. I knocked him out in the first round. And you and Army stood up on the bar and you shouted . . . you shouted, "Everybody take a drink on Harlan McClintock, the next champ." [*He looks from one to the other.*] Remember? That was the night you give me the name "Mountain."

ARMY [*Quietly*.]: I remember.

MC CLINTOCK: Sure. You asked me where I was from and I told you. I told you I lived in Tennessee on a mountain. And that's when . . . that's when Maish here says, "That's what we'll call ya. We'll call ya Mountain." [*He looks around the room again.*] How many nights we come in here, Maish? How many nights?

ARMY: A lot of 'em.

MC CLINTOCK: Couple of hundred, I guess? Couple of hundred nights. We could just sit and talk here by the hour about this fight or that fight, or some other fighter, or a fight we were gonna get. By the hour.

MAISH [*A little disjointedly*.]: It's the breaks, that's all. It's the breaks.

MC CLINTOCK: All of a sudden I . . . I'm sittin' here and it becomes different. Like . . . like right now even . . . I'm on the outside lookin' in. Like . . . I didn't belong with you guys any more. [*Then suddenly his face becomes a mask as realization seems to flood into it, and he slowly gets up on his feet.*]

ARMY: Look, Mountain—

MAISH: Why don't you sit down and have another drink? It's early—

MC CLINTOCK [*Shakes his head*.]: I think I'll just . . . I'll just take a walk. I'll see you later. [*He turns to go and is suddenly aware of the little knot of men in the back of the room still talking about fights. He looks at them for a moment, almost winces, and then to nobody in particular, says:*] That's no way. That's no way at all.

ARMY: What did you say, Mountain?

MC CLINTOCK [*As if awakened suddenly*.]: Nothin'. Nothin', Army. I'll see you later.

[MC CLINTOCK *turns and walks down the room to the door and goes out. The* BARTENDER *comes over with a tray and places it on the table in front of* MAISH *and* ARMY.]

BARTENDER: How about you, Army? You want something? [ARMY *doesn't answer him. He is staring toward the door.* MAISH *drops a coin on the tray and makes a motion with his head for the* BARTENDER *to get lost. The* BARTENDER *walks back towards the bar*.]

MAISH: Hey, Army.

ARMY [*Without looking at him*.]: What?

MAISH: Look at me when I'm talking to yuh, will yuh? I don't like talking to a guy's neck.

ARMY [*Reluctantly turns toward him*.]: How'd you lose the dough?

MAISH: How do you think?

ARMY: You bet against him, didn't you?

MAISH [*Not meeting his eyes*.]: Something like that.

ARMY: You don't sidestep very good.

MAISH: You want it clearer, huh?

ARMY: A little bit.

MAISH: I said he wouldn't go seven.

ARMY [*Smiles a crooked little smile*.]: Big disappointment, huh?

MAISH: There was another way? The minute they tell me he was matched against Gibbons I figure we should throw in the towel while he's signing the contract. Save wear and tear. Gibbons! Thirty-one fights and thirty-one wins. He's got a lit fuse in each hand, and they match him against the Mountain.

ARMY: They match him?

MAISH: Did I? I just go through the motions. Good fast brawl they said. Couple of nice crowd-pleasers in a pier six. Harlan Mountain McClintock, ex-leading heavyweight contender. Ex is right. Very ex. Eight years ex.— He's past prime, Army. I take what I can find—you know that. They say fight Gibbons, I say okay. They say Marciano. I say bring on Marciano.

ARMY: You coulda told 'em—

MAISH: Tell 'em, tell 'em, tell 'em. Tell 'em what? Tell 'em I've got a dead weight has-been on my back? That he shouldn't fight any more? And then what do I do? Put in for a pension?

[*At this moment a* MAN *walks up to the table, nods briefly at* ARMY, *and then smiles broadly at* MAISH.]

MAN: What's the good word, Maish?

MAISH [*Staring straight ahead.*]: Blow. That's a good word. I don't want any.

MAN: How do you know what I'm selling?

MAISH: So pitch. I'm busy.

MAN: Mr. Henson sent me.

[MAISH'S *hand hits the ashtray nervously and knocks it off the table.* MAISH *bends down to pick it up.*]

[*Cut to: Tight close-up of the* MAN'S *foot on* MAISH'S *hand.* MAISH *looks up from the floor, his face dead white.*]

MAN: Now you pitch. Tell me when Mr. Henson can expect his dough.

MAISH: Soon.

MAN: How soon is soon?

MAISH: Three weeks.

MAN: You said two, didn't you? [MAISH *bites his lips. The* MAN'S *foot remains on his hand.*]

MAISH [*His voice a croak.*]: Two weeks. [*The* MAN *lifts his foot, picks up the ashtray, sets it back on the table.*]

MAN: You dropped something, Mr. Loomis. I'll see you in two weeks.

[*He turns and walks away.* ARMY *stares across the table at* MAISH. MAISH *takes out a handkerchief and wipes his face. Then reaches for a half-smoked cigar he pulls out of his pocket. Then he pats around for a match.*]

MAISH: Got a match?

ARMY: You and a mouse. That's a match.

MAISH: Who am I, Atlas? These guys play for real, Army, you know that. This is no bank transaction. If I welsh, you can take a spoon, scoop what's left of me off the wall and put it in a cup. That's how serious they look on bets. And if they don't go to that trouble . . . they'll get my license so quick they'll blur the ink. I won't be able to sell peanuts at a fight, so I'm licked either way.

ARMY: Who told you to bet?

MAISH: Who told me I hadda eat?

ARMY: You picked the sport.

MAISH: This isn't a sport. If there was headroom, they'd hold them in sewers. So what do I do?

ARMY [*Very quietly*.]: What does the Mountain do?

MAISH: You tell me. That's this precious business of ours. He gives them a million dollars' worth of fighting for fourteen years. And then they're not interested in paying for the dump truck to cart 'im away. The sport. The sport and the precious crowd.

ARMY: *You* ever buy him a ticket back to Tennessee?

MAISH: Don't stick it on me. All I do is curry the horses. I'm one of the stable boys. I don't set up the rules. I get sucked in just like he does. [*He stares at the chair* MOUNTAIN *was sitting in.*] He asks me. . . . He sits there and he asks me, "What'll I do, Maish?" He asks *me* what he's gonna do. Like I was the Book of Knowledge, and I'm supposed to tell him. I don't know what to tell him. I'm so scared right now, Army, that—

ARMY: Stop it. You lost a bank roll and a meal ticket. But this poor beat-up kid—did you ever figure out what he lost tonight?

MAISH: You don't think I feel sorry for him? I don't want to hurt that kid, Army. I swear I don't want to hurt him. He thinks he's the only one that's got a memory. I got a memory, too. I remember him like he was. Like the first day he comes into my office. All hands and feet and his mouth full of teeth, and he talks like General Lee. [*He shakes his head.* MAISH *pats in his pocket again for a match.* ARMY *lights his cigar.*]

ARMY: Take one on me. [*Long pause.*] You talk about memories, Maish. Remember Christmas 1945? Right at this table. We had six bucks between us. Four of it you spent on a beefsteak and a new tie for him. Remember that, Maish?

MAISH [*Nods.*]: Sure. That horrible-lookin' tie. He wore it until there wasn't anything left of it.

ARMY: I remember a lot of times like that. That time in Scranton when that big Swede knocked him out. Remember? We couldn't get him back on his feet. They took him to a hospital that night. I remember waiting outside in the corridor with you. [MAISH *nods*.] You cried that night, Maish.

MAISH: All right, knock it off.

ARMY: Okay. But you hear me out now, Maish. I'm telling you this now. I'm telling you that I love this guy like he was of my flesh. And I figure if I don't watch for him and weep for him now nobody else will, least of all you for some reason. So be careful, Maish. That's what I'm telling you now. Be careful.

[ARMY *rises, leaves the table, goes across the room and out the door.* MAISH *watches him for a moment and then rises after him. He starts to walk slowly toward the door.*]

[*Dissolve to: The alley outside of the fight area. We see* MC CLINTOCK *very slowly walking into the alley, aimlessly without direction. Once in the center of the alley, he leans against the wall, his back touching one of the torn posters. The crowd noise comes up momentarily loud and sharp.* MC CLINTOCK'S *head goes up. He slowly turns so that he is face to face with the picture of a boxer on the poster with his hands up. And then for no rhyme or reason,* MC CLINTOCK *starts to spar with the picture. First lightly as if he knew it were a joke, then much more seriously until pretty soon his hands flick out in short jabs, they hit the wall, and they hurt. He suddenly draws back with his right as if to smash at the poster when suddenly a hand comes down on his shoulder. He stops. His head goes down. We pull back to see* MAISH *standing near him.*]

MAISH: Mountain, take it easy.

MOUNTAIN [*Nods slowly, numbly.*]: Yeah. Yeah. Maish. Take it easy.

MAISH: The world didn't end tonight. Remember that. The world didn't end because you left the ring. It didn't end for you either.

MC CLINTOCK: Sure. Sure, Maish. Just . . . just stick around for a little, will ya? I could always depend on you, Maish. I always . . . I always needed to depend on you.

[MAISH *nods slowly, pats his arm, but as he does so his eyes travel down the wall to another poster showing a big, stupid Arabian Prince in a wrestling costume. And there is a big sign "Wrestling" over the top of it.* MAISH'S *eyes slowly move from the poster to* MC CLINTOCK, *who stares up at him hopefully like a pet dog desperately needing reassurance.*]

MAISH [*Wets his lips.*]: C'mon let's get out of here.

[*The two men slowly walk away and down the alley. Slow fade to black.*]

ACT II

[*We dissolve to: An anteroom of a small office with a sign on the door: "New York State Employment Office." Sitting on a bench are* MC CLINTOCK *and* ARMY, *the former appearing nervous and fidgety. He is constantly running a finger through his collar that is much too tight as are his suit, shirt and everything else that he wears. He looks helplessly at* ARMY, *who pats his arm reassuringly.*]

ARMY: You look fine. Don't worry. You look just great.

MC CLINTOCK [*In a whisper.*]: But what do I say, Army?

ARMY: What d'ya mean, what d'ya say? Just tell her you want a job, that's all. It's simple.

MC CLINTOCK: But what kind of a job?

ARMY: You don't have to worry about that. You just tell her the sort of thing you can do, and it's up to them to find you one.

MC CLINTOCK: Army, in the past two days I've been thirty-five places already. Most of these jokers won't even let me in the door.

ARMY: It's different here. This place is official. They're here just to get people jobs. People like you that can't find them easy on their own.

[*At this moment a young woman appears at the door of the inner office.*]

GRACE: Mr. McClintock, please.

[MC CLINTOCK *bolts to his feet, almost upsetting* ARMY.]

MC CLINTOCK: That's me! That's me!

GRACE [*Smiles.*]: In here please, Mr. McClintock.

[MC CLINTOCK *turns to* ARMY *and grabs his arms.*]

ARMY [*Firmly removes his fingers.*]: I'm right here at ringside, but I can't go in to fight for you. Go ahead.

[MC CLINTOCK, *with another journey of his finger through*

his collar, walks hesitantly after the young woman. We pan with them into her office as the door closes. He turns around with a start at its closing.]

GRACE: Sit down, Mr. McClintock. Right over here please, near the desk.

MC CLINTOCK: Thanks. Thank you very much. [*He sits down with another eye toward the door. They both start to speak together.*] I was—

GRACE: Now, Mr. McClintock—

MC CLINTOCK: I was just wondering if—Oh I beg your pardon.

GRACE: You were going to say?

MC CLINTOCK: I was just wondering if my friend could come in?

GRACE: Is he looking for employment, too?

MC CLINTOCK: No. No, not exactly but—well, he's kind of my handler.

GRACE: I beg your pardon?

MC CLINTOCK [*Wets his lips.*]: It's okay, he'll stay out there.

[*Then she looks at him and smiles, looks through a sheet of paper.*]

GRACE: Harlan McClintock. Your age is—

MC CLINTOCK: Thirty-three.

[*She makes a little notation with a pencil.*]

GRACE: Place of birth?

MC CLINTOCK: Kenesaw, Tennessee.

GRACE: I see. Your education? [*She looks up at him.*] Mr. McClintock, you left that blank here.

MC CLINTOCK: My education? You mean school?

GRACE: That's right.

MC CLINTOCK: Ninth grade.

GRACE: Then you left, is that it?

MC CLINTOCK [*Nods.*]: Then I left.

GRACE: Now your field of interest.

MC CLINTOCK: I beg your pardon?

GRACE: Your field of interest. What do you like to do?

MC CLINTOCK: Most anything. I don't much care.

GRACE [*Looks down at his sheet and frowns slightly.*]: Past employment record, Mr. McClintock. You have nothing written down there. [*Then she looks up at him.*] Who've been your past employers?

MC CLINTOCK: Well . . . you see . . . I really haven't

had past employers. I mean past employers like you mean down on that sheet. I've always been kind of on my own except you might say I've been working for Maish.

GRACE: Maish?

MC CLINTOCK: You see, all I've been doing the past fourteen years is fightin'.

GRACE: Fighting?

MC CLINTOCK: That's right. You know, in the ring.

GRACE: You mean a prizefighter.

MC CLINTOCK [*Smiles.*]: That's right. Prizefighter.

GRACE: A professional prizefighter.

MC CLINTOCK [*Delightedly.*]: Yeah, that's it. You catch on. A professional prizefighter. Heavyweight.

[GRACE *stares at him for a moment, and we cut to a tight close-up of* MC CLINTOCK'S *face as he becomes conscious of her stare. He almost unconsciously puts one hand across his face to hide the scar tissue. He turns his face away ever so slightly.* GRACE *notices this and turns away herself, and then looks down again at the paper.*]

GRACE: That sounds like interesting work, Mr. McClintock.

MC CLINTOCK [*Looks up at her.*]: Well it's . . . it's a living. I don't want you to go to no trouble. Army says I should just tell you that . . . well, anything you got's jake with me. Dishwashing, anything.

[*She looks at him again for a long moment.*]

GRACE [*Kindly.*]: Let's see if we can't examine something else, Mr. McClintock—something you might like even more. How about factory work?

MC CLINTOCK [*Shakes his head.*]: I never worked in a factory. I wouldn't know anything about it.

GRACE: No sort of assembly-like work, blueprint reading, anything like that? [*He shakes his head, wets his lips.*] Anything in sales, Mr. McClintock? There's a lot of openings in that sort of thing now. Department-store work? Anything like that?

MC CLINTOCK [*Shakes his head.*]: I . . . I couldn't do anything like that. I couldn't sell nothin'. [*Then with a kind of a lopsided grin.*] With my face I'd scare away the customers. [*He laughs lightly at this, and when he looks up, she is staring at him, not laughing with him at all. He becomes embarrassed now and half rises to his feet.*]

Look, Miss, I don't want to take up your time. [*And now in his hopelessness, the words come out; he forgets his embarrassment.*] The only reason I come is because Army said I should come. I've been answering all these ads like I told you, and I've been getting no place at all. Maish needs the dough real bad, and I can't do nothin' for him any more, and I got to. I got to get some kind of a job. Don't make any difference what I do. Anything at all.

GRACE: Mr. McClintock—

MC CLINTOCK [*Unaware of her now.*]: A guy goes along fourteen years. All he does is fight. Once a week, twice a week, prelims, semifinals, finals. He don't know nothin' but that. All he can do is fight. Then they tell him no more. And what's he do? *What's he supposed to do?* What's he supposed to know how to do besides fight? They got poor Maish tied up by the ears, and I got to do somethin' for him—[*He looks down at his hands. Then he pauses for a moment, then sits down hesitantly in a chair.*]

GRACE [*Quietly.*]: Mr. McClintock, we handle a lot of placements here. I'm sure we can find you something—

MC CLINTOCK: I know you're going to do the best you can . . . but . . . [*He points to the paper on her desk.*] I don't fit in any of the holes. I mean that question there. Why did you leave your last job? State reason.

GRACE: That's question nine. You see, Mr. McClintock— what that means—

MC CLINTOCK: I understand it but what do I write down? What do I write down that would make sense? I left my last job because I got hit so much that I was on my way to punchy land and I'd probably go blind. How would that read there?

GRACE [*Eyes narrow.*] Punchy land?

MC CLINTOCK: Sure. You fight so long and then you walk around on your heels listening to the bells. That's what happens to you. Doc looks at my eyes—says one or two more, I might go blind.

GRACE [*Very softly.*]: I see.

MC CLINTOCK [*Getting excited again.*]: And that's not fair. It's a dirty break, that's all. In 1948 they ranked me number five. I'm not kidding ya. Number five. And that wasn't any easy year neither. There was Charles and

Wolcott and Louis still around. And they had me up there at number five. Maish was sure that—

GRACE: Maish? Who's Maish, Mr. McClintock?

MC CLINTOCK: Maish is my manager. And where does it leave him? That's a nice thing to do to a guy who's kept you going for fourteen years. You stop cold on him. So it's a bum break. It ain't fair at all. [*Then he rises, and he turns his back to her and he slowly subsides.*] I'm sorry . . . I'm real sorry, Miss. I didn't mean to blow up like that. You ought to kick me out of here. Honest, I'm real sorry.

GRACE [*Again quietly.*]: That's perfectly all right, Mr. Mc-Clintock. As long as you've got your address down here, we'll contact you if anything comes up, and we'll— [*She stops, staring across the room at him. At the big shoulders that are slumped in front of her and the big hands down by his sides that clench and unclench. A certain softness shows in her face. A pitying look. . . . She wets her lips and then forces a smile.*] Right after the war I did a lot of work with disabled veterans—[*As soon as she has said this she is sorry. His head jerks up and he turns slowly toward her.*]

MC CLINTOCK: Yeah? Go on.

GRACE: I meant . . . I meant you'd be surprised the . . . different kinds of openings that come up for— [*She struggles for a word.*]

MC CLINTOCK: For cripples. For those kind of guys?

GRACE: I didn't mean just that. I meant for people who have special problems.

MC CLINTOCK: I've got no special problems. [*He takes a step toward her.*] There wasn't no place on that question sheet of yours. But I was almost the heavyweight champion of the world. I'm a big, ugly slob and I look like a freak—but I was almost the heavyweight champion of the world. I'd like to put that down someplace on that paper. This isn't just a punk. This was a guy who was almost the *heavyweight champion of the world.*

[*He slams his fists on the desk. And then as quickly as the anger came it leaves. Very slowly he takes his hand from off the desk. He looks at it briefly, closes his eyes and turns away again. He looks down at his hand, feels the bruise over his eye, and stands there looking away from her.* GRACE *is staring at him all the time.*]

GRACE: Did you hurt your hand, Mr. McClintock?

MC CLINTOCK [*Looks at his hand.*]: I guess I did. That's the . . . that's the thing of it. When you go for so long, the hurt piles up and you don't even feel them. You get out of the ring, and you go back to a dressing room, and you look in the mirror. You look like somebody just ran over you with a tractor—but somehow it doesn't seem to hurt. There's always a reason for it. You know that . . . you know that you just took another step up. Then after the last one—when the wad's all shot, and you're over the hill and there aren't going to be any more—then suddenly you do start to hurt. The punches you got fourteen years ago—even then. And when Maish and the Doc and Army—they were all standing around me that night and I heard somebody say—he's wound up. Then it hurts. Then it hurts like you've got to scream. Like now. It hurts now. Before at least—before, every little piece of skin they took off you—was part of the bill you had to pay. And then all of a sudden one night you have to throw all the fourteen years out into an alley and you know then that you've been paying that bill for nothing.

[*We cut to: A very tight close-up of GRACE's face as she comes around from behind her desk. She touches his arm tentatively.*]

GRACE: Mr. McClintock . . . I think . . . I think we can get you something you'll like. Just give us time.

MC CLINTOCK [*Looks at her.*]: Something I'll like? Do that, Miss. I don't want much. Just . . . the heavyweight championship of the world. That's all.

[*He stares at her, and you can see in his face that he wants to say something . . . wants to apologize . . . wants to explain to her that this is a bitterness directed at no one, but it can't come out, it can't be articulated. He turns slowly and walks out of the room. She stands there watching him through the open door. We see ARMY rise, the two men exchange words and then they both leave. GRACE slowly closes the door, goes back to her desk pensively. Slow fade out on her face.*]

[*Fade on: A shot of Maish's hotel room—night. In the*

semidark room MAISH *and* ARMY *play cards.* MAISH *slaps down a card with tremendous vigor.*]

MAISH: Jack of Spades.

[ARMY *goes through a series of facial and body movements, shrugging left and right, opening and closing his mouth, drumming on the bridge of his nose with his fingers.*]

ARMY: That's good to know. That's very good to know.

[*He draws a card, throws it down.* MAISH *draws another, he throws it down.*] Queen of Spades.

MAISH: That's what it looks like, doesn't it?

ARMY [*Nods.*]: That's good to know. That's very good to know. [*He goes through the series of motions again.*] That's very good to know.

MAISH [*Looks up at him.*]: Army, would you not say that any more, please?

ARMY: Say what?

MAISH: "It's good to know. It's good to know. It's good to know." Everything is good to know with you.

[ARMY *grins, draws a card, throws it face down, lays out his hand, throws a single card across the table.*]

ARMY: I'll knock for two.

MAISH: You've got me. I've got a jack and eight free. You've got me . . .

ARMY That's good to know. [*Then he ducks away jokingly.* MAISH *rises and flings the cards at him across the table.*] C'mon, I'll play you another hand.

MAISH: Don't do me any favors. [*He rises and pats around his pockets.*]

ARMY [*Points to an ashtray.*]: It's over here. [MAISH *walks across the room, takes a half-smoked cigar out of an ashtray, lights it.*] One inch shorter you'd be smoking your nose.

MAISH: So does it hurt you?

ARMY: Wanna watch television? There's a fight on.

MAISH: You don't get enough of that, huh?

ARMY: It's somethin' to do.

MAISH: If it's somethin' to do, go to a bar, will ya. I get my gut full of it nine, ten hours a day. I don't like it in my hotel room.

ARMY: Cards?

MAISH: How about ice skating. You bored, Army? [*He*

chomps nervously on the cigar.] What am I going to do?

ARMY [*Shrugs.*]: Ask 'em for another week.

MAISH: Ask 'em, ask 'em, ask 'em—do you think it'll cut ice with them? They want their money. [*The phone rings and* MAISH *nervously and quickly picks it up. On the phone.*] Hello. Yeah. [*A pause.*] Well when he gets in, tell him I want to talk to him, will ya? No. I can't talk to you. I want to talk to Parelli himself. Thanks. [*He puts down the receiver and finds* ARMY *staring at him.*] Well, you want to lodge a complaint? You look it.

ARMY: Parelli handles wrestling.

MAISH: Is that a secret?

ARMY: What do you want with a wrestling promoter?

MAISH: You got the longest nose in the business.

ARMY: You gonna answer, Maish?

MAISH [*With an enforced matter-of-factness.*]: For a kick, Army. We'll let the kid wrestle a few.

ARMY: Mountain?

MAISH: Why not? They pay good for that stuff, just like they pay actors or somethin'. I could work up a routine for him—ya know? We could make him something like —well you know, like Gorgeous George and the Mad Baron—he'd be . . . he'd be Mountain McClintock the Mountaineer. We could dress him up in a coonskin hat and a . . . a . . . costume of some kind, and we could bill *his as* . . . [*He stops abruptly. He sees* ARMY *staring at him.*] It's money, ain't it?

ARMY: It's money sure, but what kind of money is it, Maish?

MAISH: What difference does it make what kind of money it is?

ARMY: A guy like him don't take getting laughed at.

MAISH [*Whirls around at him.*]: What're you talking about —a guy like him? So what is he? A prima donna? All of a sudden he's sensitive! All of a sudden he's very fragile like precious china or something. Since when does a guy like him get sensitive all of a sudden!

ARMY: Since when? Since we knowed him! That's since when. You never see things like that, Maish.

MAISH: Maybe I got no time. Ever look at it that way? Maybe I'm too busy stitching him up so he can show the next week. Maybe I'm too busy on my hands and knees pleading with a promoter to use him so we can get groceries. Maybe I've got no time to hold the poor sensitive boys on my lap.

ARMY: Hey, Maish—you stink.

MAISH: Sure, I stink. I'm a crummy, selfish louse—because for fourteen years I nurse along a pug, and instead of three square meals for my old age, I got nothing but debts and a headache. You want to know who owes who? Okay. Just check the records. Look at the wins and losses. The Mountain comes in at the short end. He owes me. I figure it's as simple as that. What do I ask of this guy? Stick on a costume and make a few people laugh a couple of minutes. Is that going to curdle his sensitive insides?

ARMY [ARMY's *voice has a barely perceptible tremor in it.*]: He's only got one thing left, Maish, that's his pride. You don't want to job that off. . . . [MAISH *doesn't answer.* ARMY *walks over to him and grabs him.*] . . . Leave something, will you? You talk about him when he was number-five contender in *Ring Magazine*. You want to remember him that way. Leave it so that's the way he'll remember himself. Not a . . . not a clown. Not like somebody who takes a pie in the face so he can eat that day. He was a somebody, Maish. Let it go at that. Don't turn him into a geek.

[MAISH *looks intensely at* ARMY. *He can't vocalize his frustration any more than he can put into words the sense of the truth that he gets from what* ARMY *has told him, and it is a truth that* MAISH *cannot answer. Finally he kicks at a table, upsetting a lamp.*]

MAISH: So I'm selling his soul on the street! So weep for him! So rip your clothes a little. So I may take an inch off his pride, but, by everything holy, I'll have a full gut to show for it. You can starve to death, wise guy. [*He turns almost aimlessly, not knowing what to do, and finally goes out the door and slams it. Dissolve out.*]

[*Fade on: With a shot of the squared circle bar as in Act I. It is midevening and the place is only partially filled. At the far end of the room the same group of old fighters stand in a semicircle around one of the others.* MC CLINTOCK *stands on their fringes listening, and as the men talk* MC CLINTOCK *studies their faces. All of them are scarred, ring-battered, and there's a kind of sameness in each face.*]

FIGHTER #1: That was Keister. Willie Keister. Used to fight out of Philly. Lightweight.

FIGHTER # 2: He wasn't never no lightweight. He always fought middle. I remember him good.

FIGHTER #1: Middleweight, your bleeding ears. He never weighed more than 135 pounds in his life.

[*This talk continues underneath as the camera moves away to take in a shot of the bar and the archway that adjoins the lobby of the little hotel. . . . From out of the lobby we see* GRACE *enter the bar. She looks around.*]

BARTENDER: Sorry, Miss, unescorted ladies ain't permitted.

GRACE: I was looking for Mr. McClintock. The man at the desk said he'd be in here.

BARTENDER: McClintock? The Mountain you mean. That's him. [*He points toward the end of the room.*]

GRACE: Thank you.

[*She walks very slowly toward the group of men in the rear, and when she gets close, we can then pick up what they are saying.*]

FIGHTER #1: So it's round four. He come out real slow like he always does.

FIGHTER #2: Yeah. He always did come out slow.

FIGHTER #1: He jabs a couple of times. Remember how he used to do that? From way up high on the shoulder. You could hardly see it coming.

FIGHTER #2: You hardly ever could.

FIGHTER #1: He touches me a couple of times up on the forehead. I back off. He keeps coming after me. I want him to lead. Now this is a guy you got to let lead, because he's the best counterpuncher in the business.

FIGHTER #2: Yeah. He can always counterpunch. Man, could that boy counterpunch. I remember one time in Chicago—

FIGHTER #3: Go ahead, Steve, go ahead.

FIGHTER #1: So, we keep sparring like that right on through the round. He don't hurt me, I don't hurt him. [*He continues to speak underneath as* MC CLINTOCK *turns and sees* GRACE. *He reacts, leaves the group and walks over to see her hurriedly.*]

MC CLINTOCK: Miss Carrie, what're you doin' here?

GRACE: Well I . . .

[*She is suddenly conscious of the rest of the men looking at her, and* MC CLINTOCK *sees this, too. He takes her arm.*]

MC CLINTOCK: Let's go over here and sit down. [*He takes her across to a booth, and they sit down. The men move away chuckling with an occasional glance at them.*]

GRACE: A friend of mine and I had dinner over at Mc-Cleary's. It isn't very far from here. She got a headache and went on home, and I—

MC CLINTOCK: Yeah?

GRACE: And I remembered your giving me your hotel and—

MC CLINTOCK: It was real nice of you to look me up. [*She looks around the room and smiles a little embarrassedly.*]

GRACE: You know—I've never been around here before.

MOUNTAIN [*Nods.*]: No change. If you're here once, you've seen it all.

GRACE [*Smiles.*]: Atmosphere.

MC CLINTOCK: Yeah, you might call it atmosphere. [*She looks over his shoulder at the men in the back of the room. One fighter is going through the motions of a battle.* GRACE *looks questioningly at him and then at* MC CLINTOCK.]

MC CLINTOCK: That? That goes on all the time around here. Maish says this part of the room is a graveyard. And those guys spend their time dying in here. Fighting their lives away inside their heads. That's what Maish says.

GRACE: That's . . . that's kind of sad.

MC CLINTOCK: I suppose it is.

GRACE [*With a smile leans toward him.*]: I've got a confession to make. I didn't eat at McCleary's, I ate at home. I came on purpose. I asked for you at your hotel. I've been thinking about you a lot, Mr. McClintock. [*There is a long pause.*] I was just wondering—

MC CLINTOCK: Yeah? Go ahead.

GRACE: I was just wondering if you ever thought of working with children. [*There's a long pause.*]

MC CLINTOCK: What?

GRACE: Work with children. Like a summer camp. You know, in athletics.

MC CLINTOCK: I—I never give it much thought.

GRACE: Do you like children?

MC CLINTOCK: Children? Well, I haven't had much to do with kids, but I've always liked them. [*Then thoughtfully, going over it in his mind.*] Yeah I like kids a lot. You were thinking of a summer camp or something—

GRACE: That's right. That sort of thing. In a month or so, there'll be a lot of openings. I was thinking . . . well, perhaps you ought to give that some thought.

MC CLINTOCK [*His hand goes to his face.*]: But they'd have to see me and listen to me talk and—

GRACE: Why not? You've got to begin someplace. You've got to give it a try.

MC CLINTOCK: Sure, I'm going to have to. [*Then he stares at her intently.*] Why did you come here tonight?

GRACE [*Looks away.*]: I've been thinking about you. I want to help—if I can. [*Then as if to dispel the seriousness of the mood, she cocks her head, grins very girllike.*] How about it, Mr. McClintock—could I have a beer?

MC CLINTOCK: A beer? You mean here?

GRACE: I kind of like it here.

MC CLINTOCK [*Grins at her.*]: Why sure. [*He stands up and calls to the* BARTENDER, *who is passing.*] Hey, Charlie! Two beers, huh? [*The* BARTENDER *acknowledges with a wave, goes back toward the bar.* MC CLINTOCK *sits down again and looks across the table at her.*]

GRACE [*Points to the jukebox.*]: How about music?

MC CLINTOCK: What?

GRACE: Don't you like to listen to music when you drink beer?

MC CLINTOCK: Music? Why . . . I never even gave it much thought. Sure. Sure, we can play music. [*He rises, fishes in his pocket, takes out a coin, puts it in the jukebox.*]

[*Cut to: A tight close-up of* FIGHTER #2 *across the room, a toothless, terribly ugly little man.*]

FIGHTER #2 [*Smiles.*]: Hey, Mountain—play "My Heart Tell Me."

[*There's laughter at this.* MC CLINTOCK *quickly turns his face away, shoves a coin in the slot, indiscriminately punches a few buttons, then returns to the booth.* BAR-TENDER *brings over two bottles of beer, slops them down in front of them.*]

MC CLINTOCK: How about a glass, Charlie, for the lady?

BARTENDER [*Over his shoulder as he heads back to the bar.*]: Fancy-schmancey. [*There's another moment's pause.*]

GRACE: Pretty.

MC CLINTOCK [*Listens for a moment.*]: Yeah. Yeah, it is kind of pretty. Them are violins.

GRACE [*Smiles.*]: Beautiful.

MC CLINTOCK: I never paid much attention to music before. I never had much time.

GRACE: What's that?

MC CLINTOCK: Music. Just plain old music. [*He looks away thoughtfully for a moment.*] The only music I know by heart really is the National Anthem because they play it before every fight. The National Anthem. [GRACE *smiles at this.*] Oh, yeah—there was Smiley Collins, too.

GRACE: Who's Smiley Collins?

MC CLINTOCK: He was a fighter. He used to play a violin. [*A pause.*] That's funny, ain't it? He was a fighter, but he used to play a violin. [*As* MC CLINTOCK *talks, we can see him losing himself in the conversation and in the sheer delight of having a girl across from him.*]

GRACE: He used to play the violin? Seriously?

MC CLINTOCK: Real serious. Oh, I don't know nothin' about his violin playing—but, oh man, did that boy have a right hand. Like dynamite. He could knock down a wall with it.

GRACE: What about his violin—

MC CLINTOCK [*Interrupts her, not even hearing her.*]: I remember his last fight. He fought a guy by the name of Willie Floyd. Floyd had twenty pounds on him.

[*At this moment the* BARTENDER *brings a glass, puts it down in front of* GRACE, *then walks away.* MC CLINTOCK *picks up her bottle and pours the beer for her.*]

GRACE [*Smiles.*]: Thanks.

MC CLINTOCK: They don't have many ladies here—that's the reason he forgets to put glasses out. [*He holds up his bottle to her glass.*] Drink hearty. That's what Maish always says. Drink hearty.

GRACE [*Smiles.*]: Drink hearty. Drink hearty, Mr. Mc-Clintock. [*The two of them drink. His eyes never leave her face. She notices this and smiles again.*] You think a lot of Maish, don't you?

MC CLINTOCK: He's number one. They don't come like him.

GRACE: He was your manager.

MC CLINTOCK [*Nods.*]: Yeah, for fourteen years. He's been a real great friend, not just a manager. In the old days . . . in the old days when I was just getting started —Maish would stake me to everything from clothes to chow. He's a real great guy. [*Then he stops abruptly and stares at her.*] Why ain't you married?

GRACE [*Laughs.*]: Should I be?

MC CLINTOCK [*Nods.*]: You're pretty. Not just pretty— you're beautiful.

GRACE: Thank you.

MC CLINTOCK: Pretty as a young colt. That's what my old man used to say.

GRACE: Your father?

MC CLINTOCK [*Nods.*]: Yeah. A girl's as pretty as a young colt, so he used to tell me.

GRACE [*Very interested.*]: Go ahead, Mountain—

MC CLINTOCK: About my father? Big guy. Nice old guy, too. I remember once—I fought a guy named Jazzo. Elmer Jazzo. And looked just like my old man. Spittin' image. And in the first round I didn't even want to hit him. Then in round two I shut my eyes and I—

GRACE [*Interrupts.*]: Mountain.

MC CLINTOCK [*Looks at her.*]: Yeah?

GRACE: There isn't much else, is there—besides fighting?

MC CLINTOCK [*Very thoughtfully looks away.*]: No. No, there isn't, I guess. I'm . . . I'm sorry . . .

GRACE: Don't be. It's just that there is so much more for you that you'll be able to find now.

[*They look at each other and both smile. The music is playing, and they are both aware of it suddenly.*]

GRACE: Hey, Mountain—

MC CLINTOCK: Yeah?

GRACE: Them are violins.

[*They both laugh. The camera pulls away from them as*

they start to talk, lost in an awareness of each other and in the pleasantness of being together. We continue a slow dolly away from them, and then a slow fade-out to black.]

[*Fade on: With a shot of the alley outside the arena.* GRACE *and* MC CLINTOCK *walk slowly away from the door toward the street. They walk slowly, looking around.*]

MC CLINTOCK [*Kicks a can out of the way.*]: A garden, ain't it?

GRACE: Where are the flowers?

MC CLINTOCK [*Flicks his ear.*]: Right here. [GRACE *smiles a little forcedly.*]

GRACE: It's late, Mountain. I've got to go home.

MC CLINTOCK: I'll get you a cab. [*She starts to walk off.*]

MC CLINTOCK: Grace—[*She turns to him.*] I . . . I've had a good time.

GRACE: I have, too.

MC CLINTOCK: You know, when we came out of the bar I heard Charlie say that I had a pretty date.

GRACE [*Smiles.*]: Thank Charlie for me.

MC CLINTOCK: It wasn't just that he thought you were pretty, he said that I had a date. It's like with the music, I don't even think I ever had a real date in all this time. A real one. Not somebody I liked. Somebody I wanted to be with.

GRACE: I think that's a compliment.

MC CLINTOCK: One time . . . one time Army had a girl friend living in St. Louis. She had a friend. Army fixed me up. We were supposed to meet after the fight. These two girls were waitin' for us outside. This girl that I was supposed to go with—she takes one look at me and she . . . she—

GRACE: She what, Mountain?

MC CLINTOCK: She turned around and she ran away. She looked at my face and she turned around and ran away. [GRACE *instinctively touches his arm and holds it tightly.*] That shouldn't have hurt. I should have been used to it. I know what I look like. I know what I sound like, too. But it . . . it did hurt. I didn't want it to happen again so I never let it happen.

[*Cut to: A tight close-up of* GRACE *as she stares at him and wonderingly shakes her head, feeling that acme of tenderness a woman can feel for a man.*]

GRACE [*Softly.*]: The cab, Mountain. It's late.

MC CLINTOCK: Sure.

[*The two start walking again toward the opening of the alley.*]

GRACE: Remember to think about what I told you. I think you'd like working with children.

MC CLINTOCK: I'll think about it. I'll think about it a lot. Don't build me up none, Miss Carrie. Don't say I'm anything special. [*Pause.*] Tell 'em . . . tell 'em I fought a hundred and eleven fights. Tell 'em I never took a dive. I'm proud of that.

[GRACE *looks at him intently for a moment, and there's a continuing softness on her face.*]

GRACE [*Whispers.*]: Sure, you are, Mountain. You must be very proud.

[*She quickly kisses him on the side of his face, studies him for a moment and hurriedly walks away from him. He stands there touching his face, looking after her.*]

[*We take a slow dissolve out to: A shot of Maish's hotel room, the same night. The door opens,* MC CLINTOCK *enters. In the room are* MAISH, ARMY *and a fat man who has been sitting in a corner of the room. Fat man rises.*]

MAISH: It's about time. Army was lookin' for ya. Somebody said you left the bar with a girl.

MC CLINTOCK [*Grins broadly.*]: I want to tell you all about it, Maish. No kiddin', she's a wonderful girl. Her name is—

MAISH: Tell me later. We've got business to attend to here.

MC CLINTOCK [*Filled to overflowing.*]: Army, it's the girl from the employment office. Miss Carrie.

ARMY: Pretty kid.

MC CLINTOCK: Beautiful. Beautiful girl.

PARELLI: How about it, Maish? I ain't got all night.

MAISH: Right away. Mountain, I'd like you to meet somebody. This is Mr. Parelli. Mr. Parelli promotes wrestling matches at Mathew's Arena.

MC CLINTOCK: I'm gladda know you.

PARELLI: Likewise. So get with it, Maish.

MAISH: We've got ourselves a nice deal here, Kid. Want to tell him, Mr. Parelli?

PARELLI: There isn't much to tell. Maish here thinks you might be a good draw. Your name's pretty well known. I've seen you fight a couple of times myself. [MC CLINTOCK *smiles*.] Yeah, I think I can line you up with some matches. I think it might be worth both our while.

MC CLINTOCK [*His smile fades somewhat.*]: Maish didn't tell ya. I'm not supposed to fight any more. I don't think I can get my license back.

[PARELLI *looks at* MAISH *questioningly, and* MAISH *forces a smile.*]

MAISH: We're not talking about boxing now, Kid. This is for wrestling. I told ya, Mr. Parelli promotes wrestling matches.

MC CLINTOCK: Wrestling matches? I don't know how to wrestle.

PARELLI [*Laughs.*]: You don't have to know how. Couple hours and you can learn the holds. There's really only two big things you've got to learn in my business, Kid. That's how to fake, make it look real, and that's how to land without hurting yourself. That's about it.

MC CLINTOCK: I don't get it.

MAISH: What do you mean, you don't get it? He's laying it out for you. And listen to what else, Mountain. I've got a funny idea. We'll dress you up in a coonskin hat, see, and you're going to be billed as the Mountaineer. How about that, huh? Just like old times. Even buy you some kind of a big long squirrel gun or something. [*Then there's a long, dead silence as* MC CLINTOCK *turns away.*] Well?

PARELLI: I don't think he goes for it, Maish.

MAISH: What're you talkin' about, he don't go for it? Mountain, what've you got to say?

MC CLINTOCK: I'd lose you a fortune, Maish. I can't wrestle. I don't think I could win a match. [PARELLI *laughs.*]

MAISH: What do you mean, win a match? These are all set up, Kid. One night you win, the next night the other guy wins.

PARELLI: It depends on who plays the heavy.

MC CLINTOCK: A tank job.

MAISH: Will you talk sense? This is an entirely different thing. Everybody knows there's a fix on in these things. It's part of the game.

MC CLINTOCK: I never took a dive for anybody. A hundred and eleven fights. I never took one single dive.

PARELLI: It's like Maish says. These aren't exactly dives —[*Then there's a long pause.*] Well, look, I'll tell you what, you guys talk it over. Give me a call, Maish, by tomorrow. I've got to know by tomorrow.

MAISH: You get the contract ready. We'll be ready to sign in the morning.

PARELLI: Sure. Nice meeting you, Mountain.

[MC CLINTOCK *nods.* PARELLI *goes out. There is the off- stage sound of the door closing.* MC CLINTOCK *stares at* MAISH. MAISH *averts his glance.*]

MAISH [*With his back to him.*]: I figure you owe it to me. [*Then a pause.*] What do you figure?

MC CLINTOCK [*Nods.*]: I guess I do.

MAISH: So there's nothing more to it, then.

[MC CLINTOCK *turns, his face shows an anguish we haven't seen before.*]

MC CLINTOCK: But, Maish—I was almost heavyweight champion of the world.

[MAISH *turns, walks over to him and grabs him tightly. His voice is fierce and intent.*]

MAISH: Then you remember just that. When I stick you in a silly costume, you just remember you were almost heavyweight champion of the world. And I'll remember I was the guy who managed you. We'll do this one with our eyes closed. [*Then he releases him. He breathes a little heavily.*] Army, take him home. [*He turns his back to them.* ARMY *walks over to* MC CLINTOCK.]

MC CLINTOCK: Never mind, Army. I'll go home by myself. [MC CLINTOCK *exits.*]

MAISH: He's upset—that's all. He just don't know.

ARMY: He knows. Believe me, he knows.

MAISH: But he'll come around.

ARMY: Sure, he will. You'll fix it that way. You gotta knack, Maish. You violin him to death. And if that don't work—squeeze him a little. Back him up. Twist it up a little for him. What a knack you got. [*He turns to go.* MAISH'S *voice is soft . . . pleading.*]

MAISH: Army, stick, will ya?

ARMY: Stick?

MAISH: Help me with him. Just stay alongside.

ARMY [*Understanding now.*]: Partners again, huh? If he sees me, he'll move faster—that the idea?

MAISH: He'll want both of us. It'll help him, Army, a lousy one-night stand.

ARMY: Stop it! You break him into a dummy harness once—he'll stay with it. [*Pounds his fists silently.*] It ain't enough I gotta watch him go down all these years. Now you want me in the pit. I gotta officiate at the burial.

MAISH: It don't have to be that way.

[*And now desperately groping for the words and for the first time we're listening to the mind of this man.* ARMY *grabs him by the lapels and holds on to him very tightly.*]

ARMY: This is a slob to you, Maish. This is a hunk. This is a dead-weight has-been. This is a cross you got to bear? I'll tell you what he is, Maish, this boy. This is a decent man. This is a man with a heart. This is a somebody flesh and blood, now, Maish. You can't sell this on the market by the pound, because if you do, if you do, you'll rot in hell for it. You understand me, Maish, you'll rot. [*He cries uncontrollably . . . and then stops.*]

MAISH: Please, Army, for him at least. Don't leave him alone.

ARMY: Of course not. I can't leave him alone. He'll do it for you even if I'm not there. So I'll *be* there [*A pause.*] Why is it, Maish . . . tell me . . . why is it . . . so many people have to feed off one guy's misery? Tell me, Maish . . . doesn't it . . . doesn't it make you want to die? [*Fade out.*]

ACT III

[*Fade on: With a tight close-up of a suit of buckskin, the coonskin hat, and an old relic of a muzzle-loading Long Tom rifle, a powder horn, and a few other accoutrements. Then we pull back for a corner shot of the room. It is a small dressing room very similar to the one in Act I.* PARELLI *is looking over the costume and chuckling softly through his cigar. He picks up one of the legs of the trousers, examines it, laughs again, tosses it aside, then starts toward the door as it opens.* MAISH *enters.*]

PARELLI [*Nods.*]: Looks good. Where is he?

MAISH: He's coming.

PARELLI: The guy at the gym says he don't have those holds down at all. Didn't understand them.

MAISH: He will. Give him a little while.

PARELLI: He knows just what to do, doesn't he?

MAISH: Yeah, he's all zeroed in.

PARELLI: And this is important. When the other guys gets a lock on him or any other kind of a hold—have him look in pain, you understand? That's important. He's got to look as if he's giving up the ghost. [*Then with a grimace.*] Pain, you understand, Maish. Real pain. Torture. Agony.

MAISH [*Sardonically.*]: He'll die out there for ya. [*Then he looks out toward the open door.*] How's the house?

PARELLI: The usual. Not good, not bad. They want action. It don't have to be good action, but it's got to be action. So tell your boy to move around.

MAISH: I told you he knows all about it.

PARELLI: Okay.

[*He starts to walk by him, and* MAISH *pinches his sleeve with two fingers.*]

MAISH: The dough, Parelli.

PARELLI: It'll be waiting for you after the fight. I don't know how you talked me into an advance. Most people can't.

MAISH [*With a grin.*]: With me, it's an art.

PARELLI: It must be. [*He looks at his watch.*] He better get here soon. [*Then with a grin.*]: It's going to take him a long time to get into that outfit.

MAISH He'll be right along. I just talked to him.

PARELLI: Okay. I'll see you later.

[*He goes out of the room. He closes the door.* MAISH *walks over to the table that the costume is on. He picks up the pieces one by one and looks at them. He has a dull, emotionless look on his face. When he gets to the gun he picks it up, and the door opens.* ARMY *enters.*]

ARMY: What's the season—grouse? What you huntin', Maish?

MAISH: Right now I'm huntin' a wrestler named McClintock. Have you seen him?

ARMY [*Shakes his head.*]: Not since last night.

MAISH [*Slams a fist against his palm.*]: He's late.

ARMY: That's good to know. [*He kicks the door shut and walks over to* MAISH. *He looks down at the paraphernalia.*]

MAISH [*Stares at him.*]: Enough to make a fuss over? [*He points to the clothes.*] Is it, Army?

ARMY [*Shrugs.*]: I don't have to wear it.

MAISH: If you did—it would break your heart, huh?

[*At this moment there's the sound of the crowd from up above and both men look up and then look at one another.*]

MAISH: Army.

ARMY: Go.

MAISH: You know me, Army.

ARMY: You bet I do.

MAISH: I don't mean just that way. I mean you know me inside. You know how I hate this. You know how it keeps me from sleeping. You know how it eats away my stomach, Army—

[*At this moment,* MC CLINTOCK *enters. He smiles at* ARMY.]

MC CLINTOCK: I looked for ya. I was afraid you wasn't gonna come.

MAISH: He's here. You better get into this thing.

MC CLINTOCK: Sure, Maish, sure. [*Then suddenly his eyes fall on the coonskin cap and costume and the gun leaning against the wall. His face goes numb. He walks over to them, lifts them up one piece at a time, then stares down at them.*]

MAISH [*Wets his lips, forces a smile.*]: Ain't that a lark, Kid? It's gonna kill 'em. Gonna knock 'em dead. [MC CLINTOCK *nods dumbly. Continuing, hurriedly.*] You know you take it off when you get in. You walk around the ring a couple of times and you take it off. You don't have to wear it very long. [*His words tumble out in a torrent.*] And underneath you wear Long Johns, and it isn't until after the bout you've got to put the stuff back on—[*He stops abruptly as* MC CLINTOCK *turns to him.*]

MC CLINTOCK: Clown.

MAISH [*Points to* ARMY.]: He called it that. You're taking it from him. Can't you think a thought for yourself?

MC CLINTOCK [*Shakes his head.*]: He called it that but I call it that, too. [*He nods toward the hallway.*] And everybody out there will call it that, too. Clown. [*He puts the flats of both hands on the table, and bends his head far down so that his face cannot be seen.*] Maish—*don't* make me!

[*Cut to: A very tight close-up of* MAISH. *What we see on his features is a look of pain—a kind of sudden, personal agony, and then he composes his features almost one by one and his voice comes out loud again and shrill along with a laugh.*]

MAISH: What do you mean, don't make you? What am I, your father? Don't make you. You don't do nothin' you don't want to do. If you don't think you owe it to me. Okay. [*There's a knock on the door.*] Yeah?
[*The door opens and* PARELLI *is standing there. Behind him a photographer.*]

PARELLI [*Grins into the room.*]: How about a couple of pictures, Maish? We ain't had any with the costume yet.

MC CLINTOCK [*His head goes up.*]: Pictures?

PARELLI: Part of the build-up, Kid. One picture is worth a million words. That's what the Greeks say. [*Then to the photographer*:] How about it? You want 'em in here or out in the hall?

PHOTOGRAPHERS: Out in the hall. I've got more room.

[*There's a long pause.* PARELLI *waits expectantly.*]

PARELLI: So? What's he waiting for—a valet? Let's hurry it up.

[*He goes out closing the door.* MC CLINTOCK *rises, looks quickly at* ARMY *and then at* MAISH, *then turns back to the table and picks up the coonskin hat, puts it on his head. Then he puts his arms into the coat and slowly puts it on.* MAISH *turns away. We are looking from close-up at him and at his face and features as they work, and a little of the agony returns. Over his shoulder we see* MC CLINTOCK *buttoning the jacket, then he takes the gun, looks at it.* MC CLINTOCK *goes to the door, stops with his hand on the knob. Stands there motionless, his eyes closed.*]

VOICE: McClintock's on next. Let's go!

MC CLINTOCK [*Almost a whisper.*]: Tell 'em to go away, Maish.

MAISH: What're you talking about?

[*There's a loud knock on the door and this time* PARELLI'S *voice.*]

PARELLI: What's going on in there? What're you trying to pull off here, Maish? Get your boy out there. Photographer's waitin' for him, and his match is on.

MAISH [*Raises his voice but it still comes out weakly.*]: He'll . . . he'll be right out, Parelli. He'll be right there. [*Then he turns to* MC CLINTOCK.] Mountain, you cross me now—and I'm dead. Understand? I'm dead.

[MC CLINTOCK *shakes his head back and forth, back and forth.*]

MC CLINTOCK: Can't. Can't, Maish. Can't.

MAISH [*Grabs him and holds him tightly by the shirt front.*]: You got a debt, mister. You owe me.

MC CLINTOCK: Maish—

MAISH: I mean it, Mountain. I've got my whole life on the line now. I can't afford to let you cross me. [MC CLINTOCK *shakes his head. His voice desperate.*] I swear I'll beat you to a pulp myself! I wouldn't have been in this jam if it weren't for you.

MC CLINTOCK [*Looks up.*]: Maish, I'll do anything you want but—

MAISH: But it bothers you too much. Well, it didn't bother you last week to stand up in a ring with your hands down at your sides and let Gibbons beat you to a pulp. That didn't bother you a bit *It didn't bother you that I had every nickel in the world tossed on a table to say that you wouldn't go seven!*
[*Then there's a long, long pause as* MC CLINTOCK'S *face shows a gradual understanding, and* MAISH *on the other hand look like a man whose tongue has suddenly gotten red-hot in his mouth.*]

MC CLINTOCK: Maish . . . Maish, you bet against me. [MAISH *doesn't answer him, and there's another pause.* MC CLINTOCK *takes a step toward him.*] Maish, why'd you bet against me?

MAISH: Would it make any difference, Mountain, if I hocked my left foot to bet on you—would it have made any difference? You're not a winner any more, Mountain. And that means there's only one thing left . . . make a little off the losing.
[MC CLINTOCK *takes another step toward him, and* MAISH, *whose back has been to him, turns to face him.* MC CLINTOCK *stares at him and his lips tremble.*]

MC CLINTOCK [*Finally.*]: You fink! You dirty fink, you, Maish! Dirty, lousy fink. [MAISH'S *face goes white but he doesn't say anything.*] And because I wouldn't go down—because I stood up and took it for ya—I've got to pay for it like this. [*He pulls at the costume.*] Like this, Maish, huh? [*He turns and walks away from him, shaking his head, trying to articulate, desperate to let something that he feels now come out without quite knowing how to let it come out.*] In all the dirty, crummy fourteen years I fought for you—I never felt ashamed. Not of a round . . . not of a minute. [*Then he turns to* MAISH, *looks down at himself, then across to* MAISH.] But now all of a sudden you make me feel ashamed. You understand, Maish? You make me feel ashamed. I'd have gone into any ring barehanded against a guy with a cleaver . . . and that wouldn't have hurt me near as much as this.

ARMY: Mountain, listen to me . . .
[MC CLINTOCK, *suddenly unable to control himself any more, raises his hand and with the flat of it smashes* ARMY *against the face.* ARMY *goes backward, falling*

against a table and winding up on his hands and knees.
MAISH *starts toward him.*

ARMY [*Picks up his head.*]: Get away, Maish. Get away.
[*Then very slowly he rises to his feet, rubs his jaw
briefly, looks at* MC CLINTOCK.]

MC CLINTOCK [*In a whisper.*]: Army . . . Army—

ARMY: You didn't hit me, Kid. It didn't come from you.
[*He turns accusingly towards* MAISH.] Go on, Kid. Go
on and leave. Take what precious little you've got left
and get out of here. [MC CLINTOCK *turns slowly and
walks out of the room. After a few moments' pause,*
ARMY *turns and goes to the door, looks down the corridor
and says*—] Good night, Mountain. [*Then a pause.*]
Good-by, Mountain.
[*From down the hall at this moment comes a shouting,
fuming, sweating* PARELLI. *He arrives at the door almost
too excited to speak.*]

PARELLI: He's walkin' out! The boy's walkin' out! What's
with this? What's with it? [*Then* PARELLI *walks over to*
MAISH, *sticks his finger in his chest, and prods him.*]
You know what I'm gonna do to you for this, don't you?
[MAISH *keeps his head down*—PARELLI *shouts.*] I'm
gonna see to it that you don't get a license to walk a
dog from now on. You don't think I will? You don't
think I will, Maish? Well let me tell ya—[ARMY *slams
the door in his face.*]

[*Dissolve to: The bar. Dolly down through it until we
reach the rear and a group of men talking fight talk, all
of them living in a little round-by-round dream world.*
MC CLINTOCK *stands a few feet away from the fringes,
staring at them and listening. Finally one of them says
loudly enough to be heard:*]

FIGHTER #1: That wasn't his name, Stevie. His name was
Hacker. Charles Hacker. And he never fought Louis.
[*Then he looks up over the crowd and sees* MC CLIN-
TOCK.] How about that, Mountain? You know him.
Hacker. Charles Hacker. He never fought Louis, did he?
[*The crowd turns and stares toward* MC CLINTOCK, *who
takes a step toward them.*]

MC CLINTOCK: No, he never fought Louis. He fought me,
though.

FIGHTER #2: No kiddin', Mountain? No kiddin'? How'd you do?

[MC CLINTOCK *takes another step and the men make way for him until he is standing almost in their midst.*]

MC CLINTOCK: It went three rounds. He was always strong in the beginning.

FIGHTER #2: Yeah, yeah. He was always strong.

MC CLINTOCK: He come in at me and he don't box none. He never did—[*Then he stops abruptly and he stares around the circle of faces. We pan with his eyes to take in a shot of each face, and then winding up on a tight close-up of his own as he suddenly slowly shakes his head.*] I . . . I don't remember it. I'm sorry but I don't remember it. [*He turns and walks away from them and goes over to the bar.*] Give me a beer, will you?

BARTENDER: Sure, Mountain . . . comin' up.

[*The camera pulls away from the shot of* MOUNTAIN *sitting at the bar until he is framed in the window. It continues to pull away until we pick up a shot of* ARMY *across the street staring toward the window. Then we see* GRACE *approaching him.*]

ARMY [*Turns to her.*]: I'm over here, Miss.

GRACE [*Approaches him.*]: You're . . . you're Army?

ARMY: That's right. Thanks for coming.

GRACE: Tell me what happened—

ARMY: What happened is that he walked out of a match. But I want to make sure he keeps walking. I didn't want him to stop at that graveyard over there.

GRACE: How can I help?

ARMY: You can help him by not conning him. He's been conned by experts. He's riddled. He'll listen to you. When he gets out of there, head him toward Grand Central Station and give him this. [*He takes out an envelope and hands it to* GRACE.]

GRACE: What's that?

ARMY: That's a train ticket to Kenesaw, Tennessee.

GRACE [*Studies the envelope for a moment.*]: Is that home?

ARMY [*Very quietly.*]: It was once. Maybe it'll be again. [*Then there is a long pause.*] Do you love him, Miss?

GRACE: I don't know. I feel so sorry for him though, I want to cry.

ARMY [*Touches her arm gently.*]: You tell him that, Miss. Tell him you think he's a decent guy, and you like him.

But tell him, for the time being, you don't come with a
kiss. He's been chasing a ghost too long now—and the
next thing he's got a hunger for—he oughta get. It's
only fair. Thanks very much, Miss. [*Then there is a
long pause.*] You're a brick.
[*He walks away and as he does so,* MOUNTAIN *comes out
of the bar.* GRACE *walks over across the street to him.
The camera stays with* ARMY *looking at the two of them
over his shoulder. We can see them talking but can't
hear them. Then we see* GRACE *hand* MOUNTAIN *the
envelope. He takes it in his hands, they exchange a few
more unintelligible words, and then* MOUNTAIN *starts to
walk away.* GRACE *turns, starts across the street, and
then stops.*]

[*Cut to: Very close shot of* GRACE *as she whirls around.*]

[*Cut to: Very tight close-up of* MC CLINTOCK'S *face in
the lamplight of the street. The broken nose, the mis-
shapen ears, scar tissues, bruises that never healed and
never will any more. The battered ugliness that is a
legacy of the profession.*]
GRACE: Mountain!
[MOUNTAIN *stops, turns to her.* GRACE *runs over to him
and very lightly kisses him.* MOUNTAIN *reaches up and
touches his face wonderingly.*]
MC CLINTOCK: Thanks for that. [*Then hesitantly, terribly unsure, he kisses her back.*] Thanks for not running
away.
GRACE: When you get home, when you get settled—write
me and tell me what's happened.
MC CLINTOCK: When I get home? [*He looks down at the
ticket.*] I'll go there—but . . . I don't know if it's home
any more.
GRACE: Go find out. You look for it, Mountain. Because
wherever home is—it's not over there. [*She points
toward the bar. Then she hands him a slip of paper.*]
It's my home address, Mountain. Write me.
[*He very tentatively takes the paper and then slowly
shakes his head. He crumples it in his fist. She grabs his
hand and guides it into his pocket.*]
GRACE: Good-by, Mountain.
[*He turns and walks slowly away.* GRACE *watches him

for a moment and then starts to cross the street toward the camera. Halfway across the street her head goes down, and her hands are down at her sides. She blinks her eyes and very quietly she begins to cry.]

[*Dissolve out on her face to: Cover shot of the dressing room in semidarkness.* MAISH *sits alone by the rubbing table. The only light comes from the bulbs out in the hall.* ARMY *appears at the door, peers inside, sees* MAISH *and enters.*]

ARMY: You gonna stay here all night?

MAISH: That's a thought.

ARMY: Fox is out there with some other guys.

MAISH: It comes, I figured.

ARMY: If it comes, it comes. Get it over with, Maish.
[MAISH *studies* ARMY *intently.*]

MAISH: Hey, Army, what are you going to do?

ARMY [*Smiles.*]: Tomorrow, I'll be for hire. You know, Maish—you said so yourself—I'm the best cut man in the business. And after I patch up my millionth cut, maybe somebody'll give me a gold watch.

MAISH: You're needed, aren't you?

ARMY [*Nods.*]: A little bit. There's a lot of hurt in this business, Maish. I'll help the ones on the outside.

MAISH: What about the inside, Army?

ARMY: You want to know, Maish? [*He nods toward the door.*] Go out and take your beating. Then take a train like the Mountain. And you look for a home. Come on, Maish, I'll be alongside.
[*The two men walk out into the hall.* FOX *and two other men are waiting.*]

FOX: Maish—[MAISH *stops dead in his tracks, staring straight ahead.* FOX *comes up behind him.*] This ain't a payoff, Maish, relax.

MAISH: You here to give me a medal? [*Looks at the other two men.*] It must be heavy.

FOX: We're here to give you a proposition. This is Mr. Arnold.
[*A heavy-set man comes up alongside. He is the same man we saw in the bar.*]

MAISH: Mr. Arnold and I have met. You work for Henson?

MAN: Yeah.

FOX: Here's the proposition, Maish. It's a sweetie, a real sweetie.

[*With this he propels the other man to the front and into the light. He is a young fighter in his late teens. At first sudden glance there is a striking resemblance between this boy and* MOUNTAIN—*as* MOUNTAIN *must have appeared very early in the game.* MAISH *looks at him briefly.*]

MAISH: What's he want . . . a haircut?

FOX: Mr. Henson would like him managed. Managed good.

MAN: Groomed—that's the word.

MAISH: Why me? That's the question.

FOX: He wants a nice, dependable guy with know-how, Maish, and you're it. Some guy who knows his business —and who'll go along.

MAISH: I know my business—

MAN: And you'll go along.

MAISH: I've got a choice, huh?

MAN: Yeah, you've got a choice. You take this kid and make a fighter out of him—or the Commissioner gets a phone call that a certain manager's been making bets.

FOX: That's against the law, Maish.

MAISH: Is that a fact?

FOX [*Seriously.*]: You know it is. Pari mutuels at race or harness tracks—that's the only place betting is permitted. They'd take away your license, Maish. It wouldn't be just a suspension, Maish—it'd be permanent.

[MAISH *takes a step closer to the young* FIGHTER *and studies his face in the light.*]

MAISH: Where're you from, Kid?

FOX [*Interjects.*]: It's an amazing coincidence. It really is, Maish. He's from Kentucky. You could call him Mountain—

FIGHTER: Who's Mountain?

MAISH [*His lip trembles perceptibly.*]: He was a good, fast kid. All hands and feet with his mouth full of teeth, and he talked like General Lee. Like you do—like you look. You better go back there and work in a drugstore. [*He turns away.*]

MAN: Is that what I tell Mr. Henson?

MAISH: No. Tell him thanks. Thanks for getting me out. C'mon, Army. [*He walks slowly down the aisle. He pauses by a poster, a torn, beat-up aged poster. There is a picture of Mountain in ring togs posing.* MAISH *pauses by it, walks over to it, rips Mountain's name off the bottom of the poster and crumples it up. Then he whirls around at the young* FIGHTER.] Check this. There's eight champions in this business. Everybody else is an also-ran. There's the good and the bad in it. The good's great—the bad stinks; I hope you make out. [*He opens up his fist and unravels the piece of poster with Mountain's name on it and stares at it. Very softly.*] I hope you make out, Kid. [*Then he flings the crumpled paper away, and he and* ARMY *walk slowly down the corridor. The camera pans down to the piece of poster on the floor.*

[*We lap-dissolve to: A film clip of a train and a section of a car.* MC CLINTOCK *sits across from a* WOMAN *and a little* BOY.]

BOY [*Suddenly leans over to him.*]: Hiya.

MC CLINTOCK [*Looks down in surprise.*]: Hiya.

[BOY *picks up one of* MC CLINTOCK'S *big hands and examines it.*]

BOY: You're a fighter, aren't you?

MC CLINTOCK [*Looks down at him.*]: Yeah. I was a fighter.

BOY: I can tell by your ears. You got big ears.

[*There is a long pause and very slowly* MOUNTAIN *grins.*]

MC CLINTOCK: Yeah, cauliflower ears.

[*The* BOY *returns his grin, and we can see* MOUNTAIN *relaxing for the first time.*]

BOY: How do you get ears like that? I'd like ears like that.

WOMAN: Jeffey, don't be rude—

MC CLINTOCK: That's all right, Ma'am.

[*The* BOY *goes over to sit next to* MC CLINTOCK.]

BOY [*Suddenly assuming a fight position.*]: Like this? This is the way you do it?

MC CLINTOCK [*Straightens the boy's hands.*]: No, you hold your right down, keep that left up, hunch your shoulder like this. Okay. Now lead. No, no, no—with the left, and don't drop your right. Okay, now lead again.

[*The* BOY *does all this, delighted.*]

WOMAN: I hope he's not bothering you—

MC CLINTOCK: Not a bit, Ma'am. I like it.

WOMAN: Where are you heading for?

[*There is a long pause.* MC CLINTOCK *reaches in his pocket and takes out the slip of paper that* GRACE *has given him, unfolds it and smoothes it out.*]

MC CLINTOCK: Home. I'm heading for home. I don't know for how long. 'Cause I . . . 'cause I'll probably be taking a job one of these days soon. Work with kids like Jeffey here.

BOY [*Impatiently.*]: C'mon, Champ. Let's you and me spar.

MC CLINTOCK: Okay, Champ. Now lead again. That's right. Right from the shoulder. Okay, now cross with the right. No, no, no—don't drop your left. That's right. [*The camera starts to pull away very slowly from them until their voices cannot be heard, and all we can see is the pantomime of* MOUNTAIN MC CLINTOCK *and the little* BOY *fighting the Mountain's greatest fight. We take a very slow dissolve to the film clip of the train as it disappears into the night. A slow fade to black.*]

TWELVE ANGRY MEN

by Reginald Rose

Copyright © 1956 by Reginald Rose.

The notes on characters are extremely brief, since it is felt that what they are and who they are will be revealed in their dialogue and actions during the course of the film.

FOREMAN: *35 years old. Assistant high-school football coach. A small, petty man who is at first wary of, and then impressed with the authority he has. Handles himself quite formally. Not overly bright, but dogged.*

JUROR #2: *38 years old. Bank clerk. A meek, hesitant man who finds it difficult to maintain any opinions of his own. Easily swayed and usually adopts the opinion of the last person to whom he has spoken.*

JUROR #3: *40 years old. Head of messenger service. A very strong, very forceful, extremely opinionated man within whom can be detected a streak of sadism. A humorless man who is intolerant of opinions other than his own, and accustomed to forcing his wishes and views upon others.*

JUROR #4: *50 years old. Stockbroker. A man of wealth and position. A practiced speaker who presents himself well at all times. Seems to feel a little bit above the rest of the jurors. His only concern is with the facts in this case and he is appalled with the behavior of the others. Constantly preening himself, combing his hair, cleaning his nails, etc.*

JUROR #5: *25 years old. Mechanic. A naïve, very frightened young man who takes his obligations in this case very seriously but who finds it difficult to speak up when his elders have the floor.*

JUROR #6: *33 years old. Housepainter. An honest, but dull-witted man who comes upon his decisions slowly and carefully. A man who finds it difficult to create positive opinions, but who must listen to and digest and accept these opinions offered by others which appeal to him most.*

JUROR #7: *42 years old. Salesman. A loud, flashy, glad-handed salesman type who has more important things to do than to sit on a jury. He is quick to show temper, quick to form opinions on things about which he knows nothing. He is a bully, and, of course, a coward.*

JUROR #8: *42 years old. Architect. A quiet, thoughtful, gentle man. A man who sees many sides to every question and constantly seeks the truth. A man of strength tempered with compassion. Above all, a man who wants justice to be done, and will fight to see that it is.*

JUROR #9: *70 years old. Retired. A mild, gentle old man, long since defeated by life, and now merely waiting to die. A man who recognizes himself for what he is, and mourns the days when it would have been possible to be courageous without shielding himself behind his many years. From the way he takes pills whenever he is excited, it is obvious that he has a heart condition.*

JUROR #10: *46 years old. Garage owner. An angry, bitter man. A man who antagonizes almost at sight. A bigot who places no values on any human life save his own. A man who has been nowhere and is going nowhere and knows it deep within him. He has a bad cold and continually blows his nose, sniffs a benzedrine inhaler, etc.*

JUROR #11: *48 years old. Watchmaker. A refugee from Europe who has come to this country in 1941. A man who speaks with an accent and who is ashamed, humble, almost subservient to the people around him, but a*

*man who will honestly seek justice because he has
suffered through so much injustice.*

JUROR #12: *30 years old. Advertising man. A slick, bright
advertising man who thinks of human beings in terms
of percentages, graphs and polls, and has no real understanding of people. A superficial snob, but trying to
be a good fellow. Throughout the play he doodles on a
scratch pad.*

and

THE JUDGE
THE COURT CLERK
THE GUARD
THE TWO ALTERNATE JURORS

and (if desired)

THE COURT STENOGRAPHER

[*N. Y. Court of General Sessions. Day. A large, imposing building, gray, impressive as a background for the
comings and goings of a number of ordinary people on
an ordinary day. The lobby is seething with activity,
people of all kinds walking swiftly, purposefully to and
from elevators, newsstands, etc., others standing, waiting.
Guards stationed at various posts. A number of people
crowd into an elevator. The door closes.*
[*A long corridor upstairs. The elevators on left. Many
doorways to various courtrooms on right. Each door
marked with a hanging sign. The first sign reads "Court
of General Sessions. Part I." The second sign reads
"Court of General Sessions. Part II," etc. An elevator
door opens and a number of people exit and walk down
the corridor. Other people, men and women, stand in
the corridor talking. The whole feeling is one of movement, activity, intense concentraion. Everyone has a
purpose. People peel off from the group at various doors.
At each door stands a guard. People move in and out
of the doors. A guard stands in front of door marked
"Part VI" impassively. No one else is in front of the
door, as compared to the knots of whispering people
in front of all the other doors. The case going on in
"Part VI" obviously has very little general interest.*

*Through the glass window of the door we can see, far
in the background, the* JUDGE *at his bench. He is facing
to his left, and talking. We hear nothing. He stops and
turns to his right. He raises his hand as if calling a
waiter.*

[*An empty water glass on a tray. From the noise of the
corridor we are now in the deathlike stillness of a court-
room. A hand places a freshly filled pitcher of water on
the tray. A pair of hands fills a glass from the pitcher.*
JUDGE *drinks water. He finishes, puts the glass down,
and turns to his left again. He clears his throat. Then he
begins to speak.*]

JUDGE: Pardon me, gentlemen. [*Gravely.*] To continue,
you've heard a long and complex case. Murder in the
first degree . . . premeditated homicide . . . is the most
serious charge tried in our criminal courts.
[*We see the jury seated in the jury box, listening intently
to the* JUDGE. *We see the 14 members of the jury. This
includes the two alternates, who sit on the far right side
of the jury, one behind the other. The jury sits in nu-
merical order reading from left to right: the foreman
through #6 in the front row, #7–#12 in the rear row.*
JUDGE: You've listened to the testimony, and you've had
the law read to you and interpreted as it applies to this
case. It now becomes your duty to sit down to try and
separate the facts from the fancy. One man is dead. The
life of another is at stake. I urge you to deliberate honestly and thoughtfully. [*#7 fidgets endlessly. #10 sniffs
as if he has a cold. #3 looks coldly off in the direction
in which the* DEFENDANT *sits. All other jurymen watch
the* JUDGE, *listening intently.*] If there is a reasonable
doubt in your minds as to the guilt of the accused . . .
a reasonable doubt . . . then you must bring me a verdict
of not guilty. If, however, there is no reasonable doubt,
then you must, in good conscience find the accused
guilty. However you decide, your verdict must be unani-
mous. In the event you find the accused guilty, the bench
will not entertain a recommendation for mercy. The
death sentence is mandatory in this case. [*The* JUDGE
pauses for a moment. There is a stillness in the room.]

I don't envy you your job. You are faced with a grave responsibility. Thank you, gentlemen.

[*There is a pause. The* JUDGE *turns away from the jury and nods in another direction, at the* COURT CLERK.]

CLERK: The alternate jurors are excused. [*All of the heads of the jurymen turn to camera right. Self-consciously, the two* ALTERNATES *rise and move awkwardly out of the jury box. When they are gone, we hear the* CLERK.] The jury will retire.

[*The members of the jury look hesitantly at each other, each reluctant to be the first to stand. Finally #3 stands up. Then the others begin to rise and file slowly off left until the jury box is empty. They file through a long corridor, then through one door, then another. They are silent, serious. All we hear is the sound of their footsteps.*]

[*The jury room. The room is empty, silent save for the sounds of traffic twelve floors below. In center of room is a large scarred table and twelve chairs. There are four other chairs against the wall opposite the windows. Along one wall are three windows through which we can see the New York skyline. On the opposite wall is an electric clock and an electric fan. At one end of the jury room is a coat rack, on either side of which is a door, one lettered "men" and the other lettered "women." Against the fourth wall is an old-fashioned water cooler. There are pencils, pads, ashtrays on the table. Nothing else. The room is drab, bare, in need of a painting. The door is opened by a uniformed* GUARD. *On the door are lettered the words "Jury Room." The* GUARD *stands against the door, holding it open, as the members of the jury file into the room. He holds a clipboard and pencil, and we can see his lips moving, counting the jurymen as they enter. Four or five of the jurymen light cigarettes immediately. They move into the room.* JUROR #2 *goes to the water fountain.* JUROR #9, *the old man, enters hastily and goes toward the men's room.* JUROR #7 *enters the room last. The* GUARD *steps into the room and closes the door. Again he begins to count the jurors. #7 walks across the room toward the windows. The* FOREMAN *has seated himself at the head of the table. #11 and #4 also sit at the table. #11 begins to make notes in a little pad. #4 reads the newspaper. The others move awkwardly about the room. They are ill at ease, do not really know each other to talk to, wish they were anywhere but here. There is no conversation for a moment. #7 reaches the window. He and #6 look out at the skyline. #7 offers a stick of gum to him. He shakes his head. #7 offers the gum to #8 who also looks out window. #8 smiles.]*

#8: No thanks.

[#7 mouths the gum, and mops his brow.]

#7 *[To #6.]:* Y'know something? I phoned up for the weather this morning. This is the hottest day of the year. *[#6 nods and continues to look out window.]* You'd think they'd at least air condition the place. I almost dropped dead in court.

[He reaches over and opens the window wider.]

GUARD *[Finished counting.]:* Okay, gentlemen. Everybody's here. If there's anything you want I'm right outside. Just knock.

[He exits, closing the door. JUROR #5, the youngest juryman, watches the door. We hear the lock click. #5 half grins, self-consciously.]

#5: I never knew they locked the door.

#10: Sure they lock the door. What'd you think?

#5: I don't know. It just never occurred to me.

[#10 gives him the look of a professional know-it-all, and then turns and takes off his jacket. He walks across room to coat rack. He passes the FOREMAN, who stands at the head of the table tearing up little slips of paper for ballots, and he stops.]

#10: Hey, what's that for?

FOREMAN: Well, I figured we might want to vote by ballots.

#10 *[Grinning.]:* Great idea! Maybe we can get him elected senator.

[#10 laughs until he begins to cough. He moves off to the coat rack, coughing. The FOREMAN laughs, not appreciatively, and stops as #10 walks off. He continues to tear slips. He looks at his watch now, and then up at the wall clock, comparing times. It reads 4:35. #2 sits in a chair against the wall, thinking about the trial.

#3 *passes by him carrying a paper cup of water from water cooler. He stops in front of* #2 *and looks around the room, sipping the water.* #2 *looks at him a bit self-consciously.* #3 *looks down at him.* #2 *smiles and nods.*]

#3: How'd you like it?

#2 [*Mildly.*]: I don't know, it was pretty interesting.

#3 [*Pleasantly.*]: Yeah? I was falling asleep.

#2: I mean I've never been on a jury before.

#3: Really? I don't know. I've sat on juries, and it always kind of amazes me the way these lawyers can talk, and talk and talk, even when the case is as obvious as this one, I mean, did you ever hear so much talk about nothing?

#2: Well, I guess they're . . . entitled.

#3: Sure they are. Everybody deserves a fair trial. [*He balls up his paper cup and flips it at the water cooler.*] That's the system. Listen, I'm the last one to say anything against it, but I'm telling you sometimes I think we'd be better off if we took these tough kids and slapped 'em down hard *before* they make trouble, you know? Save us a lot of time and money.

[#2 *looks at him nervously, nods, gets up and walks to the water cooler. He pours himself a drink and stands alone sipping it. We hear movement in the room during all of this, and quiet ad lib conversation.* #2 *is sipping his water.* #3 *is hanging up his jacket.* #6 *and* #8 *are looking out windows.* #4, #11 *and the* FOREMAN *are seated at table.* #7 *and* #10 *are at far end of room, talking quietly.* #7 *lets out a raucous laugh.* #9 *is still in men's room.* #5 *walks toward water cooler.* #12 *is walking over to windows.* #7 *calls out to* FOREMAN. #12 *stops walking.*]

#7: Hey, how about getting started here.

#3: Yeah, let's get this over with. We've probably all got things to do.

FOREMAN: Well, I was figuring we'd take a five-minute break. I mean, one gentleman's in the bathroom . . .

[#7 *shrugs, and turns back to* #10. #5 *walks over to the* FOREMAN *as* #12 *continues over to* #8 *at the window.* #3 *continues business of hanging up his jacket, and goes to sit at table.*]

#5 [*Hesitantly*.]: Are we going to sit in order?

FOREMAN [*Looking up*.]: What? I don't know. I suppose so.

[*#8 is thinking hard, biting his fingernail. #12 looks out the window over his shoulder*.]

#12: Not a bad view. [*#8 nods*.] What'd you think of the case? [*#8 looks at him questioningly*.] It had a lot of interest for me. No dead spots, know what I mean. I'll tell you we were lucky to get a murder case. I figured us for a burglary or an assault or something. Those can be the dullest. Say, isn't that the Woolworth Building?

#8: That's right.

#12: Funny, I've lived here all my life and I've never been in it.

[*#8 looks out the window. #12 looks at him for a moment and then walks away. He stares out the window. We hear #7 laugh again*.]

#7: Yeah! And what about the business with the knife. I mean asking grown-up people to believe that kind of bushwash.

[*#8 turns during these lines to look at #7. #10 sits in a chair not at table, #7 stands over him mopping his brow*.]

#10: Well, look, you've gotta expect that. You know what you're dealing with.

#7: Yeah, I suppose. [*#10 blows his nose vigorously*.] What's the matter, you got a cold?

#10: And how. These hot-weather colds can kill you. [*He tilts his head back slightly*.] I can hardly touch my nose. Know what I mean?

[*#7 nods sympathetically*.]

#7: I just got over one. [*There is an awkward pause. #7 looks at his watch. Then he looks up at FOREMAN, who is standing at head of table*.] What d'ya say, Mr. Foreman? [FOREMAN *standing at head of table. #7, #10 in background. #3, #4 seated at left at table.* FOREMAN *looks around at the wall clock. #3 leans over to scan #4's newspaper*.]

#3: Anything exciting going on? [*#4 looks up at him. #3 smiles*.] I didn't get a chance to look at the papers today.

#4: I was just wondering how the market closed.

#3 [*Pleasantly.*]: I wouldn't know. Say, are you on the Exchange or something.

#4: I'm a broker.

#3: Well, that's very interesting. Listen, maybe you can answer a question for me. I have an uncle who's been playing around with some Canadian stuff . . .

[*The* FOREMAN *turns around and, as if it is an effort, calls out loudly to the others.*]

FOREMAN: All right, gentlemen. Let's take seats.

[*There is a slow movement toward the table.* #3 *shrugs at* #4 *and turns to the* FOREMAN.]

#7: This better be fast. I got tickets to a ball game tonight. Yanks-Cleveland. We got this new kid, Modjelewski, or whatever his name is, going. He's a bull, this kid! [*He shoots his hand forward and out to indicate the path of a curve ball.*] Shhhhooooom. A real jug handle. [*To* FOREMAN.] Where d'ya want us to sit?

[*When* FOREMAN *gets used to this minor authority he will enjoy it. Right now he is still nervous.*]

FOREMAN: Well, I was thinking we ought to sit in order, by jury numbers. [*He points with each number.*] Two. Three. Four, and so on. If that's okay with you gentlemen.

#10: What's the difference?

#4: I think it's reasonable to sit according to number.

#10: Let it be.

[FOREMAN *has looked back and forth a bit anxiously at this exchange. Now he relaxes and sits down.* #2, #3, #4, #5 *are seated.* #6 *is hanging his coat on the coat rack.* #7 *is draping his over the chair.* #8 *still stares out the window.* #9 *is in bathroom.* #10 *is walking toward his seat, mopping his brow.* #11, #12 *are seated.*]

#12 [*to* #11.]: What was your impression of the prosecuting attorney?

[#11 *looks at him.*]

#11 [*German accent.*]: I beg pardon?

#12: I thought he was really sharp. I mean the way he hammered home his points, one by one, in logical sequence. It takes a good brain to do that. I was very impressed. . . .

[#8 *stares out window, thinking.*]

#11 [*To* #12.]: Yes, I think he did an expert job.

#12: I mean, he had a lot of drive, too. Real drive.

#7 [*Calling, off.*]: Okay, let's get this show on the road.

FOREMAN [*Standing, to* #8.]: How about sitting down. [#8 *doesn't hear the* FOREMAN. *He stares out window.*] The gentlemen at the window. [#8 *turns startled.*] How about sitting down.

#8: Oh. I'm sorry. [#8 *heads for a seat.*]

#10: [*Across table to* #4.]: It's pretty tough to figure, isn't it? A kid kills his father. Bing! Just like that.

#12 [*Butting in.*]: Well, if you analyze the figures . . .

#10 [*Ploughing ahead.*]: It's the element. I'm tellin' you they let those kids run wild up there. Well, maybe it serves 'em right. Know what I mean?

[*This is an annoying characteristic of* #10*'s, this forcing an answer with* "*know what I mean?*"*, as if he is saying* "*Listen, you better answer me, because I'm somebody, see?*" #4 *reacts by looking squarely at* #10*, nodding and turning back to his paper.* #8 *has sat down quietly by this time.* #11 *has looked curiously from* #10 *to* #12 *during this exchange.*]

FOREMAN: Is everybody here?

#6 [*Gesturing toward bathroom.*]: The old man's inside.

FOREMAN: Would you knock on the door.

[#6 *gets up and starts for the bathroom.*]

#7 [*To* #5 *as* #6 *goes by.*]: Hey, you a Yankee fan?

#5: No. Baltimore.

#7: Baltimore! Oh, the suffering! That's like being hit in the head with a crowbar once a day! Listen, who they got . . .

[#6 *reaches the bathroom door and is about to knock when* #9 *opens the door.*]

#6 [*Apologetically.*]: I was just coming to get you.

#7: I'm asking you, who they got besides great groundskeepers?

FOREMAN: We'd like to get started.

#9: Forgive me, gentlemen. I didn't mean to keep you waiting. [*He begins to walk toward his seat, as does* #6.]

#7: Baltimore!

[FOREMAN *is still standing. He looks around. This is the moment for his big speech.*]

FOREMAN [*Nervously.*]: All right. Now you gentlemen can handle this any way you want to. I mean, I'm not going to make any rules. If we want to discuss it first and then vote, that's one way. Or we can vote right now to see how we stand. [*He pauses and looks around.*] Well . . . that's all I have to say.

#4: I think it's customary to take a preliminary vote.

#7: Yeah, let's vote. Who knows, maybe we can all go home.

FOREMAN [*From opposite end of the table.*]: It's up to you. Just let's remember we've got a first-degree murder charge here. If we vote guilty, we send the accused to the electric chair. That's mandatory.

#4: I think we all know that.

#3: Come on, let's vote.

#10: Yeah. Let's see who's where.

FOREMAN: Anybody doesn't want to vote? [*He looks around the table. There is no answer.*] All right. This has to be a twelve-to-nothing vote either way. That's the law. Okay, are we ready? All those voting guilty, raise your hands. [*Seven or eight hands go up immediately. Several others go up more slowly. Everyone looks around the table as the* FOREMAN *begins to count hands. #9's hand goes up now, and all hands are raised, save #8's.*] . . . nine . . . ten . . . eleven. That's eleven for guilty. Okay. Not guilty. [*#8 slowly raises his hand.*] One. Right. Okay, eleven to one, guilty. Now we know where we are. [*#8 lowers his hand.*]

#10: Boy-oh-boy. There's always one.

[*#8 doesn't look in his direction.*]

#7: So what do we do now?

#8: Well, I guess we talk.

#10: Boy-oh-boy.

#3 [*Leaning across to #8.*]: Well, look, do you really think he's innocent?

#8: I don't know.

#3 [*Smiling.*]: I mean, let's be reasonable. You sat right in court and heard the same things we did. The man's a dangerous killer. You could see it.

#8: He's nineteen years old.

#3: Well, that's old enough. He knifed his own father. Four inches into the chest.

#6 [*To #8.*]: It's pretty obvious. I mean I was convinced from the first day.

#3: Well, who wasn't? [*To #8.*] I really think this is one

of those open and shut things. They proved it a dozen
different ways. Would you like me to list them for you?

#8: No.

#10 [*Annoyed.*]: Then what do you want?

#8: Nothing. I just want to talk.

#7: Well, what's there to talk about? Eleven men in here
agree. Nobody had to think about it twice, except you.

#10 [*Leaning over toward #8.*]: I want to ask you some-
thing. Do you believe his story?

#8: I don't know whether I believe it or not. Maybe I
don't.

#7: So what'd you vote not guilty for?

#8: There were eleven votes for guilty. It's not so easy
for me to raise my hand and send a boy off to die without talking about it first.

#7: Who says it's easy for me?

#8 [*Turning.*]: No one.

#7: What, just because I voted fast? I think the guy's
guilty. You couldn't change my mind if you talked for
a hundred years.

#8: I'm not trying to change your mind. It's just that
we're talking about somebody's life here. I mean, we
can't decide in five minutes. Supposing we're wrong?
[*There is a pause. #7 looks at #8.*]

#7: Supposing we're wrong! Supposing this whole build-
ing fell on my head. You can suppose anything.

#8: That's right.

#7: What's the difference how long it takes? We honestly
think he's guilty. So supposing we finish in five minutes?
So what?

#8: Let's take an hour. The ball game doesn't start till
eight o'clock.
[*#7 looks angrily at him for a moment, and then suddenly breaks into a smile as if to say, "What am I heat-
ing myself up over you for?" #7 makes the curve-ball
motion with his hand again.*]

#7 [*Smiling.*]: Shhhooom! [*He settles back in his chair,
smiling. No one says a word for a moment.*]

FOREMAN [*Hesitantly.*]: Well, who's got something to say?
[*He looks at #2. #2 shrugs.*]

#2: Not me.
[FOREMAN *looks around the table. Some of them shrug,
others merely sit. He looks at #9.*]

#9: I'm willing to sit for an hour.

#10: Great. [*A pause.*] I heard a pretty good story last night . . .

#8 [*Sharply.*]: That's not what we're sitting here for.

[*#10 and #8 speak across #9, who turns from one to the other. Camera shoots over shoulders of #4 and 5.*]

#10: All right, then you tell me. What are we sitting here for?

[*#8 looks at him, trying to phrase the following. They wait.*]

#8: Maybe for no reason. I don't know. Look, this boy's been kicked around all his life. You know, living in a slum, his mother dead since he was nine. He spent a year and a half in an orphanage while his father served a jail term for forgery. That's not a very good head-start. He's a wild, angry kid and that's all he's ever been. You know why he got that way? Because he was knocked on the head by somebody once a day, every day. He's had a pretty terrible nineteen years. I think maybe we owe him a few words. That's all. [*He looks around the table. #9 nods slowly.*]

#10: I don't mind telling you this, mister. We don't owe him a thing. He got a fair trial, didn't he? What d'you think that trial cost? He's lucky he got it. [*Turning to #11.*]: Know what I mean? [*Now looking across table at #'s 3, 4, 5.*] Look, we're all grown-ups in here. We heard the facts, didn't we? [*To #8.*] Now you're not going to tell us that we're supposed to believe that kid, knowing what he is. Listen, I've lived among 'em all my life. You can't believe a word they say. You know that. [*To all.*] I mean they're born liars.

[*There is a pause.*]

#9 [*Slowly.*]: Only an ignorant man can believe that.

#10: Now, listen . . .

#9 [*To #10.*] Do you think you were born with a monopoly on the truth? [*To all.*] I think certain things should be pointed out to this man.

[*#3 is annoyed at this argument.*]

#3: All right. It's not Sunday. We don't need a sermon in here.

#9 [*To all.*]: What he says is very dangerous. . . .

#10 [*Loudly.*]: All right, that's enough!

[*He glares at #9. #9 half rises, but then feels #8's*

hand firmly on his arm, gently pulling him down. He sits down, turns away from #10 and looks briefly at #8. #8 looks calmly, firmly back, and in his look there is understanding and sympathy.]

#4: I don't see any need for arguing like this. I think we ought to be able to behave like gentlemen.

#12: Right!

#4 [*Calmly.*]: If we're going to discuss this case let's discuss the facts.

FOREMAN: I think that's a good point. We have a job to do. Let's do it.

[*#2 rises and walks around end of table. #2 goes off to his jacket to get a package of cough drops, and returns during the next lines. #12 doodles steadily on his pad. #11 watches him. He draws a cereal box.*]
Maybe if the gentleman who's disagreeing down there could tell us why. You know, tell us what he thinks, we could show him where he's probably mixed up.

[*#12 looks at #11 and sees him watching his doodling. He holds up his drawing for him to see.*]

#12 [*To #11 confidentially.*]: Rice Pops. It's one of the products I work on at the agency. "The Breakfast with the Built-in Bounce." I wrote that line.

[*#11 smiles in spite of himself.*]

#11: It's very catchy.

FOREMAN [*Annoyed, to #12.*]: If you don't mind.

#12: I'm sorry. I have this habit of doodling. It keeps me thinking clearly.

FOREMAN: We're trying to get someplace here. Y'know, we can sit here forever . . .

#12: Well look, maybe this is an idea. I'm just thinking out loud, but it seems to me it's up to us to convince this gentleman [*indicating #8*] that we're right and he's wrong. Maybe if we each took a minute or two. Mind you, this is just a quick idea. . . .

FOREMAN: No, I think it's a good one. Supposing we go once around the table.

#7: Anything. Let's start it off.

FOREMAN [*To #7.*]: Okay. How about you going first?

#7: Not me. I think we oughta go in order. [*He takes his gum out of his mouth and looks for a place to throw it. Finally he lets fly. We hear a thin clank. He seems satisfied.*]

FOREMAN: That sounds all right. In order, a coupla minutes apiece. [*To* #2.] I guess you're first.

#2: Oh. Well. . . . [*He pauses nervously.*] Well, it's hard
to put into words. I just . . . think he's guilty. I thought
it was obvious from the word go. I mean nobody proved
otherwise.

#8 [*Quietly.*]: Nobody has to prove otherwise. The bur-
den of proof is on the prosecution. The defendant
doesn't have to open his mouth. That's in the Constitu-
tion. You've heard of it.

#2 [*Flustered.*]: Well, sure I've heard of it. I know what
it is. I . . . what I meant . . . well, the man is guilty. I
mean somebody saw him do it. . . . [*He looks around
helplessly, and then looks down.*]

#3: Okay. Now here's what I think, and I have no per-
sonal feelings about this. I'm talking about facts. Number one: let's take the old man who lived on the second floor right underneath the room where the murder
took place. At ten minutes after twelve on the night of
the killing he heard loud noises in the apartment upstairs. He said it sounded like a fight. Then he heard
the kid shout out, "I'm gonna kill you." A second later
he heard a body fall, and he ran to the door of his apartment, looked out, and saw the kid running down the
stairs and out of the house. Then he called the police.
They found the father with a knife in his chest. . . .

FOREMAN: And the coroner fixed the time of death at
around midnight.

#3: Right. I mean there are facts for you. You can't re-
fute facts. This boy is guilty. I'm telling you. Look, I'm
as sentimental as the next guy. I know the kid is only
nineteen, but he's still got to pay for what he did.

#7: I'm with you.

FOREMAN: All right. Next.

[*#3 and 5 listen closely to #4, a quiet, imposing, metic-
ulous man. He takes off his eyeglasses, waving them as
he talks.*]

#4: It was obvious, to me anyway, that the boy's entire
story was flimsy. He claimed he was at the movies during
the time of the killing and yet one hour later he couldn't
remember what films he saw, or who played in them.

#3: That's right. Did you hear that? [*To* #4.] You're
absolutely right.

#4: No one saw him going in or out of the theater. . . .

#10 [*Impatiently in #8's direction.*]: Listen, what about that woman across the street? If her testimony don't prove it, nothing does.

#11: That's right. She was the one who actually saw the killing.

FOREMAN: Let's go in order here.

[*#10 rises, handkerchief in hand.*]

#10 [*Loudly.*]: Just a minute. Here's a woman . . . [*He blows his note.*] Here's a woman who's lying in bed and can't sleep. [*He begins to walk around the table, wiping his tender nose and talking.*] She's dying with the heat. Know what I mean? Anyway, she looks out the window and right across the street she sees the kid stick the knife into his father. The time is 12:10 on the nose. Everything fits. Look, she's known the kid all his life. His window is right opposite hers, across the el tracks, and she swore she saw him do it. [*#10 is now standing behind #6 and looking across table at #8. #10 wipes his nose.*]

#8: Through the windows of a passing elevated train.

#10 [*Through the handkerchief.*]: Right. This el train had no passengers on it. It was just being moved downtown. The lights were out, remember? And they proved in court that at night you can look through the windows of an el train when the lights are out and see what's happening on the other side. They proved it!

#8 [*To #10.*]: I'd like to ask you something. You don't believe the boy. How come you believe the woman? She's one of "them" too, isn't she?

[*#10 is suddenly angry.*]

#10: You're a pretty smart fellow, aren't you?

[*He takes a step toward #8. #8 sits calmly there. #10 strides toward #8. The FOREMAN rises in his seat. #3 and 5 jump up and move toward #10.*]

FOREMAN [*Nervously.*]: Hey, let's take it easy.

[*#3, 5, and 10 stand behind #7. #3 and 5 have reached #10, who looks angrily at #8. #3 takes #10's arm.*]

#10 [*Angrily.*]: What's he so wise about? I'm telling you . . .

#3 [*Strongly*]: Come on. Sit down. [*He begins to lead #10 back to his seat.*] What are you letting him get you all upset for? Relax.

FOREMAN: Let's calm down now. I mean we're not gonna get anywhere fighting.

[*#3 and* 10 *reach* #10's *seat.* #10 *sits down.* #3 *remains standing now. Until his next lines, he walks around the room, takes a drink at the fountain, etc.*]

FOREMAN [*Standing.*]: Okay. Let's try to keep it peaceful in here. [*He looks down the table.*] Whose turn is it?

#12 [*Pointing at* #5.]: His.

FOREMAN: Okay. You've got two minutes.

[#5 *looks around nervously.*]

#5: I'll pass it.

FOREMAN: That's your privilege. How about the next gentleman?

#6: I don't know. I started to be convinced, uh . . . you know, very early in the case. Well, I was looking for the motive. That's very important. If there's no motive, where's the case? So anyway, that testimony from those people across the hall from the kid's apartment, that was very powerful. Didn't they say something about an argument between the father and the boy around seven o'clock that night? I mean, I can be wrong.

#11: It was eight o'clock. Not seven.

#8: That's right. Eight o'clock. They heard an argument, but they couldn't hear what it was about. Then they heard the father hit the boy twice, and finally they saw the boy walk angrily out of the house. What does that prove?

[*Any time* #6 *is working on his own ideas he feels himself on unsteady ground, and is ready to back down. He does so now.*]

#6: Well, it doesn't exactly prove anything. It's just part of the picture. I didn't say it proved anything.

#8: You said it revealed a motive for this killing. The prosecuting attorney said the same thing. Well, I don't think it's a very strong motive. This boy has been hit so many times in his life that violence is practically a normal state of affairs for him. I can't see two slaps in the face provoking him into committing murder.

#4 [*Quietly.*]: It may have been two too many. Everyone has a breaking point.

[#8 *is looking across at* #4, *and realizing instantly that this will probably be his most powerful adversary.* #4

*is the man of logic, and a man without emotional at-
tachment to this case.*]

FOREMAN [*To* #6.]: Anything else?

#6: No.

[*#6 gets up and walks a few paces from the table to
stretch. #3 is standing at the water fountain, listening.
All others are seated.*]

FOREMAN [To #7.]: Okay. How about you?

#7: Me? [*He pauses, looks around, shrugs, then speaks.*]
I don't know, it's practically all said already. We can
talk about it forever. It's the same thing. I mean this
kid is five for oh. Look at his record. He was in children's court when he was ten for throwing a rock at his
teacher. At fifteen he was in reform school. He stole a
car. He's been arrested for mugging. He was picked up
twice for knife-fighting. He's real swift with a knife,
they said. This is a very fine boy.

#8: Ever since he was five years old his father beat him
up regularly. He used his fists.

#7 [*Indignantly.*]: So would I! A kid like that.

[*#3 walks over from the water fountain toward #7. He
stands behind #7, talks to #8.*]

#3: And how. It's the kids, the way they are nowadays.
Listen, when I was his age I used to call my father "sir."
That's right. Sir! You ever hear a boy call his father
that anymore?

#8: Fathers don't seem to think it's important any more.

#3: No? Have you got any kids?

#8: Three.

#3: Yeah, well I've got one, a boy twenty-two years old.
I'll tell you about him. When he was nine he ran away
from a fight. I saw him. I was so ashamed I almost
threw up. So I told him right out: "I'm gonna make a
man outa you or I'm gonna bust you in half trying."
Well, I made a man outa him all right. When he was
sixteen we had a battle. He hit me in the face! He's big,
y'know. I haven't seen him in two years. Rotten kid. You
work your heart out . . . [*He stops. He has said more
than he intended and more passionately than he intended
it. He is embarrassed. He looks at #8, and then at all
of them. Then loud.*] All right. Let's get on with it. [*He
turns and walks angrily around the table to his seat. He*

sits down. #4 looks at #3 and then across the table.]

#4: I think we're missing the point here. This boy, let's say he's a product of a filthy neighborhood and a broken home. We can't help that. We're here to decide whether he's guilty or innocent, not to go into the reasons why he grew up this way. He was born in a slum. Slums are breeding grounds for criminals. I know it. So do you. [*#5 reacts to the following.*] It's no secret. Children from slum backgrounds are potential menaces to society. Now, I think . . .

#10 [*Interrupting.*]: Brother, you can say that again. The kids who crawl outa those places are real trash. I don't want any part of them, I'm telling you.

[*The face of #5 is angry. He tries to control himself. His voice shakes.*]

#5: I've lived in a slum all my life. . . .

[*#10 knows he has said the wrong thing.*]

#10: Oh, now wait a second . . .

#5 [*Furious.*]: I used to play in a back yard that was filled with garbage. Maybe it still smells on me.

#10 [*Beginning to anger.*]: Now listen, sonny . . .

[FOREMAN *has risen.*]

FOREMAN [*To #5.*]: Now, let's be reasonable. There's nothing personal . . .

[*#5 shoots to his feet.*]

#5 [*Loud.*]: There is something personal! [*He looks around at the others, all looking at him. Then, suddenly he has nothing to say. He sits down, fists clenched. #3 gets up and walks to him, pats him on the back. #5 doesn't look up.*]

#3: Come on now. He didn't mean you, feller. Let's not be so sensitive.

#11 [*Softly.*]: This sensitivity I can understand.

[*The* FOREMAN *looks at #11, and his face shows distaste for him in spite of himself. #12 gets up and walks to the window.*]

FOREMAN: All right, let's stop all this arguing. We're wasting time here. [*Pointing to #8.*] It's your turn. Let's go.

#8: Well, I didn't expect a turn. I thought you were all supposed to be convincing me. Wasn't that the idea?

#12: Check. That was the idea.

FOREMAN: I forgot about that. He's right.

#10 [*Annoyed with* #12.]: Well, what's the difference! He's the one who's keeping us in here. Let's hear what he's got to say.

FOREMAN: Now just a second. We decided to do it a certain way. Let's stick to what we said.

#10 [*Disgusted.*]: Ah, stop bein' a kid, willya!

FOREMAN: A kid! Listen, what d'you mean by that?

#10: What d'ya think I mean? K-I-D, kid!

FOREMAN: What, just because I'm trying to keep this thing organized? Listen . . . [*He gets up.*] You want to do it? Here. You sit here. You take the responsibility. I'll just shut up, that's all.

#10: Listen, what are you gettin' so hot about? Calm down, willya.

FOREMAN: Don't tell me to calm down! Here! Here's the chair. [*Gesturing toward his empty chair.*] You keep it goin' smooth and everything. What d'ya think it's a snap? Come on, Mr. Foreman. Let's see how great you'd run the show.

#10 [*Grinning helplessly.*]:   Did y'ever see such a thing?

FOREMAN [*Loud.*]: You think it's funny or something?

[#12 *walks over to him from the window.*]

#12: Take it easy. The whole thing's unimportant.

[FOREMAN *glares up at* #12.]

FOREMAN: Unimportant? You want to try it?

#12: No. Listen, you're doing a beautiful job. Nobody wants to change.

[*The* FOREMAN *turns away from* #12 *and looks at the rest of the jury. He is embarrassed now. For a moment he tries to think of something to say. Then, abruptly he sits down. He looks down at the table.*]

[#8, 9, 10 *all look in direction of* FOREMAN. *There is a pause. Then:*]

#10: All right. Let's hear from somebody.

[*There is another pause.*]

#8: Well, it's all right with me if you want me to tell you how I feel about it right now.

[FOREMAN *looks down at table.*]

FOREMAN [*Softly.*]: I don't care what you do.

[#8 *waits for a moment, and then begins. As he speaks,* #12 *walks up and stands behind* #9.]

#8: All right. I haven't got anything brilliant. I only

know as much as you do. According to the testimony the boy looks guilty. Maybe he is. I sat there in court for six days listening while the evidence built up. You know everybody sounded so positive that I started to get a peculiar feeling about this trial. I mean nothing is that positive. I had questions I would have liked to ask. Maybe they wouldn't have meant anything. I don't know. But I started to feel that the defense counsel wasn't conducting a thorough enough cross-examination. He let too many things go. Little things.

#10 [*Interrupting*.]: What little things? Listen, when these guys *don't* ask questions that's because they know the answers already, and they figure they'll be hurt.

#8: Maybe. It's also possible for a lawyer to be just plain stupid, isn't it? It's possible.

#6: You sound like you met my brother-in-law once.

[*A few of the jurors laugh.*]

#8 [*Smiling*.]: I kept putting myself in the place of the boy. I would have asked for another lawyer, I think. I mean if I was on trial for my life, I'd want my lawyer to tear the prosecution witnesses to shreds, or at least to try. Look, there was one alleged eyewitness to this killing. Someone else claims he heard the killing and then saw the boy running out afterward. There was a lot of circumstantial evidence, but actually those two witnesses were the entire case for the prosecution. We're dealing with a human life here. Supposing they were wrong?

[#12 *stands behind* #8 *and looks down at him.*]

#12: What do you mean supposing they were wrong? What's the point of having witnesses at all?

[#12 *stands behind* #8. #8 *is turned to look up at him.* #9 *listens carefully.*]

#8: Could they be wrong?

#12: They sat on the stand under oath. What are you trying to say?

#8: They're only people. People make mistakes. Could they be wrong?

#12: I . . . No! I don't think so!

#8: Do you know so?

#12: Well, now listen, nobody can *know* a thing like that. This isn't an exact science. . . .

[#8 *turns away from* #12, *satisfied.*]

#8 [*Quietly.*]: That's right. It isn't.

[*There is silence for a moment. #12 walks back to his seat. #3 gets up angrily and strides down to a position behind #5.*]

#3 [*To #8.*]: All right. Let's try to get to the point here. What about the switch-knife they found in the father's chest?

#2 [*Nervously.*]: Well, wait a minute. I think we oughta . . . There are some people who haven't talked yet. Shouldn't we . . .

#3 [*To #2.*]: Look, they can talk whenever they like. Now just be quiet a second, willya please. [*#2, wounded at being slapped down by #3, looks down at table. To #8.*] Okay what about the knife? You know, the one that fine upright boy admitted buying on the night of the murder. Let's talk about that.

[*#8 appears just a bit pleased at this turn of conversation.*]

#8: All right. Let's talk about it. Let's get it in here and look at it. I'd like to see it again. [*He turns toward* FOREMAN.] Mr. Foreman?

[FOREMAN *looks at #8 for a moment. Then he gets up and moves to the door.*]

#3 [*Off.*]: We all know what it looks like. I don't see why we have to look at it again.

[*The* FOREMAN *knocks on the door. The door opens and the* GUARD *pokes his head into the room. #3 still stands behind #5. He looks at door where* FOREMAN *stands whispering to the* GUARD. *Then #3 turns to table.*] What are we gonna get out of seeing the knife again?

#5 [*Looking up.*]: You brought it up.

#3 [*Giving him a look and then turning to #4.*]: What do you think?

#4: The gentleman has a right to see exhibits in evidence. [*#3 shrugs and turns away.*]

#4 [*Across to #8.*]: The knife, and the way it was bought, is pretty strong evidence. Don't you think so?

#8: I do.

#4: Good. Now supposing we take these facts one at a time. One. The boy admitted going out of his house at 8 o'clock on the night of the murder after being punched several times by his father.

#8: He didn't say "punched." He said "hit." There's a

difference between a slap and a punch.

#4 [*Doggedly.*]: After being *hit* several times by his father. Two. The boy went directly to a neighborhood junk shop where he bought a . . . what do you call these things?
[*Simultaneously.*]

#3: Switch-knives.   #4: A switch-blade knife.
                                      [*To* #3.] Thanks.

#4: Three. This wasn't what you'd call an ordinary knife. It had a very unusual carved handle. Four. The store-keeper who sold it to him identified it and said it was the only one of its kind he had ever had in stock. Five. At oh, about 8:45 the boy ran into some friends of his in front of a tavern. Am I correct so far?

#8: Yes, you are.

#3 [*To* #8.]: You bet he is. [*To all.*] Now, listen to this man. He knows what he's talking about.

#4: The boy talked with his friends for about an hour, leaving them at about 9:45. During this time they saw the switch-knife. Six. Each of them identified the death-weapon in court as that same knife. Seven. The boy arrived home at about 10 o'clock. Now this is where the stories offered by the boy and the state begin to di-verge slightly.
[*#8 listens quietly, patiently, waiting his turn.*]

#4: He claims that he stayed home until 11:30 and then went to one of those all-night movies. He returned home at about 3:15 in the morning to find his father dead and himself arrested. Now, what happened to the switch-knife? This is the charming and imaginative little fable the boy invented. He claims that the knife fell through a hole in his pocket sometime between 11:30 and 3:15 while he was on his trip to the movies, and that he never saw it again. Now there is a tale, gentlemen. I think it's quite clear that the boy never went to the movies that night. No one in the house saw him go out at 11:30. No one at the theatre identified him. He couldn't even remember the names of the pictures he saw. What actually happened is this. The boy stayed home, had another fight with his father, stabbed him to death with the knife at ten minutes after twelve and fled from the house. He even remembered to wipe the knife clean of fingerprints.

[*The door opens. The* GUARD *enters carrying a curiously designed knife with a tag hanging from it.* #4 *walks into the shot and takes the knife from the guard. He turns and moves back to his seat as the* GUARD *exits. He stands behind his seat holding the knife.*]

#4 [*Leaning over to* #8.]: Everyone connected with the case identified this knife. Now are you trying to tell me that it really fell through a hole in the boy's pocket and that someone picked it up off the street, went to the boy's house and stabbed his father with it just to be amusing?

#8: No. I'm saying that it's possible that the boy lost the knife, and that someone else stabbed his father with a similar knife. It's possible.

[#4 *flicks open the blade of the knife and jams it into the table. Jurors* #2, 5, 10, 11, 12 *get up and crowd around to get a better look at it.*]

#4: Take a look at that knife. It's a very unusual knife. I've never seen one like it. Neither had the storekeeper who sold it to the boy. Aren't you trying to make us accept a pretty incredible coincidence?

#8: I'm not trying to make anyone accept it. I'm just saying that it's possible.

[#3, *standing next to* #4, *is suddenly infuriated at* #8*'s calmness. He leans forward.*]

#3 [*Shouting.*]: And I'm saying it's not possible.

[#8 *stands for a moment in the silence. Then he reaches into his pocket and swiftly withdraws a knife. He holds it in front of his face, and flicks open the blade. Then he leans forward and sticks the knife into the table next to the other. The two ornately carved knives stick into the table, side by side, are each exactly alike. There is an immediate burst of sound in the room.*]

[*Simultaneous*]

#7: What is this? #6: What is it?

#12: Where'd that come from? #2: How d'you like that!

[*The jurors cluster around the knives.* #8 *is standing away from the table, watching.* #3 *looks up at him.*]

#3 [*Amazed.*]: What are you trying to do?

#10 [*Loud.*]: Yeah! What's going on here? Who do you think you are?

[#6 *has taken the knife out of the table and is holding it.*]

#6: Look at it! It's the same knife!

[#8 *watches them closely, a few steps back from the group. The ad lib hubbub still goes on.*]

#4: Quiet! Let's be quiet!

[*The noise begins to subside.* #4 *takes the knife from* #5's *hand and speaks to* #8, *who stands at left of frame.*]

#4: Where'd you get it?

#8: I was walking for a couple of hours last night, just thinking. I walked through the boy's neighborhood. The knife comes from a little pawnshop three blocks from his house. It cost two dollars.

#4: It's against the law to buy or sell switch-blade knives.

#8: That's right. I broke the law.

[#3 *pushes in next to* #4. *He is much too angry for the situation. Others look at him peculiarly as he speaks.*]

#3: Listen, you pulled a real bright trick here. Now supposing you tell me what you proved. Maybe there are ten knives like that. So what?

#8: Maybe there are.

[#3 *is silent for a minute. He knows that a tiny dent has been made in the case. He splutters.*]

#3: So what does that mean? What do you think it is? It's the same kind of knife. So what's that? The discovery of the age, or something?

#11 [*Quietly.*]: This does not change the fact that it would be still an incredible coincidence for another person to have made the stabbing with the same kind of knife.

#3: That's right! He's right.

#7: The odds are a million to one.

#8: It's possible.

[#4 *looks calmly at* #8, *and speaks quietly.*]

#4: But not very probably.

[#8 *looks steadily at* #4.]

FOREMAN: Listen, let's take seats. There's no point in milling around here.

[*They begin to move back to their seats.* #4 *flips the knife back into the table and sits down. There is quiet ad libbing as most of the jurors take seats.* #8 *stays on his feet, watching them. #2 turns to the* FOREMAN *with a nervous half-smile.*]

#2: It's interesting that he'd find a knife exactly like the one the boy bought. . . .

FOREMAN [*Ignoring him, speaking to all.*]: Okay. Now what?

#3 [*To #2.*]: What's interesting? You think it proves anything?

#2: Well, no. I was just . . .

#3 [*Turning away.*]: Interesting! [#3 *suddenly has an idea. He points at #8.*] Listen, how come the kid bought the knife to begin with?

#8: Well, he claims that . . .

#3: I know. He bought it as a present for a friend of his. He was gonna give it to him the next day, because he busted the other kid's knife dropping it on the pavement.

#8: That's what he said.

#7: Boloney!

#9: The friend testified that the boy did break his knife.

#3: Yeah. And how long before the killing? Three weeks. Right? So how come our noble lad bought this knife one half hour after his father smacked him, and three and a half hours before they found it shoved up to here in the father's chest?

#7 [*Grinning.*]: Well, he was *gonna* give the knife to his friend. He just wanted to use it for a minute.

[*There is scattered laughter. #8 waits till the laughter dies down.*]

#8 [*To #3.*]: Look, maybe you can answer this. It's one of the questions I wanted to ask in court. If the boy bought the knife to use on his father, how come he showed what was going to be the murder weapon to three friends of his just a couple of hours before the killing?

[*There is silence. The silence holds for a minute. #8 watches them, and then walks to the window and looks out. The following speeches are simultaneous.*]

#10: So maybe he decided to knife his old man when he got home.

FOREMAN: He never told his friends he bought the thing as a present.

[#3 *gets to his feet.*]

#3 [*Angry.*]: Listen, all of this is just talk. The boy lied and you know it.

[#8, *at window, turns, waits a beat, and then walks toward table.*]

#8: He may have lied. [*He reaches* #10 *and puts his hand on* #10*'s shoulder.*] Do you think he lied?

#10: Now that's a stupid question. Sure he lied!

#8 [*To* #4.]: Do you?

#4: You don't have to ask me that. You know my answer. He lied.

#8 [*To* #5.]: Do you think he lied?

[#5 *can't answer immediately. He looks around nervously.*]

#5: Well . . . I don't know. . . .

#3: Now, wait a second! [*He starts to stride around table past* #4, 5, 6.] What are you, the kid's lawyer or something? Who do you think you are to start cross-examining us? Listen, there are still eleven of us in here who think he's guilty. [#3 *is standing behind* #7 *now.*]

#7: Right! What do you think you're gonna accomplish? You're not gonna change anybody's mind. So if you want to be stubborn and hang this jury, go ahead. The kid'll be tried again and found guilty sure as he's born.

[#8 *walks back to his seat. He stands behind it.* #3 *stands behind* #7*'s seat.*]

#8: You're probably right.

#7: So what are you gonna do about it? We can be here all night.

#9: It's only one night. A boy may die.

[#7 *glares at* #9, *but has no answer.* #8 *sits down.*]

#7: Brother! Anybody got a deck of cards?

[*There is silence.* #3 *starts a walk over to the coat rack to get some cigarettes from his jacket. The room is quiet.*]

#2 [*To* FOREMAN.]: I don't think he ought to joke about it.

FOREMAN [*Annoyed.*]: What do you want me to do?

[#2 *would like to say something to* #7, *but daren't.* #10 *slams his hand down on the table.*]

#10: Listen, I don't see what all this stuff about the knife has to do with anything. Somebody *saw* the kid stab his

father. What more do we need? You guys can talk the
ears right offa my head. Know what I mean? I got three
garages of mine going to pot while you're talking! Let's
get done and get outa here!

#11 [*Mildly.*]: The knife was very important to the district
attorney. He spent one whole day . . .

#10 [*Mad.*]: He's a fifteenth assistant, or something.
What does he know?

[*#10 blows his nose loudly. #11 shifts in his seat away
from #10. #10 glares at him over the handkerchief.*]

FOREMAN: Okay. I think we oughta get on with it now.
These side arguments only slow us up. [*He leans down
to #8.*] What about it?

[*#8 sits in his seat quietly.*]

#11: You're the only one.

[*#8 nods. He still sits silently, thinking. Then he looks
around the table for a moment. Finally he seems to have
made his decision.*]

#8: I have a proposition to make to all of you. [*#2, 5, 9,
listen closely.*] I want to call for a vote. I'd like
you eleven men to vote by secret written ballot. I'll ab-
stain. there are still eleven votes for guilty I won't
all al. We'll take a guilty verdict in to the judge
But if anyone votes not guilty we'll stay and
out. [*There is a pause.*] Well that's all.
If   try it, I'm ready.

#7:   let's do it.

FOREMAN: hat sounds fair. Is everyone agreed? [*Some
of the urors nod their heads.*] Anyone doesn't agree?
[*There is silence.*] Okay. Pass these along.

[*The FOREMAN begins to pass out slips of paper. #8
gets up and walks over to the window. He stands with
his back to it. The jurors pass the slips along. And finally
each of them begins to write. #8 watches, waiting. Now
some of them begin to fold up their slips, and pass them
back to the FOREMAN. When all the slips are back, the
FOREMAN stacks the slips on the table next to him. Then
he looks over at #8, who looks back at FOREMAN, waiting. FOREMAN looks from #8 down to table. He picks
up the first slip, opens it, and reads.*]

FOREMAN: Guilty. [*The FOREMAN opens another slip and
reads it.*] Guilty. [*No one moves. Each man waits tense-*]

ridicule of others, even when there's a worthy cause. [#7 *raises his eyes to heaven, shakes his head in disgust, and gets up. He turns his back on #9 and heads for the men's room. #9 stands up and speaks spiritedly to his back.*] So he gambled for support, and I gave it to him. I respect his motives. The boy on trial is probably guilty. But I want to hear more. Right now the vote is ten to two. [*The bathroom door slams shut. #9 takes one step toward it, furious at #7's arrogance, and shouts.*] I'm talking here! You have no right to . . . [*But he is stopped by #8's hand on his shoulder. He turns to #8.*]

#8 [*Gently.*]: He can't hear you. He never will. Let's sit down.

[*#9 nods and slowly takes his seat, spent with his effort. #8 remains standing, looking down at him.*]

#3: Well, if the speech is over, maybe we can go on.

FOREMAN: I think we ought to take a break. One man's inside there. Let's wait for him.

[*The* FOREMAN *stands up; he walks around the table to where the two knives are stuck into table. He plucks the tagged one out, and closes it. #4 opens up his newspaper and begins to read it. #3 gets up and, standing behind his chair, stretches. We hear murmured ad lib conversations, and the sound of several other jurors getting up. The* FOREMAN *goes to the door. He knocks. The door opens and the guard pokes his head in. The* FOREMAN *hands him the knife. The* GUARD *closes the door.* FOREMAN *walks back to his seat. #2 sits at table cleaning his glasses. #11 and 12 are still seated. Their heads are turned toward each other. In background, #3 stands near door, thinking. He watches #5, and while we hear the following dialogue between #11 and 12, #3 watches as #5 gets up, crosses in front of him, and goes to far end of room. #3 obviously wants the right opportunity to talk with him alone.*]

#12: Looks like we're really hung up here. I mean that thing with the old man was pretty unexpected. [#11 *nods and shrugs.*] I wish I knew how we could break this up. [*Suddenly smiling.*] Y'know in advertising—I told you I worked at an agency, didn't I? [#11 *nods.*] Well, there are some pretty strange people . . . not strange really . . . they just have peculiar ways of expressing themselves, y'know what I mean? [#11 *nods again*.] Well, it's probably the same in your business, right? What do you do?

#11: I'm a watchmaker.

#12: Really? The finest watchmakers come from Europe, I imagine. [#11 *bows slightly*.] Anyway, I was telling you, in the agency, when they reach a point like this in a meeting, there's always some character ready with an idea. And it kills me, I mean it's the weirdest thing in the whole world sometimes the way they precede the idea with some kind of phrase. Like . . . Oh, some account exec'll say, "Here's an idea. Let's run it up the flagpole and see if anyone salutes it." [#12 *laughs*.] I mean it's idiotic, but it's funny. . . .

[#3 *walks over to* #5, *who stands at the water fountain.* #5 *looks up at him over a cup of water*.]

#3: Look, I was a little excited. Well, you know how it is, I . . . I didn't mean to get nasty or anything. [#5 *finishes the water and tosses the cup in the basket*.] I'm glad you're not the kind who lets these emotional appeals influence him. [#10 *stands next to* #5, *sniffing*.] I'm telling you there's always someone who wants to give a proven criminal another chance. [*Thumbing in* #8's *direction*.] Like this guy . . .

#10: They're old women. Waddya expect? [*To* #5.] Look, nobody meant anything before, y'know? It's just sometimes ya get heated up. Listen, intelligent people gotta stick together here to see that justice is done. That's the most important. You stay with us, hear?

[#10 *claps* #5 *on the back, and looks off across the room.* #8 *stands alone against the window at far end of room, watching* #3, 5, 10. *He watches for a moment and then turns and walks toward men's room. He opens door and enters. The scene now changes to the men's room.* #7 *is at sink drying his hands and face on a paper towel. He looks up into the mirror now, and we see his face in mirror, looking at* #8. #7 *turns and steps away from sink.* #8 *goes to sink and runs water.* #7, *still drying, watches him*.]

#7: Say, are you a salesman?

#8 [*Looking at him in mirror*.]: I'm an architect.

#7: You know what the soft sell is? [#8, *his face dripping now, looks at him again in the mirror*.] You're pretty good at it. I'll tell ya. I got a different technique. Jokes. Drinks. Knock 'em on their tails. I made twenty-seven thousand last year selling marmalade. That's not bad. [#8 *bends to rinse his face.* #7 *watches him for a moment.*] What are ya getting out of it, kicks? [#8 *looks up at him.*] The boy is guilty, pal. Like the nose on your face. So let's go home before we get sore throats.

[#8 *turns off the water, and turns to* #7. #7 *hands him a paper towel and waits.* #8 *starts to dry his face, watching* #7.]

#8 [*Through the towel.*]: What's the difference whether you get it here or at the ball game?

[#7 *looks at him narrowly, and then smiles.*]

#7: No difference, pal. No difference at all.

[#7 *exits, letting the door slam.* #8 *slowly dries his face. A moment later the door opens. We hear a loud laugh from outside.* #6 *enters the bathroom. The door closes.* #6 *walks over to the sink, turns on the water. During this next exchange, he lets it run over his wrists.*]

#6 [*Sarcastically.*]: Nice bunch of guys.

#8: I guess they're the same as any.

#6: That loud, heavy-set guy, the one who was tellin' us about his kid . . . the way he was talking . . . boy, that was an embarrassing thing.

#8 [*Smiling.*]: Yeah. [#8 *stands watching* #6 *cool his wrists.*]

#6: What a murderous day. [*He looks at* #8 *in the mirror, then pointedly.*] You think we'll be much longer?

#8: I don't know.

#6: He's guilty for sure. There's not a doubt in the whole world. We shoulda been done already. [#8 *doesn't answer him.*] Listen, I don't care, y'know. It beats workin'. [*He laughs, and* #8 *smiles. Then* #6 *pointedly looks at* #8. *His smile vanishes.*] You think he's not guilty?

#8: I don't know. It's possible.

#6 [*Friendly.*]: I don't know you, but I'm bettin' you've never been wronger in your life. Y'oughta wrap it up. You're wastin' your time.

#8: Supposing you were the one on trial?

[#6 *looks at him seriously. There is a pause. He takes a towel and dries his hands.*]

#6: I'm not used to supposing. I'm just a working man. My boss does the supposing. But I'll try one. Supposing you talk us all outa this, and the kid really did knife his father?

[*#6 looks at #8, and then exits. #8 stands there alone for a few moments, and we know that this is the problem which has been tormenting him. He doesn't know, and never will. Finally he exits. The scene returns to the jury room.*]

FOREMAN: Okay. Let's take seats.

[*The twelve jurymen move for their seats. Finally all are seated. #2 settles his glasses on his nose and turns to look up at the wall clock. He turns to* FOREMAN.]

#2: Looks like we'll be here for dinner.

[FOREMAN *scowls at #2, then turns and addresses the group.*]

FOREMAN: Okay. Let's get down to business. Who wants to start it off?

[*There is a pause. #4 and 6 start to speak at the same time.*]

#6: Well, I'd like to make a point. . . . [*To #4.*] Pardon me.

#4: Maybe it would be profitable if we . . . [*To #6.*] I'm sorry. go ahead.

#6: I didn't mean to interrupt. . . .

#4: No. Go ahead. It's all right.

#6: Well . . . I was going to say, well, this is probably a small point, but anyway . . . [*Across to #8.*] The boy had a motive for the killing. You know, the beatings and all. So if he didn't do it, who did? Who else had the motive? That's my point. I mean nobody goes out and kills someone without a motive, not unless he's just plain nuts. Right? [*He sits back rather proudly.*]

#8: As far as I know, we're supposed to decide whether or not the boy on trial is guilty beyond a reasonable doubt. We're not concerned with anyone else's motives here. That's a job for the police.

#4: Very true. But we can't help letting the only motive we know of creep into our thoughts, can we? And we can't help asking ourselves who else might have had a motive. Logically, these things follow. [*Nodding at*

#6.] This gentleman is asking a reasonable question. Somebody killed him. If it wasn't the boy, who was it?

#3 [*Grinning.*]: Modjelewski.

#7 [*Mock indignance.*]: You're talking about the man I love! The world's fastest rookie . . .

#3 [*Still grinning.*]: He's got a rubber arm!
[*We hear a few laughs.*]

#4 [*Angry.*]: I don't see what's funny about this. If you haven't got anything to add besides jokes, I suggest you listen.

#3 [*Still grinning.*]: Okay. It's just letting off steam. I'm sorry. Go ahead. [#3, *as always, shows real respect for* #4. *The grin fades from his face.*]

#4 [*Across to* #8.]: Well, maybe you can answer me. Who else might have killed the father?

#8: Well, I don't know. The father wasn't exactly a model citizen. The boy's lawyer brought this out pretty clearly, I thought. He was in prison once. He was known to be a consistent horse bettor. He spent a lot of time in neighborhood bars and he'd get into fist fights sometimes after a couple of drinks. One of them was over a woman no one could seem to remember. He was a tough, cruel, primitive kind of a man who never held a job for more than six months in his life. So here are a few possibilities. He could have been murdered by any one of many men he served time with in prison. By a bookmaker. By a man he'd beaten up. By a woman he'd picked up. By any one of the characters he was known to hang out with. . . .

#10 [*Blustering.*]: Boy-oh-boy, that's the biggest load 'a tripe I ever . . . Listen, we know the father was a bum! So what has that got to do with anything?

#8: I didn't bring it up. I was asked who else might have killed him. I gave my answer.

#9 [*Mildly, pointing across table.*]: That gentleman over there asked a direct question.

#10: Everyone's a lawyer!
[#3 *points down at* #9.]

#3: Listen, as long as you've joined the discussion, supposing you answer this question. The old man . . .

#8 [*Firmly.*]: There's no need to be sarcastic. [*He looks unwaveringly at #3. #3's face hardens. He stares at #8.*]

#3 [*Controlled now.*]: Would you please answer this question for me . . . [*Then, sarcastically.*] Sir . . . [*He pauses.*] The old man who lived downstairs heard the kid yell out, "I'm going to kill you." A split second later he heard a body hit the floor. Then he saw the kid run out of the house. Now what does all that mean to you?

[*#8 is still standing. He looks down at #9. #9 doesn't have an answer, obviously. He looks up at #8, then down at table. #8 looks across at #3.*]

#8: I was wondering how clearly the old man could have heard the boy's voice through the ceiling.

#3: He didn't hear it through the ceiling. His window was open and so was the window upstairs. It was a hot night, remember?

#8: The voice came from another apartment. It's not that easy to identify a voice, especially a shouting voice.

FOREMAN: He identified it in court. He picked the boy's voice out of five other voices, blindfolded.

#8: That's not the same. He knows the boy's voice very well. They've lived in the same house for years. But to identify it positively from the apartment downstairs. Isn't it possible that he was wrong . . . that maybe he thought the boy was upstairs, and automatically decided that the voice he heard was the boy's voice?

#4: I think that's a bit farfetched.

#10: You said a mouthful! [*To #8.*] Look. He heard the father's body falling, and then he saw the boy run out of the house 15 seconds later. He saw the boy!

#12: Check. And don't forget the woman across the street. She looked right into the open window and saw the boy stab his father. I mean, isn't that enough for you?

#8: Not right now. No, it isn't.

#7 [*Exasperated.*]: How do you like him? It's like talking into a dead phone!

[*#4 appears to be a bit impatient now. He gestures with a nail clipper with which he has been clipping his nails. #3 gets up during these lines and strides restlessly around the table.*]

#4: The woman saw the killing through the windows of a moving elevated train. The train had six cars and she saw it through the windows of the last two cars. She remembered the most insignificant details. I don't see how you can argue with that.

[*There is silence for a moment. #3 looks down at #8. #12 doodles busily on a scrap of paper.*]

#3 [*In #8's direction.*]: Well, what have you got to say about it?

#8 [*Doggedly.*]: I don't know. It doesn't sound right to me.

#3: Well, supposing you think about it. [*He looks down at #12, who has drawn a crude picture of an elevated train.*] Lend me your pencil.

[*#12 gives it to him. #3 bends over #12 and starts to draw a tic-tac-toe pattern on the same sheet of paper upon which #12 has drawn the train.*]

#5: Y'know, I don't think he would've shown the knife to his friends that time . . .

#7: Listen, what difference does that make?

[*#3 has finished the tic-tac-toe pattern. He fills in an X, hands the pencil to #12.*]

#3: Your turn. We might as well pass the time.

[*#8 watches this tic-tac-toe business, suddenly angry for the first time.*]

#5 [*To #7.*]: Well, I don't know if it makes a difference or not. Listen, this boy . . .

[*#8 is up on his feet, walking fast toward #12's seat. #12 has just finished making an O and is handing pencil to #3. #8 reaches down and snatches the paper off the table. #3 whirls around.*]

#3 [*Furious.*]: Wait a minute.

#8 [*Hard.*]: This isn't a game!

#3 [*Shouting.*]: Who do you think you are?

[*He lunges at #8, but is caught by #11 and 12. The FOREMAN hops into it, taking him by the arm. #8 stands calmly near him, watching. The three jurors move #3 around the table toward his seat. Other jurors are on their feet suddenly, watching, some crowding around. #3 is furious.*]

#12 [*To #3.*]: All right, let's take it easy.

FOREMAN [*To #3.*]: Come on, sit down now. . . .

[*#3 is urged around the table. He shakes off #11 and 12.*]

#3: I've got a good mind to walk around the table and belt him one!

FOREMAN: Now, please. I don't want any fights in here. [*He reaches for #3's arm. #3 shakes him off.*]

#3: Did you see him? The nerve! The absolute nerve!

#10: All right. Forget it. It's not important. Know what I mean?

#3: This isn't a game. Who does he think he is? [*#8 stands calmly alone, holding the paper he has snatched from #12, looking steadily at #3, who glares angrily at #8. Then, finally he sits down in his seat.*]

FOREMAN: Come on now. It's all over. Let's take our seats. [*Slowly they all move to their seats, save #8. #8 looks at the paper in his hand, and suddenly something seems to click for him. He begins a walk around the table toward #3's seat. When he reaches #3's seat, #3 is busy fixing his tie. #8 stands behind him, looking at the paper. Then suddenly he leans over #3 and throws the paper in front of him onto the table. #3 half rises, angry again. #4 puts a hand on his arm. He sits down.*]

#8: Take a look at that sketch. I wonder if anybody has an idea how long it takes an elevated train going at medium speed to pass a given point?

#4: What has that got to do with anything?

#8: How long? Take a guess.

#4: I wouldn't have the slightest idea.

#8 [*To #5.*]: What do you think?

#5: I don't know. About ten or twelve seconds maybe.

#3: What's all this for?

#8 [*Ignoring #3.*]: I'd say that was a fair guess. Anyone else?

#11: That sounds right to me. [*#10 looks at him and then across at #8.*]

#10: Come on, what's the guessing game for?

#8 [*To #2.*]: What would you say?

#2 [*Shrugging.*]: Ten seconds is about right.

#4: All right. Say ten seconds. What are you getting at?

#8: This. A six-car el train passes a given point in ten seconds. Now say that given point is the open window of the room in which the killing took place. You can almost reach out of the window of that room and touch the el tracks. Right? [*#2 nods.*] All right. Now let me ask you this. Has anyone here ever lived right next to the el tracks?

#6: Well, I just finished painting an apartment that overlooked an el line. I'm a house painter, y'know. I was there for three days.

#8: What was it like?

#6: What d'ya mean?

#8: Noisy?

#6: Brother! Well, it didn't matter. We're all punchy in our business, anyway.

[#6 *laughs and is joined by others*.]

#8: I lived in a second-floor apartment next to an el line once. When the window's open and the train goes by, the noise is almost unbearable. You can't hear yourself think.

#3: Okay. You can't hear yourself think. Will you get to the point!

#8: I will. Let's take two pieces of testimony and try to put them together. First, the old man in the apartment downstairs. He says he heard the boy say, "I'm going to kill you," and *a split second later* he heard the body hit the floor. One second later. Right?

#2: That's right.

#8: Second, the woman across the street claimed positively that she looked out of her window and saw the killing through the last two cars of a passing elevated train. Right? The last two cars.

#3: All right, what are you giving us here?

#8: Now, we agreed that an el takes about 10 seconds to pass a given point. Since the woman saw the stabbing through the last two cars, we can assume that the body fell to the floor just as the train passed by. Therefore, the el had been roaring by the old man's window for a full ten seconds before the body hit the floor. The old man, according to his own testimony, "I'm going to kill you," body falling a split second later, would have had to hear the boy make this statement while the el was roaring past his nose. It's not possible that he could have heard it!

[*There is silence as they digest this. Then* #3 *angrily turns around in his chair*.]

#3: That's idiotic. Sure, he could have heard it.

#8: Do you think so?

#3: He said the boy yelled it out. That's enough for me.

#8: If he heard anything at all, he still couldn't have identified the voice with the el roaring by. . . .

[#3 *shoots to his feet. He glares at* #8.]

#3 [*Furious.*]: You're talking about a matter of seconds here. Nobody can be that accurate!

[#3 *stands next to* #8 *now.*]

#8 [*Quietly.*]: Well, I kind of think that testimony which could put a human being into the electric chair should be reasonably accurate.

[#3 *moves away from* #8 *down toward* #5. #5 *turns around in his seat.*]

#5: I don't think he could have heard it.

#6 [*Turning around.*]: Maybe he didn't hear it. I mean with the el noise . . .

#3: What are you people talking about?

#5: Well, it stands to reason . . .

#3: You're crazy! Why would he lie? What's he got to gain?

#9 [*Softly.*]: Attention, maybe.

#3: You keep coming up with these bright sayings. Why don't you send one in to a newspaper? They pay three dollars!

[#9 *seems to shrink in his seat. He looks down at the table.* #3 *stares at the old man.* #5 *looks at* #3. #6 *rises, and faces* #3. *He stares at him with frank disgust. He looks ready for almost any trouble* #3 *can name. He speaks quietly, but with great strength, heightened by his slow-witted sincerity. This is a man who is rarely aroused, but when he is, is afraid of nothing.*]

#6: What're ya talking to him like that for?

[#3 *looks at him and then turns disgustedly away.* #6 *reaches out and turns* #3 *firmly around by the arm, looks into his face.*] A guy who talks like that to an old man oughta really get stepped on, y'know.

#3: Get your hands off me.

[#5 *rises and makes a move toward* #6. #6 *looks at him briefly. He stops.* #6 *looks back to* #3.]

#7: Hey, let's not get into any fist fights in here.

#6 [*Riding over* #7's *lines.*]: You oughta have some respect, mister.

#3: I said let go of me . . .
[#6 *pulls* #3 *firmly, strongly toward him.* #3 *help-lessly stands there.*]

#6 [*Very low.*]: If you say stuff like that to him again . . . I'm gonna lay you out. [#6 *releases* #3 *and steps away from him.* #3 *continues to stare harshly at him.* #6 *quietly turns in the direction of* #9. *Softly.*] Go ahead. You can say anything you want. Why do you think the old man might lie?
[#9 *looks up and seems to take strength.* #10 *shows disgust.*]

#9: It's just that I looked at him for a very long time. The seam of his jacket was split under the arm. Did you notice it? I mean to come into court like that. [#9 *pauses, and* #10 *deliberately yawns.*] He was a very old man with a torn jacket, and he walked very slowly to the stand. He was dragging his left leg, and trying to hide it because he was ashamed. I think I know him better than anyone here. This is a quiet, frightened, in-significant old man who has been nothing all of his life, who has never had recognition, his name in the news-papers. Nobody knows him, nobody quotes him, nobody seeks his advice after seventy-five years. That's a very sad thing, to be nothing. A man like this needs to be recognized, to be listened to, to be quoted just once. This is very important. [*All listening to* #9. *Only* #8 *shows pity.* #6 *half understands.* #3 *is furious,* #7 *in-credulous.*] It would be so hard for him to recede into the background when there's a chance to be . . .

#7 [*Superior.*]: Now, wait a minute. Are you trying to tell us he'd lie just so that he could be important once?

#9: No. He wouldn't really lie. But perhaps he'd make himself believe that he'd heard those words and recog-nized the boy's face.
[#3 *looks at* #6, *and then turns to* #9.]

#3: Well, that's the most fantastic story I've ever heard! How can you make up a thing like that? What do you know about it?

#9 [*Softly.*]: I speak from experience.
[*He lowers his head, embarrassed.* #3's *jaw hangs open. He stares at* #9. *There is absolute silence, punctuated only by the honking of a horn in the street. Then, ab-*

ruptly #3 *whirls about and stalks back to his seat. The entire jury is frozen for a moment now as* #3 *sits down.* #2 *clears his throat, and begins to unwrap a cough drop.* #12 *lights a cigarette.* #6 *begins to tap the dottle out of his pipe. But no one speaks.* #9 *sits with head bowed.* #10 *looks at him as if he were a bug on a pin.*]

#10 [*Shaking his head.*]: Boy-oh-boy. That's what I call a hot one! [*He lets out a short, mocking laugh.* #5 *looks at* #10, *wishing he could crack him across the mouth.*]

FOREMAN: Okay. Is there anything else?

[#5*'s spell of contained anger is broken. He looks in the direction of the* FOREMAN.]

#5 [*Hesitantly.*]: Yeah, I'll tell you, I was figuring I'd like to . . .

#4 [*Interrupting.*]: Listen! I think it's about time we stopped behaving like kids in here. We can't continue to allow these emotional outbursts to influence us. Gentlemen, this case is based on a reasonable and logical progression of facts. Let's keep it there.

#11: Facts are sometimes colored by the personalities of the people who present them. . . .

[#4 *gives* #11 *a somewhat sour look. There is silence for a moment. Then,* #2 *haltingly breaks the silence.*]

#2: *Anybody* . . . want a . . . cough drop?

[*There is an awkward silence again.* #2 *holds out the cough drops to the* FOREMAN. *The* FOREMAN *looks away, annoyed. The only man standing is* #8. *He walks from his position behind* #6 *toward* #2, *obviously thinking of something. He reaches* #2.]

#8: I'll take one. [#2 *almost gratefully offers him the box. He pops a cough drop into his mouth.*] Thanks. [*Then he continues his walk around the table, sucking the cough drop.*]

#12 [*Embarrassed.*]: Say what you like, I still don't see how anybody can think he's not guilty.

[*He looks around, and his statement hangs emptily in the air. He looks around for confirmation, and then begins to doodle again.* #10 *gets up and begins a cross which will leave him behind* #3 *for his next lines. He blows his nose gingerly as he walks.* #8 *is standing near the window.*]

#8: There's another thing I wanted to talk about for a

minute. I think we've proved that the old man couldn't have heard the boy say, "I'm going to kill you," but supposing . . .

#10 [*Interrupting.*]: You didn't prove it at all. What are you talking about?

#8 [*Steadily.*]: But supposing he really did hear it. This phrase, how many times has each of us used it? Probably hundreds. "I could kill you for that, darling." "If you do that once more, Junior, I'm going to kill you." "Come on Rocky, kill him!" We say it every day. It doesn't mean we're going to kill someone.

#3 [*Angry.*]: Wait a minute. What are you trying to give us here? The phrase was, "I'm going to kill you," and the kid screamed it out at the top of his lungs. Don't tell me he didn't mean it. Anybody says a thing like that the way he said it, they mean it.

#2 [*Hesitantly.*]: Well gee, I don't know. I remember I was arguing with the guy I work next to at the bank a couple of weeks ago, so he called me an idiot, so I yelled at him . . .

#3 [*Interrupting.*]: Now listen, this guy [*Indicating* #8] is making you believe things that aren't so. The kid said he was going to kill him, and he did kill him!

#8: Well, let me ask you this: Do you really think the boy would shout out a thing like that so the whole neighborhood would hear it? I don't think so. He's much too bright for that.

#10 [*Exploding.*]: Bright? He's a common ignorant slob. He don't even speak good English!

#11 [*Quietly.*]: He *doesn't* even speak good English.
[#10 *glares at* #11 *furiously. There is silence for a moment.* #5 *looks anxiously around the table for a moment. Then he clears his throat.*]

#5: I'd like to change my vote to not guilty.

#7: You what?
[#5 *turns his head toward* #7 *and looks firmly at him.*]

#5: You heard.
[#3 *starts to get up, trying to control his anger.* #4 *stares at* #5. #5 *sits stiffly, waiting to be bombarded.*]

FOREMAN: Are you sure?

#5: Yes. I'm sure.

FOREMAN: The vote is 9 to 3 in favor of guilty.

[*#3 stalks off past #5 on his way around to the windows. As he passes #7, #7 speaks, two beats after* FOREMAN *finishes above line.*]

#7: Well, if that isn't the livin' end!

[*#3 moves as #7 speaks. He reaches the windows and finds himself next to #8. #8 is calm, #3 furious but controlled. They exchange one look, and it is as if at that moment this entire room has become a battleground for these two men, who have never known each other before. This is the battle of good against evil, of compassion against brutality. #3 turns away from #8, and looks out the window. During all of this #7 speaks.*]

#7: What are you basing it on? Stories this guy made up! He oughta write for *Amazing Detective Monthly.* He'd make a fortune. [*To #5.*] Listen, there are facts staring you right in your face. Every one of them says this kid killed his old man. For cryin' out loud, his own lawyer knew he didn't stand a chance right from the beginning. His own lawyer. You could see it!

#8: It's happened before that a lot of facts somehow fall into place and all of a sudden it looks like a murderer has been caught. But every once in a while you read about a convict who's freed ten years after the crime because someone else has confessed.

[*#7 and 9 in their seats, #3 at window, #8 standing behind #9.*]

#7 [*To #8.*]: I'm talkin' to him. [*Indicating #5.*] Not to you! [*To all.*] Boy, this guy is really something. [*To #8.*] Listen, the kid had a lawyer, didn't he? The lawyer presented his case, not you. How come you've got so much to say?

#5: Lawyers aren't infallible.

[*#7 swings around to #5, gives him a look.*]

#8: He was court-appointed.

[*#7 swings back to #8.*]

#7: So what does that mean?

#8: Well, it could mean a lot of things. It could mean he didn't want the case. It could mean he resented being appointed. It's the kind of case that brings him nothing. No money. No glory. Not even much chance of winning. It's not a very promising situation for a young lawyer. He'd really have to believe in his client to make a good fight. As you pointed out a minute ago, he obviously didn't.

#7: Sure, he didn't! Who in the heck could, except God come to earth or somebody.

[#8 *looks calmly at* #7. #7 *evades* #8's *eyes. He looks down at his watch and then up at the clock.*]

#7: Come on already! Look at the time!

[#11 *shows disgust with* #7's *concern for the time. Then he looks down at the table at some notes he has made on a scrap of paper.* #10 *is back in his seat.*]

#11: Pardon me, but I have made some notes here. I would like please to say something.

[*He picks up the scrap of paper, and, finding himself hampered by a lighted cigarette in his hand, looks for an ashtray in which to put it. The ashtray is in front of* #10. *He looks at* #10, *and then reaches over for the ashtray.* #10 *looks at him with obvious distaste.*]

#10: Wait a minute! Here.

[#10 *slides the ashtray over to him.*]

#11: Thank you. [*He puts out the cigarette, and looks at his notes.*] I have been listening very closely, and it seems to me that this man [*Indicating* #8.] has some very good points to make. From what was presented at the trial the boy looks guilty, on the surface. But maybe if we go deeper . . .

#10: Come on, willya. . . .

#11 [*More firmly.*]: There is a question I would like to ask. We assume that the boy committed murder. He stabbed his father in the chest, and ran away. This was at ten minutes after twelve. Now, how was he caught by the police? He came home at three o'clock or so, and was captured by two detectives in the hallway of his house. My question is, if he really had killed his father, why would he come back home three hours later? Wouldn't he be afraid of being caught?

[#3 *stands at window, listening.*]

#3 [*As if talking to a child.*]: Look . . . he came home to get his knife. It's not nice to leave knives around sticking in people's chests.

#7: Yeah, especially relatives.

[#3 *looks in his direction and grins appreciatively.*]

#4 [*In* #7's *direction.*]: I don't see anything funny about it. [*To* #11.] The boy knew that there were people who could identify the knife as the one he had just bought. He had to get it before the police did.

#11: But if he knew the knife could be identified, why did he leave it there in the first place?

#4: Well, I think we can assume he ran out in a state of panic after he killed his father, and then when he finally calmed down, he realized that he had left his knife there.

#11: This then depends on your definition of panic. He would have had to be calm enough to see to it that there were no fingerprints on the knife. Now where did his panic start and where did it end?

[#3 *walks up behind* #11, *annoyed.*]

#3: Look, you can forget all that other stuff. He still came home to dig out his knife, and get rid of it.

#11: Three hours later?

#3: Sure, three hours later!

#11: If I were the boy and I had killed my father, I would not have come home three hours later. I would be afraid that the police would be there. I would stay away, knife or no knife.

#3: Listen, you voted guilty, didn't you? What side are you on?

#11: I don't believe I must be loyal to one side or the other. I am simply asking questions.

[#11 *looks at his notes.* #12 *clears his throat.*]

#12: Well, this is just off the top of my head, but if I were the boy, and I'd, you know, done the stabbing and everything, I'd take a chance and go back for the knife. I'll bet he figured no one had seen him and that the body probably wasn't even discovered yet. After all, it was the middle of the night. He probably thought no one would find the body till the next day.

#11: Pardon. Here is my whole point. The woman across the street testified that a moment after she saw the killing, that is, a moment after the el train went by, she screamed, and then went to telephone the police. Now, the boy must certainly have heard that scream, and known that somebody saw something. I don't think he would have gone back, if he had been the murderer.

#4: Two things. One, in his state of panic he may not

have heard the scream. Perhaps it wasn't very loud. Two, if he did hear it, he may not have connected it with his own act. Remember, he lived in a neighborhood where screams were fairly commonplace.

[#9, 10, 11, 12 *are seated.* #3 *is behind* #11. #8, *near his seat, begins a walk toward* #11.]

#3: Right! There's your answer!

#8: Maybe. Maybe he did stab his father, didn't hear the woman's scream, did run out in a panic, did calm down three hours later and come back to try and get the knife, risking being caught by the police. Maybe all of those things are so. But maybe they're not. I think there's enough doubt to make us wonder whether he was there at all during the time the murder took place.

[#10 *stands up furiously, turns to* #8.]

#10 [*To* #8.]: What d'ya mean doubt? What are you talking about? Didn't the old man *see* him running out of the house. [*He turns to all the others.*] He's twisting the facts! I'm telling you! [*He turns to* #11, *who is still seated.*] Did or didn't the old man see the kid running out of the house at 12:10? [#11 *turns away from him.* #10 *moves around to the other side of him, then harshly.*] Well, did or didn't he?

#11: He says he did.

#10: Says he did! [*To all.*] Boy-oh-boy. How do you like that. [*Bending to* #11.] Well, did or didn't the woman across the street see the kid kill his father? [*He stands up and answers for* #11, *mocking him.*] She says she did. [*To* #11.] You're makin' out like it don't matter what people say. [#11 *gets up and begins a walk to the water cooler.* #10 *looks angrily after him and then starts to pursue him, still talking.*] What you want to believe, you believe, and what you don't want to believe, so you don't. What kind of way is that? [#11 *is at the cooler now.* #10 *has stopped halfway.* #11 *takes a cup and begins to pour some water.*] What d'ya think these people get up on the witness stand for, their health? [#10 *turns to the table.*] I'm telling you men, the facts are being changed around here. Witnesses are being doubted and there's no reason for it.

#5: Witnesses can make mistakes.

#10 [*Loud.*]: Sure, when you want 'em to, they do! [*He turns to* #3.] Know what I mean?

FOREMAN: Okay. Let's hold the yelling down.

[#11, *at water cooler slowly sips, and listens as* #10 *goes to* FOREMAN. #8 *standing quietly by in foreground, watching* #11 *at water cooler in background as* #10, *halfway between them, talks.*]

#10: You keep saying that. Maybe what we need is a little yelling in here. These guys are going off every which way. Did hear the scream, didn't hear the scream. What's the difference? You people are only talking about the little details. You're forgetting the important stuff. I mean all of a sudden here everybody ...

#8: [*Quietly.*]: I'd like to call for another vote.

#10 [*Angry.*]: Listen I'm talking here!

[#8 *turns his back on* #10 *and walks out of shot toward his seat.* #10 *is visibly annoyed at this. He takes one step after* #8, *then stops.*]

FOREMAN: There's another vote called for. [#10 *burns.*] How about taking seats.

[#10 *starts for his seat.* FOREMAN *stands at his seat. The others who are standing head for seats.*]

#3: What are we gonna gain by voting again?

FOREMAN: I don't know. The gentleman asked ...

[#11 *sits in his seat.*]

#3: I never saw so much time spent on nothing.

#2 [*Mildly to* #3.]: It only takes a second.

[#3 *gives him a look, then turns away.*]

FOREMAN: Okay. I guess the fastest way is to find out who's voting not guilty. All those in favor of not guilty raise their hands.

[*There is a great deal of looking around the table as* #5, 8 *and* 9 *raise their hands.*] Still the same. One, two, three not guilty's. Nine guilty's.

[#11 *is in the process of making a very difficult decision.*]

#7: So now where are we? I'm telling you, we can yakity-yak until next Tuesday here. . . . Where's it getting us? [*There is a pause.*]

#11 [*Quietly.*]: Pardon. [*He slowly raises his hand.*] I vote not guilty.

#7: Oh, brother!

#3: Oh, now listen, what are you talking about? I mean we're all going crazy in here or something. This kid is guilty! Why dontcha pay attention to the facts! [*To* #4.] Listen, tell him, will ya? [#4 *shrugs*.] This is getting to be a joke!

[*He gets up and starts a walk down toward* #7.]

FOREMAN: The vote is eight to four, favor of guilty.

#3 [*Over* #5's *shoulder toward* #11.]: I mean everybody's heart is starting to bleed for this punk little kid like the President just declared it Love Your Underprivileged Brother week, or something. Listen, I'd like you to stand up and tell me why you changed your vote. Come on, give me reasons!

[#11 *looks straight at* #3, *and speaks strongly*.]

#11: I don't have to defend my decision to you! I have a reasonable doubt in my mind.

[#3 *stands behind* #5, *who is turned, looking at him.* #3 *looks off at* #11 *angrily*.]

#3: What reasonable doubt? That's nothing but words! [*He leans over the table, pulls the switch knife out of the table, and holds it up*.] Here, look at this! The kid you just decided isn't guilty was *seen* ramming this thing into his father! Well, look at it, Mr. Reasonable Doubt!

[#3 *flicks it angrily into the table. It quivers in the wood*.]

#9 [*Mildly*.]: That's not the knife. Don't you remember? [#3 *whirls and stares at him.* #9 *regards him steadily.* #8 *smiles openly.* #3 *is burning, but controlled*.]

#3: Brilliant!

[#3 *stares at* #9 *for another moment and then walks around past* #7. *His next lines will be taken at the window. There is a pause.* #7 *looks around*.]

#7: I'm tellin' ya, this is the craziest! [*To* #8.] I mean you're sittin' in here pulling stories outa thin air! What're we supposed to believe? [*To all*:] I'm telling ya if this guy [*Indicating* #8.] sat ringside at the Dempsey-Firpo fight, he'd be tryin' to tell us Firpo won! [*To* #8.] Look, what about the old man? Are we supposed to believe that he *didn't* get up and run to his door and see the kid tearing down the stairs fifteen seconds after the killing? He's only *saying* he did to be important, right?

I mean what's the point of the whole . . .

#5 [*Interrupting.*]: Hold it a second.

#7 [*Looking at #5 and doing a Clem McCarthy.*]: *And* the Baltimore rooter is heard from! *And* pop-ups are falling for base hits wherever we look. I tell you . . .

#5 [*Interrupting.*]: Did the old man say he *ran* to the door.

#7: Ran. Walked. What's the difference? He got there.

#6: He said he ran to the door. At least I think he did.

#5: I don't remember what he said. But I don't see how he could run.

#4: He said he *went* from his bedroom to the front door. That's enough, isn't it?

#8: Where was his bedroom again?

#10: Down the hall somewhere. I thought you remembered everything. Don't you remember that?

#8: No. Mr. Foreman, I'd like to take a look at the diagram of the apartment.

#7 [*To #8.*]: Why don't we have them run the trial over just so you can get everything straight?

#8 [*Ignoring him.*]: Mr. Foreman . . .

FOREMAN: I heard you.

[*He rises, and walks toward door. #3, standing at windows, glares at #8. We hear door opening and closing during next lines.*]

#3: All right, what's this for? How come you're the only one in the room who wants to see exhibits all the time?

#5: I want to see this one too.

[*#3 starts a walk from the windows which will lead him to a position directly behind #8.*]

#3: And I want to stop wasting time!

#4: If we're going to start wading through all that nonsense about where the body was found . . .

[*#3 is standing behind #8 now. #8 leans across table toward #4's position.*]

#8: We're not. Not unless someone else wants to. I'd like to see if a very old man who drags one leg when he walks because he had a stroke last year can get from his bed to his front door in fifteen seconds.

#3: He said twenty seconds!

#8: He said fifteen.

#3: Now I'm telling you he said twenty! What're you trying to distort . . .

#11: He said fifteen.

#3 [*Turning in that direction.*]: How does he know how long fifteen seconds is? You can't judge that kind of a thing!

[*#9 looks up at #3.*]

#9: He said fifteen seconds. He was very positive about it.

#3 [*Down to #9, furiously.*]: He's an old man. You saw him. Half the time he was confused! How could he be positive about . . . anything?

[*He looks around angrily, unable to cover up his blunder. Then he stalks around the table. The others watch. As he gets to his seat the door behind him opens. The GUARD enters carrying a large pen and ink diagram of the apartment. FOREMAN crosses to GUARD.*]

GUARD: This what you wanted?

FOREMAN: That's right. Thanks.

[*The GUARD nods and exits. FOREMAN holds up the diagram and, looking at it, crosses back toward his seat. #8 rises from his seat and walks toward FOREMAN's seat. During these crosses we hear the following.*]

#4: I don't see what we're going to prove here. The man said he *saw* the boy running out.

#8 [*Walking to FOREMAN.*]: Well, let's see if the details bear him out. As soon as the body fell to the floor, he said, he heard footsteps upstairs running toward the front door. He heard the upstairs door open and the footsteps start down the stairs. He got to his front door as soon as he could. He swore that it couldn't have been more than fifteen seconds. Now, if the killer began running immediately . . .

#12 [*Interrupting.*]: Well, maybe he didn't.

#8: The old man said he did!

#7 [*To #8.*]: Brother, I crown you king of the hairsplitters.

[*#10 laughs at this.*]

#6 [*Mildly, to #7.*]: Listen, why don't you stop making smart remarks all the time.

#7: My friend, for your three dollars a day you've gotta listen to everything.

[*There is a silence for a moment. #6 has no answer, but he hasn't liked what he heard.*]

#10 [*To #8.*]: Well, now that you've got that thing in here, what about it?

#8 [*To* FOREMAN.]: May I?

[*He takes the chart, and holds it up on a corner of the table so that everyone can see it. During #8's lines, #2, 5, 6, 11, 12 and* FOREMAN *also crowd around diagram. The diagram itself is a layout of a railroad flat. A bedroom faces the el tracks. Behind it is a series of rooms off a long hall. In the front room is an X marking the spot where the body was found. At the back of the apartment we see the entrance into the apartment hall from the building hall. We see a flight of stairs in the building hall. Each room is labeled, and the dimensions of each room are shown.*]

✗#8: This is the apartment in which the killing took place. The old man's apartment is directly beneath it, and exactly the same. [*Pointing.*] Here are the el tracks. The bedroom. Another bedroom. Living room. Bathroom. Kitchen. And this is the hall. Here's the front door to the apartment. And here are the stairs. [*Pointing to front bedroom.*] Now, the old man was in bed in this room. He says he got up, went out into the hall, down the hall to the front door, opened it and looked out just in time to see the boy racing down the stairs. Am I right so far?

[*#3 stands at his chair, watching.*]

#3: That's the story, for the nineteenth time.

#8 [*Ignoring this.*]: Fifteen seconds after he heard the body fall.

#11: Correct.

#8: His bed was at the window. It's—[*Looking closely at diagram.*] 12 feet from his bed to the bedroom door. The length of the hall is 43 feet 6 inches. Now, he had to get up out of bed, walk 12 feet, open the bedroom door, walk 43 feet and open the front door . . . all in 15 seconds. Do you think he could have done it?

[*#10, standing behind #8, barks out.*]

#10: Sure, he coulda done it!

#11 [*To* #10.]: He can only walk very slowly. They had to help him into the witness chair.

#3: You make it sound like a long walk. It's not!
[#8 *looks in* #3*'s direction, and then, laying down the diagram, begins a walk around to the other side of the table. As he walks,* #9, *who had been standing near* #8, *answers* #3.]

#9: For an old man who had a stroke it's a long walk.
[#8 *has walked directly to the empty chairs of* #2 *and* #3. *He takes one in each hand now, and swings them out into the middle of the floor, placing them side by side.* #3 *strides toward him.*]

#3: What are you doing?

#8: I want to try this thing. Let's see how long it took him.

#3: What d'you mean *you* want to try it? Why didn't the kid's lawyer bring it up if it's so important?
[*The other jurors have begun to crowd in.*]

#5: Well, maybe he just didn't think of it.

#10: What d'ya mean didn't think of it! You think the man's an idiot or something? It's an obvious thing.

#5: Did you think of it?
[#10 *moves a step or two toward* #5.]

#10 [*Angry, to* #5.]: Listen, smart guy! It don't matter whether I thought of it.

FOREMAN [*Worried.*]: Okay, now . . .

#10: He didn't bring it up because he knew the answer'd hurt his case. Now what d'ya think of that?

FOREMAN: Okay . . .

#8: It's possible that he didn't bring it up because it would have meant badgering and bullying a helpless old man, something that I don't think sits very well with a jury. Most lawyers avoid that kind of thing if they can.

#7 [*Loud.*]: So what kind of a bum is he then?

#8 [*Quietly.*]: That's what I've been asking. [#7 *shuts up, sorry that he's spoken.*] All right, let's say these chairs are the old man's bed. I'm going to pace off 12 feet, the length of the bedroom. [*He begins to do this.*]

#3: You're crazy. You can't recreate a thing like that.

#11: I'd like to see it.

#3: It's a ridiculous waste of time!

#6: Let him do it.

[#8 *has now paced off his* 12 *feet. He stands on the spot.*]

#8: Someone hand me a chair. [#6 *picks up a chair and brings it to him.* #8 *puts it down where he is standing.*] All right, this is the bedroom door. [*He looks around.*] The hall is a little over 43 feet long. I'll pace over to that wall [*Pointing.*] and back again. [*He starts to do it, counting his steps silently as he paces. He passes* #10 *after a dozen steps.*]

#10: Look, this is absolutely insane. What's the idea of wasting everybody's time here?

#8 [*Interrupting his counting.*]: Sixteen. [*He stops pacing, turns to* #10.] According to you it'll only take 15 seconds. We can spare that. [*He resumes his pacing, counting to himself. He reaches the wall. Everyone watches silently. He turns and paces back, counting off the rest of the 43 steps. As he nears the end he counts aloud.*] Thirty-nine, forty, forty-one, forty-two, forty-three. Okay, pass me another chair please. [#2 *hands him a chair. He places it down.*] This is the door to the outside hall and stairway. It was chain-locked, according to testimony.

#5: Right.

[#8 *now walks over to the two chairs he placed side by side. He sits down.*]

#8: Who's got a watch with a second-hand?

#2: I have.

#8: When you want me to start, stamp your foot. That'll be the body falling. Time me from there. [*He lies down on the two chairs.*]

#7: Anyone for charades?

#3 [*Exasperated.*]: I've never seen anything like this in my whole life!

#8: Okay. I'm ready.

[*He lies down on the chairs. They all watch carefully.* #2 *stares at his watch, waiting. There is a tense silence.*]

#2 [*Apologetically.*]: I want to wait till the second-hand reaches sixty.

[*They wait, silent, tense. Suddenly* #2 *stamps his foot.* #8 *rises to a sitting position, swings his legs to the floor. He stands up.* #2 *keeps his eyes on the watch.*]

'#8 *begins to hobble, dragging one leg, toward the chair which serves as the bedroom door. He reaches it, pretends to open it. He turns now and begins to hobble along the simulated 43-foot hallway.*]

#10: Come on. Speed it up. He walked twice as fast as that!

[#8 *continues to walk.*]

#11: This is, I think, even more quickly than the old man walked in the courtroom.

#8 [*Still hobbling.*]: If you think I should go faster, I will. [*He speeds up his pace slightly, reaches the wall and turns. He heads for the second chair, the chair simulating the door to the outer hallway.*]

#3: Come on, willya! Let's get this kid stuff over with! [*They watch as #8 reaches the last chair. He pretends to open an imaginary chain lock, and then opens the imaginary door.*]

#8: Stop!

#2: Right.

#8: What's the time?

#2: Fifteen . . . twenty . . . thirty . . . thirty-three seconds exactly.

#6: Thirty-three seconds!

[*The other jurors around #2 ad lib their surprise.*]

#8: I think this is what happened. The old man had heard the fight between the boy and his father a few hours earlier. Then, while lying in bed he heard a body hit the floor in the boy's apartment, and he heard the woman scream from across the street. He got up, tried to get to the door, heard someone racing down the stairs, and *assumed* it was the boy.

#6: I think that's possible.

[#3 *stands, furious.*]

#3 [*Shouting.*]: Assumed? Now, listen to me, you people! I've seen all kinds of dishonesty in my day . . . but this little display takes the cake! [#3 *strides swiftly toward* #8. *He reaches him, waves his hand in* #8's *face.*] You come in here with your heart bleeding all over the floor about slum kids and injustice, and you make up some wild stories, and all of a sudden you start getting through to some of these old ladies in here! Well, you're not getting through to me! I've had enough! [*To all.*] What's the matter with you people? Every one of you knows this kid is guilty! He's got to burn! We're letting him slip through our fingers here!

#8 [*Calmly.*]: Slip through our fingers? Are you his executioner?

#3 [*Furious.*]: I'm one of 'em.

#8: Maybe you'd like to pull the switch. . . .

#3 [*Shouting.*]: For this kid? You bet. I'd like to pull the switch!

#8: I'm sorry for you. . . .

#3: Don't start with me now!

#8: What it must feel like to want to pull the switch!

#3 [*Raging.*]: Listen, you shut up!

#8 [*Baiting him.*]: Ever since we walked into this room you've been behaving like a self-appointed public avenger!

#3 [*Loud.*]: I'm telling you now! Shut up!

#8: You want to see this boy die because you personally want it, not because of the facts.

#3 [*Roaring.*]: Shut up!

#8: You're a sadist. . . .

[*The jury groups around* #3 *and* 8.]

#3 [*Roaring.*]: Shut up! [*And he lunges wildly at* #8. #8 *holds his ground as* #3 *is caught by many hands and held back. He strains against the hands, his face dark with rage.*] Let me go! I'll kill him! I'll kill him!

#8 [*Calmly.*]: You don't *really* mean you'll kill me, do you?

[#3 *stops struggling with the jurors who are restraining him. Still held, he stares bitterly at* #8. *Then, finally, he shrugs off the many hands on him, adjusts his jacket and walks around the group of silent, watching men to the window. He stands at the window and there is not a sound for a moment. Then we hear the sound of the door being opened. Some of the jurors turn their heads in that direction. The* GUARD *is standing in the doorway.*]

GUARD: Is there anything wrong, gentlemen? I heard some noise.

FOREMAN: No. There's nothing wrong. [*He walks toward the door, picking up the diagram of the apartment on the way. He reaches the door.*] Just a little argument.

Everything's okay. [*He hands the* GUARD *the diagram.*] We're finished with this.

[*The* GUARD *takes it, looks carefully around the room and then exits. The* FOREMAN *turns to the others.* #3 *stands at the windows. A few of the jurors walk back to their seats. The others stand watching* #3. *He turns to look at them.*]

#3 [*Angry.*]: Well, what are you looking at?

[*Embarrassed, they turn away. He stands there for a moment and then begins the long walk back to his seat. After a moment, the other jurors begin to take their seats. There is a stiffness in the room which had not been there before. The jurors sit at the table without a sound. The* FOREMAN *clears his throat.* #10 *blows his nose. They are each waiting for some one else to break the silence.*]

#12 [*Tentatively.*]: Well . . . I suppose someone has to . . . start it off again. . . .

[*Again there is a pause.* #2 *turns elaborately in his chair and cranes his neck for a look at the wall clock.*]

#2: It's getting late. [*To* FOREMAN.] What do they do, take us out to a restaurant for supper?

FOREMAN: How do I know?

#2: I wonder if they let us go home in case we can't finish tonight. I've got a boy with mumps. [*He smiles self-consciously, gesturing with his hands around his jaws to indicate a swelling.*] He's out to here. The wife says he looks like Mussolini.

[*He subsides into embarrassed silence. No one laughs.* #2, 3, 4, 5, 6, 7 *sit silently, each trying to think of some way to break out of his own personal embarrassment. The room begins to darken perceptibly now. No one notices it.* #11 *clears his throat slightly and leans forward.*]

#11: Pardon. This fighting. This is not why we are here, to fight. We have a responsibility. This, I have always thought, is a remarkable thing about democracy. That we are, uh, what is the word? [*A pause.*] Notified. That we are notified by mail to come down to this place and decide on the guilt or innocence of a man we have never heard of before. We have nothing to gain or lose by our verdict. This is one of the reasons why we are strong. We should not make it a personal thing. [*Now fearing perhaps that he has forced his views on others a bit too passionately, #11 sits back, somewhat embarrassed, and says humbly.*]: Thank you.

[*Again there is a silence. #12 leans forward into the silence.*]

#12 [*Brightly.*]: Um, if no one else has an idea, I may have a cutie here. I mean I haven't put much thought into it. Anyway, lemme throw it out on the stoop and see if the cat licks it up.

FOREMAN: See if the cat licks it up?

#12 [*Insisting.*]: Yeah! Now, if the boy arrived home . . . [*The FOREMAN laughs and then #12 realizes that he has fallen into the trap he set for himself earlier. He stops in midsentence. #11 joins in the laughter. The edge is off the tension now, but #12 shuts up tight and begins to doodle furiously.*]

#5 [*Looking at window.*]: Look at how dark it's getting. We're gonna have a storm. [*There is a pause.*] Boy it's hot. [*He yanks open his tie and fans himself with some papers. Then idly, he turns to #4. #4 still sits there in tie and jacket, seemingly not bothered by the heat at all. #5 looks at him, then grinning.*] Don't you sweat?

#4 [*Coldly.*]: No, I don't.

[*#5, surprised at #4's coldness, turns away. There is a pause. #6 looks around a bit nervously.*]

#6: Uh, listen, I was wondering if maybe we shouldn't take another vote.

#7: Great idea. Maybe we can follow this one up with dancing and refreshments.

[*#6 gives #7 a look, and then turns to the FOREMAN.*]

#6: Mr. Foreman?

FOREMAN: It's all right with me. Anyone doesn't want to vote? [*He looks around the table. There is no answer. #12 doodles away, still annoyed with himself.*]

#3: I think we ought to have an open ballot. Call out our votes, y'know? Let's see who stands where.

FOREMAN: That sounds fair. Anyone object? [*There is no answer.*] All right. I'll call off your jury numbers. [*He takes a pencil and paper and draws a line down the middle of the paper.*] I vote guilty. [*He makes a check *on one side of the line.*] Number two?

[*#2 has a hard decision to make. He thinks for a long moment.*]

#2: Not guilty.

FOREMAN: Number 3?

[*#3 is staring at #2.*]

#3 [*Sharply.*]: Guilty.

[*#4 sits back, relaxed, at ease.*]

FOREMAN: Number 4?

#4: Guilty.

FOREMAN: Number 5?

#5: Not guilty.

FOREMAN: Number 6?

[*#6 stares down at the table, picking at a piece of cuticle on his thumb. His decision is difficult, too.*]

#6 [*Low.*]: Not guilty.

[*As soon as he speaks he puts his sore thumb in his mouth, sucks on the cuticle. #7 is looking disgustedly at #6.*]

FOREMAN: Number 7?

#7: Guilty.

FOREMAN: Number 8?

#8: Not guilty.

[*#9 is in the process of taking a pill out of a bottle.*]

FOREMAN: Number 9?

#9: Not guilty.

[*#10 is touching his tender nose appraisingly.*]

FOREMAN: Number 10?

#10 [*Loud.*]: Guilty!

[*#11 watches #10 with some distaste.*]

FOREMAN: Number 11?

#11: Not guilty.

[*#12 doodles concentric circles on a pad.*]

FOREMAN: Number 12?

[*#12's pencil stops. He stares down at the table, thinking. There is a pause.*]

FOREMAN [*Impatiently.*]: Number 12?

#12: Guilty.

[FOREMAN *tallies his marks quickly.*]

FOREMAN: Six to six.

[*#7 repeats his Clem McCarthy take-off.*]

#7: *And* we go into extra innings here!

[*He gets up and heads for the water fountain. As he passes #10, #10 starts to rise, annoyed.*]

#10: Six to six! I'm telling you, some of you people in here are out of your minds. A kid like that.

#9 [*Mildly to #10.*]: I don't think the kind of boy he is has anything to do with it. The facts are supposed to determine the case.

#10 [*Down to #9.*]: Ah, don't give me any of that! I'm sick and tired of facts. You can twist 'em any way you like. Know what I mean?

[*He walks away. #9 half rises, angrily, and calls after #10.*]

#9 [*Indicating #8.*]: That's exactly the point this gentleman has been making. I mean you keep shouting at the top of your lungs . . .

[*#8 puts his hand on #9's shoulder. #9 looks at him. #8's expression says, "He isn't worth overexciting yourself." #9 sits down, quite agitated. He takes out a handkerchief and mops his brow with it. We hear ad lib conversation at the water cooler.*]

#9: I'd like to be a little younger. That man . . . [*He stops, unable to go on. Then, trying to calm himself:*] It's very hot in here.

[*#8 nods sympathetically.*]

#8: D'you want some water?

#9: No, thanks.

[*#9 continues to mop his brow. #8 rises and walks to the window. He stands there, looking out. It has grown considerably darker now, oppressively still. The room is silent save for a murmur of voices at the fountain. #8 runs his hand over his face wearily. Then he opens his tie. At the water fountain, #3 is drinking. #7 holds a cup under the faucet. #10 waits his turn. #7 turns to the window. His cup overflows. He turns to it, steps away from the fountain and begins to drink, staring at the window. #2 walks up to wait his turn at the fountain.*]

#2: It's going to rain.

#7 [*Sarcastically.*]: No! [*#2 meekly turns away and gets a paper cup. #7 turns to him.*] How come you switched?

#2: Well, it just seemed to me . . .

#7 [*Interrupting.*]: I mean you haven't got a leg to stand on. You know that, don'tcha?

#2: Well, I don't feel that way. There're a lot of details that never came out . . .

#10 [*Interrupting.*]: Details! You're just letting yourself get bulldozed by a bunch'a what d'ya callem . . . intellectuals.

#2 [*Mildly.*]: Now, that's not so.

#10: Ah, come on. You're like everybody else. You think too much, you get mixed up. [*To* #3.] Know what I mean?

#2 [*Annoyed.*]: Now listen, I don't think you have any right to . . .

[*But* #10 *has crumpled his cup, flipped it on the floor and walked away, leaving* #2 *in the middle of a sentence.*]

#2 [*Softly.*]: Loudmouth!

[#2 *turns to* #7, *opens his mouth as if to speak, then decides not to. He walks over to the other window. He puts his head against the glass and stares out. It is darker now than before.* #8 *is still at window staring out. We see a portion of the skyline behind him, outside window. There is absolute silence in the room. There is no movement in the room. Everyone waits for the storm now. And suddenly it comes. We hear only the sound of the rain, pouring down into the silence. No lightning. No thunder. Heads turn toward the windows. There is no talk. The rain pours down as if this were a tropical storm.* #8 *steps back from the window as the rain splashes in. Then he reaches forward and closes the window. We hear the sound of the other window being closed by* #2. #8 *stares out the window. They all stare at the windows silently. The room is quite dark now. The rain pours down. Jurors' faces, in shadows for the first time, stare at the depressing spectacle of the rain. The* FOREMAN *finally gets up and walks over to the door. Next to it is a light switch. He flips it on. There is a flickering of light, and then the overhead fluorescent lamps come on full, throwing harsh white light onto the jurors. At the same moment we hear the first crack of thunder. (Throughout the remainder of the play the rain continues, and now and then there are flashes of lightning and the rumble of thunder.) The* FOREMAN *walks over to the windows now, and looks out. He stands next to* #8.]

FOREMAN [*Low.*]: Wow! [*He speaks almost to himself.*]

Look at that, will ya! [*#8 nods and continues to look out.*] Think it'll cool things off?

#8: [*Looking at him.*]: Yeah, I guess so.

FOREMAN [*Whistles.*]: Boy! Look at it go! Reminds me of the storm we had last . . . November something. What a storm! Right in the middle of the game. We're behind 7–6, but we're just startin' to move the ball, off tackle, y'know! Boom! Boom! Boom! Boy, I'll never forget that. We had this kid Slattery. A real ox. Wish I had another one like him. [*He looks up to find #8 looking at him.*] Oh. I probably forgot to tell you I'm assistant head coach at the Andrew J. McCorkle High School. That's in Queens. [*#8 nods, smiles briefly and looks out the window.*] So anyway we're movin' real nice. Their line is comin' apart. I'm tellin' ya, this Slattery! Boy! [*He chuckles.*] And all of a sudden it starts to come down cats and dogs. It was murder. I swear I almost bawled. We couldn't go nowhere!

#7: Hey, let's get this fan goin' in here. What d'ya say? [*The* FOREMAN *turns to the sound of the voice. He looks at #8 for a moment. Then he walks across the room. #7 stands under a wall fan looking up at it.* FOREMAN *walks over next to him and looks up. Then he gets a chair, pulls it over to the fan and stands up on the chair. He reaches up and turns on the fan. It starts to turn slowly. He watches it for a moment. Then he climbs down and turns around as if waiting for applause. No one speaks. His smile fades, and camera follows him as he slowly walks to his seat and sits down. #7 is back in his seat now. He looks up at the fan. Then he takes a page from his scrap pad, crumples it up and flips it up at the fan. He tears off another page and repeats this business. And another. A wad of paper hits the fan and is flung off by the blades. #3 and 4 are standing near the water fountain. The wad of paper strikes #3 on the shoulder. He turns around angrily.*]

#7 [*Calling.*]: Sorry.

[*#3 turns back to #4.*]

#3 [*Low.*]: What a stupid thing to do. [*#4 bends to get a drink of water. #3 waits till he straightens up.*] Some rain, huh? [*#4 drinking, nods.*] Well, what d'ya think of this thing? It's even Steven. [*#4 nods as he drinks.*] Kind of surprising, isn't it?

#4: Yes.

#3: Listen, that business before, you know where what's-his-name, that tall guy over there, was baiting me, I mean that doesn't prove anything. Listen, I'm a very excitable person, y'know. So where does he get off to call me a public avenger, and a sadist and everything? Anybody in his right mind'd blow his stack, wouldn't he? He was just trying to bait me.

#4 [*Wryly*.]: He did an excellent job.

[*We hear jumbled ad lib conversation in background.*]

#3 [*Missing this*.]: Now, I'm being sincere about this. I'm no small potatoes like some of these people. I run a messenger service that employs over sixty-five workers. Well, maybe that doesn't mean anything to you, but I consider myself a respectable citizen, and I'm trying to do my duty in here very sincerely. He has no call to act like that. I mean I could really've belted him one!

#10: Listen, I'll tell you what I think. [#3 *and* 4 *turn in the direction of his voice.* #10 *stands at his seat.*] We're goin' nowhere here. I'm ready to walk into court right now and declare a hung jury. There's no point in this thing goin' on any more.

[*Most of them are seated now.* #3 *and* 4 *walk back to their seats.*]

#7: I go for that, too. Let's take it into the judge and let the kid take his chances with twelve other guys.

#8: I don't think the court will accept a hung jury. We haven't been in here very long.

#7 [*Standing up*.]: Well, let's find out!

#11: I am not in favor of this.

#7 [*To* #11.]: Listen, this kid wouldn't stand a chance with another jury and you know it. [*Turning to the others*.] C'mon, we're hung. Nobody's gonna change his opinion. Let's take it inside.

#5: You still don't think there's any room for a reasonable doubt?

#7: No, I don't!

#11: Pardon. Maybe you don't fully understand the term "reasonable doubt."

[#7 *reacts strongly to this. He walks around the table until he is standing behind* #4, *speaking angrily to* #11 *as he goes.*]

#7: What d'ya mean I don't understand it? Who d'ya

think you are to talk to me like that? [*To all.*] How d'ya like this guy? I'm tellin' ya they're all alike. He comes over to this country running for his life and before he can even take a big breath he's telling us how to run the show! The arrogance of the guy!

#5 [*To #7.*]: Wait a second! Nobody around here's asking where you came from!

#7: I was born right here!

#5: Or where your father came from! [#7 *doesn't answer, but stares at #5, amazed at this unexpected outburst.*] Where does it hurt us to take a few tips from people who come running here for their lives? Maybe they learned something we don't know. We're not so perfect!

#11 [*Mildly.*]: Please. It doesn't matter. . . .

#7 [*To #5 on top of #11's lines.*]: Okay, homely philosopher . . . but lemme tell you something. Nobody around here's gonna tell me what words I understand and what words I don't. Hear? [*Pointing at #11.*] Especially him!

[#7 *stalks back to his seat. He sits down. During the* FOREMAN's *next lines, #7 indignantly looks around, feeling that he has won his skirmish, until finally his eyes meet #8's. #8 looks at him long and hard, and finally #7 breaks and turns away.*]

FOREMAN: All right. Let's stop the arguing for two minutes in here. Who's got something constructive to say?

[*There is a silence. Then #8 turns toward the others.*]

#8: I'd like to go over something, if you *gentlemen* don't mind. [*On the word "gentlemen" he looks pointedly at #7.*] An important point for the prosecution was the fact that the boy, after he claimed he was at the movies during the hours the killing took place, couldn't name the pictures he saw or the stars who appeared in them. [*Pointing across at #4.*] This gentleman has repeated that point in here several times.

#4: That's correct. It was the only alibi the boy offered, and he himself couldn't back it up with any details at all.

#8: Putting yourself in the boy's place, if you can, do you think you'd be able to remember details after an upsetting experience such as being struck in the face by your father?

#4: I think so, if there were any special details to remember. He couldn't remember the movies at the theatre he named because he wasn't there that night.

#8: According to police testimony in court, he was questioned by the police in the kitchen of his apartment while the body of his father was lying on the floor in the bedroom. Do you think you could remember details under those circumstances?

#4: I do.

#8: Under great emotional stress?

#4: Under great emotional stress.

#8: He remembered the movies in court. He named them correctly and he named the stars who played in them.

#4: Yes, his lawyer took great pains to bring that out. He had three months from the night of the murder to the day of the trial in which to memorize them. It's not hard for a lawyer to find out what played at a particular theatre on a particular night. I'll take the testimony of the policeman who interrogated him right after the murder, when he couldn't remember a thing about the movies, great emotional stress or not.

[#8 *stands up and walks slowly to a position behind* #6.]

#8: I'd like to ask you a personal question.

#4: Go ahead.

#8: Where were you last night?

#4 [*Puzzled.*]: I was home.

#8: What about the night before last?

#10: Come on, what is this?

#4 [*In* #10's *direction.*]: It's perfectly all right. [*To* #8.] I was at my office till 8:30. I went straight home and to bed.

#8: And the night before that?

#4 [*Beginning to strain.*]: That was . . . Tuesday. The night before that? I . . . was . . . oh yes. That was the night of the bridge tournament. I played bridge.

#8: And Monday night?

#7: When you get him down to New Year's Eve, 1952, lemme know.

[#10 *lets out a loud laugh, which degenerates into a phlegmy cough.*]

#4 [*Trying to remember.*]: Monday. [*There is a pause.*] Monday night. [*Remembering.*] Monday night my wife and I went to the movies.

#8 [*Fast.*]: What did you see?

#4 [*Faster.*]: *The Scarlet Circle.* [*He smiles.*] It's a very clever who-done-it.

#8: What was the second feature?

#4 [*Straining.*]: The . . . I'll tell you in a minute. The . . . *Remarkable Mrs. Something.* Mrs. . . uh . . . Bainbridge. *The Remarkable Mrs. Bainbridge.*
[*There is a pause.*]

#2: I saw that. It's called *The* Amazing *Mrs. Bainbridge.*

#4 [*Embarrassed.*]: *The . . . Amazing Mrs. Bainbridge.* Yes. I think that's right.

#8: Who was in *The Amazing Mrs. Bainbridge?*
[*There is a long pause as #4 strains for the names.*]

#4: Barbara . . . Long, I think. She's a dark, very pretty girl. Barbara . . . Lang . . . Lane . . . something like that.

#8: Who else?
[*A single drop of sweat glistens on #4's neck and then rolls down into his collar. He moves uncomfortably.*]

#4: Well, I'd never heard of them before. It was a very inexpensive second feature, with unknown . . .

#8 [*Interrupting.*]: And you weren't under an emotional strain, were you!
[*#4 doesn't answer for a long moment.*]

#4 [*Quietly.*]: No, I wasn't.

#9: I think the point is made.
[*There is a silence. #10 blows his nose.*]

#10: Big point!

#9: I think it is a big point.

#10: What? Just because he [*Indicating #4.*] can't remember the name of some two-bit movie star? I suppose that *proves* the kid was at the movies.

#9 [*Quietly.*]: No. But it indicates that no one can prove he wasn't. He might have been at the movies and forgotten what he saw. It's possible. If it's perfectly normal for this gentleman [*Indicating #4.*] to forget a few details, then it's also perfectly normal for the boy. Being accused of murder isn't necessarily supposed to give him an infallible memory.

#10 [*To #9.*]: You can talk till your tongue is draggin' on the floor. The boy is guilty. Period. Know what I mean, my friend? [*They look at each other for a moment, and then #9 turns away.*] Who's got those cough drops?

#2 [*Staring hard at* #10.]: They're all gone, my friend. [*He flips the empty box across the table. The* FOREMAN *watches it slide, and then looks up.*]

FOREMAN: Y'know, there's something we're forgetting here that I was just thinking about. Well, that's the whole business that dragged out forever, y'know with the psychiatrist, where he got all involved . . .

#10: Now, don't start with all that phoney psycho-what-ever-you-call it stuff. What a racket that is! Filling people's heads with all that junk. Listen, I've got three psychiatrists keeping their cars in one of my garages. The whole three of 'em are crazy!

FOREMAN: Listen, there's a point I'm tryin' to make here. Do you mind?

#10: I wouldn't give you a nickel for a psychiatrist's testimony.

#8 [*Meaning* #10.]: Why don't you let the man talk? You can take five minutes on the uselessness of psychiatry when he's finished.

[#10 *glares angrily at* #8 *for a moment, then turns away, and blows his nose hard.*]

FOREMAN [*Looking peculiarly at* #8.]: Thanks. [*To all.*] What I was gonna say was, the psychiatrist definitely stated that the boy had strong homicidal tendencies. I mean that he felt like killing somebody half the time. Well, not felt like, that he was, what d'ya call it, cap-able. He described all those tests, inkblots and all that stuff, and he said the kid is definitely a killer-type. Am I right?

#12: Check. I think he said something about paranoid tendencies if I'm not mistaken.

FOREMAN: Right. Whatever that is, he said it. [*To all.*] Let's not forget, we're talking about a boy who's always had murder on his mind.

#12 [*Proudly.*]: His *unconscious* mind.

FOREMAN [*Stolidly.*]: Nobody else's.

#11: I beg pardon, in discussing . . .

#10 [*Interrupting. Mimicking.*]: I beg pardon . . . What are you so polite about?

#11 [*Looking straight at* #10.]: For the same reason you are not. It's the way I was brought up. [*They stare at each other for a moment. Then* #11 *turns to the others.*] In discussing such a thing as the murder potential we should remember that many of us are *capable* of committing murder. But few of us do. We impose controls upon ourselves to prevent it. The most these psychiatric tests can accomplish along these lines is this: they can tell us that some day a particular person *may* commit a murder. That's all. They prove nothing.

#4: Then how come they're admitted in evidence?

#11: They have many uses, of course. In this case, they added to the general impression the prosecution was trying to create. Perhaps we would find that if we twelve men took the same tests, one or two of us might be discovered to have unconscious desires to kill, and the potentiality of carrying them out. Yet none of us has. To say that a man is capable of murder does not mean that he has committed murder.

#10 [*Angry.*]: But it can mean it. Listen, if they said the kid is capable of killing, he could've killed, couldn't he?
[*#7 looks at his watch and up at the wall clock disgustedly. #8 leans down to #10.*]

#8: You're the one who said, and I quote, "I wouldn't give you a nickel for a psychiatrist's testimony!"
[*#10 knows he's been trapped, and he's angry about it. He speaks through gritted teeth.*]

#10 [*To #8.*]: Boy, I'm telling you, I'd like to . . . [*He stops and slams his fist on the table. Then he gets up and walks around the table trying to control himself. Camera pans with him. When he reaches #8 he stands over him for a minute. #8 doesn't look up at him. He stands there staring at #8 blackly.*]

FOREMAN [*Nervously.*]: Listen, just let's take it easy here.
[*#10 finally walks away from behind #8. Then #8 reaches out to the middle of the table and pulls the switch-knife out of the table. He closes it. Then he flicks it open. Then he closes it. While this is happening we hear the following.*]

#6: What time is it?

#5: There's a clock on the wall right behind you.

#7 [*As #6 turns.*]: It's five of six. [*A pause.*] Man, look at that rain!
[*#10 has walked over to side of room. We see him in background as he angrily sits in a chair against the wall, where he will stay through the entire next sequence until*]

after the vote. #8 still toys with the knife. #2 looks down at #8.]

#2: Say, could I see that a second?

[*#8 closes the knife and slides it across table toward #2. While this goes on we hear the* FOREMAN's *lines.*]

FOREMAN: Well, we're still tied up six to six. Who's got a suggestion?

#12: Let's get some dinner.

[*#2 opens the knife and examines it.*]

#5: Why don't we wait till seven? Give it another hour.

#12: Okay with me.

#2: Um . . . there's something I'd like to say. I mean it's been bothering me a little, and as long as we're stuck . . . Well, there was this whole business about the stab wound and how it was made, the downward angle of it, you know?

#3: Don't tell me we're gonna start with that. They went over it and over it.

#2: I know they did, but I don't go along with it. The boy is 5 feet 7 inches tall. His father was six two. That's a difference of seven inches. It's a very awkward thing to stab *down* into the chest of someone who's more than a half a foot taller than you are.

[*#3 stands up. He points to the knife.*]

#3: Give me that. [*#2 does so.*] Look, you're not gonna be satisfied till you see it again. I'm gonna give you a demonstration. [*#3 walks to a position behind and to the left of* FOREMAN. *He looks at table.*] Somebody get up. [*There is a pause. No one moves for a moment. Then #8 stands up. He walks along the table toward #3. Finally he reaches him. They stand looking at each other for a moment. There is absolute silence in the room.*] Okay. [*Over shoulder to #2.*] Now watch this. I don't want to have to do it again. [*He turns back to #8 and looks squarely at him, measuring him. #8 waits.*] I'm six or seven inches shorter than you. Right?

#2: That's about right. Maybe a little more.

#3: Okay. Let it be more.

[*#3 flicks open the knife, changes its position in his hand and holds it aloft, ready to stab downward. He looks steadily at #8 and #8 at him. Then suddenly he stabs downward hard.*]

#2 [*Shouting.*]: Look out!

[*The blade stops about an inch from #8's chest. #8 doesn't move. #3 smiles. #8 closes his eyes for a second and opens them as we hear the following two lines over several ad lib remonstrations. Several of the jurors run over to #3 and 8.*]

#6 [*Angry.*]: That's not funny!

#5 [*Yelling.*]: What's the matter with you!

#3: Now just calm down. Nobody's hurt. Right?

#8 [*Quietly.*]: No. Nobody's hurt.

[*#3 looks at the rest of the jury challengingly. No one says anything. Then, still holding the knife at #8's chest, pointing down and in, he speaks over his shoulder to #2.*]

#3: All right. There's your angle. Take a look at it. Down and in. That's how I'd stab a taller man in the chest and that's how it was done. Now go ahead and tell me I'm wrong.

[*#2 looks at it for a moment and then, after looking up at #3 as though to say something, turns away and walks to his seat. #8 still stands there as #3 turns, flips the knife into the table and walks away. Several other jurors stand around him, including the* FOREMAN *and #12. #12 walks over to him and, using his closed hand, simulates stabbing #8 in the chest.*]

#12: Down and in. I guess there's no argument.

[*He moves to his seat as do some of the other jurors. Several jurors walk to the water cooler, and #7 goes to his jacket on the coat rack for more cigarettes. #8 turns and walks to the table. He takes the knife out of the table and closes it. He flicks the knife open, takes it by the blade with his left hand, changes its position in his right hand and makes a downward stab with it. Then quickly he closes it and turns to the table. He stands between the* FOREMAN's *seat and #2's seat.*]

#8: Has anyone in here ever stabbed a man? [*He is greeted with a few laughs. He looks at #3 as the jurors at the water cooler move to their seats.*] Have you?

#3: All right, let's not be silly.

#8: Have you or haven't you?

#3 [*Loud.*]: I haven't!

#8: Well, where do you get all your information about how it's done? Have you ever seen a knifing?

#3: How do I know!

#8: Don't you think seeing a man knifed would make a pretty vivid impression on you? [#3 *doesn't answer.*] Well, have you ever seen a knifing?

#3 [*Loud.*]: No!

#8: All right. I want to ask you something now. The boy was pretty experienced with one of these things. He was even sent to reform school for knifing some one, isn't that so?

#2: That's right.

#8: All right, take a look at this. [*He takes the knife, holds it in front of him, and releases the blade. It springs out. Then he takes the blade with his left hand while he changes the position of the knife in his right hand preparatory to stabbing in an overhanded motion. Then he stabs.*] Doesn't that seem like an awkward way to handle a knife?

#3 [*Annoyed.*]: It's the way I'd use a knife if I felt like using a knife.

[*#8 closes the knife. Holds it underhanded in front of his belly, and releases the blade. #5 stands up swiftly.*]

#5 [*Loud.*]: Wait a minute. [*Then he looks around the table, as though remembering something he had never wanted to think of again. He turns toward #8.*] Give me that. [*He reaches out for it. #8 walks up to him and gives him the knife. He takes it, closes it, holds it in his hand gingerly. He looks down at it, then low.*] I hate these things.

#8: Have you ever seen a knife fight?

#5: Yes.

#8: Where?

#5: On my stoop. In my backyard. In the lot across the street. Switch-knives came with the neighborhood where I lived. Funny, I wasn't thinking of it. I guess you try to forget those things.

#8: How do you use a switch-knife?

#5: Underhanded. [*He flicks it open, and, holding it underhanded, slashes swiftly forward and upward.*] Like that. Anyone who's ever used a switch-knife'd never handle it any other way.

#8: Are you sure?

#5: I'm sure. [*He closes the blade, and flicks it open again.*] That's why they're made like this.

#8 [*Looking at* #7.]: The boy is pretty handy with a knife, isn't he?
[#7 *looks back at* #8 *sourly.* #8 *then turns to* #5.]
Do you think he could have made the kind of wound that killed his father?

#5: Not with the experience he'd had all his life with these things. [*Holding up the knife.*] No, I don't think he could. He'd go for him underhanded. . . .

#3 [*Interrupting.*]: How do you know? What, were you standing right in the room when the father was killed?

#5: No. And neither was anyone else.

#3 [*Standing, to* #8.]: You're giving us a lot of mumbo-jumbo here! I don't believe it.

#4 [*Calmly.*]: I don't think you can determine what type of wound this boy might or might not have made simply because he knows how to handle a knife.

#3: That's right. That's absolutely right.
[#8 *walks around toward the* FOREMAN'*s end of the table. He reaches* FOREMAN'*s chair.* #8 *looks at* #12.]

#8: What do you think?
[#12 *is confused, trying to be honest. He hesitates for a moment.*]

#12: Well . . . I don't know.

#3: What d'ya mean you don't know?
[#12 *looks at him silently.* #8 *begins to walk down toward* #7. #7 *is looking up at the wall clock and comparing it with his watch.* #8 *looks at him.*]

#8: What about you?
[#7 *looks from the clock to* #8. *Then he looks around the table.*]

#4: Just a minute. According to the woman across the street . . .

#7 [*Interrupting.*]: Listen, I'll tell you something. I'm a little sick of this whole thing already. All this yakkin's gettin' us nowhere, so let's break it up here. I'm changing my vote to not guilty.

#3: You're what?
[#7 *gets up nervously, and starts to walk down past* #8, 9, 10, 11, 12.]

#7: You heard me. I've had enough.
[#7 *walks toward* #11. #3 *stands up furiously and leans across table toward* #7.]

#3: What d'you mean you've had enough? That's no answer!

[#7 *stops walking. He is behind* #10's *empty seat. He looks across at* #3.]

#7: Hey, listen you! Just worry about yourself, willya?

[#11 *turns and looks at* #7.]

#11: He's right. That is not an answer.

[#11 *stands up and faces* #7.]

#11 [*Strongly.*]: What kind of a man are you? You have sat here and voted guilty with everyone else because there are some baseball tickets burning a hole in your pocket. Now you have changed your vote because you say you're sick of all the talking here.

#7: Listen, buddy . . .

#11 [*Overriding him.*]: Who tells you you have the right to play like this with a man's life? This is an ugly and terrible thing to do! Don't you care . . .

#7 [*Loud.*]: Now wait a minute! You can't talk like that to me!

#11 [*Passionately.*]: I can talk like that to you! If you want to vote not guilty, then do it because you're convinced the man is not guilty . . . not because you've had enough! And if you think he's guilty . . . then vote that way! [#11 *reaches the peak of his rage now.* #7 *blinks at the power of him.*] Or don't you have the . . . the guts to do what you think is right?

#7: Now, listen . . .

#11 [*Hard.*]: Guilty or not guilty?

#7 [*Hesitantly.*]: I told you. Not guilty.

#11: Why?

#7: I don't have to . . .

#11: You *do* have to! Say it! Why? [*They stare each other in the eyes for a long moment. Then* #7 *looks down.*]

#7 [*Low.*]: I . . . don't think he's guilty.

[#11 *looks at him disgustedly, then sits down.* #7 *stands there defeated.*]

#8: I want another vote.

[*There is a silence in the room.*]

FOREMAN [*Quietly.*]: Okay, there's another vote called for. I guess the quickest way is a show of hands. Anybody object? [*He looks around the table questioningly. There is no answer*.] All those voting not guilty raise your hands. [*#7 is still standing. #10 still sits in the chair at side of room. #2, 5, 6, 7, 8, 9, 11 put up their hands immediately. The* FOREMAN *starts to count the upraised hands*.] One. Two. Three. Four. Five. Six. Seven. [*The seventh number is #11. #12's hand is down, but his face is a mask of indecision. As the* FOREMAN's *counting finger moves past him, he suddenly raises his hand*.] Eight. [*The* FOREMAN *stops counting and looks around the table. Slowly now, almost embarrassedly, he raises his own hand*.] Nine. [*He lowers his hand*.] All those voting guilty. [*#10 jumps to his feet, angrily raising his hand. #3 and 4 raise their hands*.] Three. [*They lower their hands*.] The vote is nine to three in favor of acquittal.

[*#10 is standing angrily now behind #4*.]

#10: I don't understand you people! I mean all these picky little points you keep bringing up. They don't mean nothing! [*He starts a walk around table. He stands behind it. He continues to talk during his walk. Everyone is seated at table now but #10*.] You saw this kid just like I did. You're not gonna tell me you believe that phoney story about losing the knife, and that business about being at the movies. Look, you know how these people lie! It's born in them! [*He whips out a handkerchief and blows his nose*.] I mean what the heck, I don't have to tell you. They don't know what the truth is! And lemme tell you, they don't need any real big reason to kill someone either! No sir! [*As #10 talks, #5 gets up from his seat and walks over to the coat rack. He stands with his back to #10*.] You know, they get drunk . . . oh they're very big drinkers, all of 'em, and bang, someone's lying in the gutter. Oh, nobody's blaming them for it. That's how they are! By nature! You know what I mean? [*Shouting it violently*.] Violent! [*#9 gets up from the table and walks to the window, stands with his back to #10 as #10 talks*.] Human life don't mean as much to them as it does to us! [*#11 gets up and walks to the other window. As he goes, #10 whirls to him*.] Hey, where are you going? [*#11 pays no attention, stands with his back to the window. #10 turns back to the table. He begins to sound slightly desperate*.] Look, these people're lushing it up and fighting all the time, and if somebody gets killed, so somebody gets killed! They don't care. Oh sure, there are some good things about 'em too. Look, I'm the first one to say that. [*#8 gets up and walks to the nearest wall, and stands with his face to it.*] I've known a couple who were okay, but that's the exception, you know what I mean? [*#2 gets up, and a moment later so does #6. They each walk to positions along the wall, and stand with their backs to #10.*] Most of 'em, it's like they have no feelings. They can do anything. What's going on here? [*Louder.*] I'm tryin' to tell you you're making a big mistake, you people. This kid is a liar! I know it. I know all about them! I mean what's happening in here? I'm speaking my piece, and you . . . [*The* FOREMAN *gets up and walks to the water cooler. #12 follows him. They stand with their backs toward #10.*] Listen to me! They're no good! There's not a one of 'em who's any good. [*#7 gets up and walks to the window, stands with his back to #10, who looks around wildly.*] Boy, are you smart! Well, I'm telling you we better watch out! This kid on trial here, his type. . . . Well don't you know about them? [*#3 gets up and, standing at his seat, turns his back on #10. #4 gets up and starts the long walk around the table toward #10 who is now hysterical.*] What are you doing? Listen to me! I'm trying to tell you something! [*#10 gesticulates wildly.*] There's a danger here! These people are wild! Don't you know about it? [*Roaring.*]: Listen to me!

[*He turns furiously, and finds himself face to face with #4. Softer.*] Listen to me!

[*#4 stares at him as he trails off into silence. There is a long pause.*]

#4 [*Quietly.*]: If you open your mouth again, I'm going to split your skull!

[*#4 stares contemptuously at #10. There is no sound, no move. Then #10 looks down at the table.*]

#10 [*Very softly.*]: I'm only tryin' to tell you . . .

[*There is a long pause. Then #4 turns and walks away from him. The only movement and sound in the room are #4's footsteps. He walks slowly back to his seat. The other ten jurors stand in various attitudes and postures around the walls of the room, their backs to #10. #4 reaches his chair. He pulls it out and sits down. Then,*]

*slowly, the jurors begin to return to their seats. #10
stands, head down, without moving, until the last of the
jurors have silently taken their seats. Then he begins a
walk which takes him to a chair at the far end of the
room against a wall. He sags into it, beaten. He lowers
his head into his hands and sits there. As is everyone
else, #8 is embarrassed. He looks around the table.
Then he clears his throat.*]

#8 [*Slowly.*]: It's very hard to keep personal prejudice
out of a thing like this. And no matter where you run
into it, prejudice obscures the truth. [*He pauses. There
is silence. #4 looks at #8 steadily. Then, softly.*] Well,
I don't think any real damage has been done here. Because I don't really know what the truth is. No one ever
will, I suppose. Nine of us now seem to feel that the defendant is innocent, but we're just gambling on probabil-
ities. We may be wrong. [*Looking at #4.*] We may be
trying to return a guilty man to the community. No one
can really know. But we have a reasonable doubt, and
this is a safeguard which has enormous value to our
system. No jury can declare a man guilty unless it's *sure*.
[*#4 listens.*] We nine can't understand how you three
are still so sure. [*He pauses for a moment.*] Maybe you
can tell us. [*#4 looks strongly at #8.*]

#4: I'll try. [*He looks at #3, and then back to #8.*]
You've made some excellent points. The last one, in
which you "proved" that the boy couldn't have made
the kind of overhand stab wound that killed his father
was very convincing. [*He stands up and stretches, and
then continues to stand.*] But I still believe the boy is
guilty of murder. I have two reasons. One: the evidence
given by the woman across the street who actually *saw*
the murder committed.

#3: And how, brother! As far as I'm concerned, that's
the most important testimony.

[*#4 looks down at #3 with some coldness.*]

#4: And two: the fact that this woman described the
stabbing by saying she saw the boy raise his arm over
his head and plunge the knife *down* into the father's
chest. She saw him do it . . . the wrong way.

#3 [*Excitedly.*]: That's right! That's absolutely right!

[*#8 listens carefully as #4 goes on, and we can see
that he has no real answer to this.*]

#4: Now let's talk about this woman for a minute. She said that she went to bed at about 11 o'clock that night. Her bed was next to the window and she could look out while lying down and see directly into the boy's window across the street. She tossed and turned for over an hour, unable to fall asleep. Finally, she turned toward the window at about ten minutes after twelve and, as she looked out, she saw the killing through the windows of the passing el train. She says that the lights went out immediately after the killing but that she got a good look at the boy in the act of stabbing his father. [*He simulates an overhand stabbing movement with his arm to accent this statement.*] As far as I can see, this is unshakable testimony.

#3: That's what I mean! That's the whole case!

#4 [*Leaning over to #8, and mimicking him.*]: What do you think? [*#8 hesitates for a moment, but doesn't answer. #4 looks in the direction of #12.*] How about you?

[*#12 has never been sold on voting not guilty, and is now swayed in the opposite direction, yet he is apprehensive about how he will look in the eyes of the other jurors if he shifts his vote again.*]

#12: Well . . . I don't know. There's so much evidence to sift. . . . [*He pauses, and chews at a fingernail.*] This is a pretty complicated business. [*He looks around indecisively.*]

#4: Frankly, I don't see how you can vote for acquittal.

#12: Well, it's not so easy to arrange the evidence in order . . .

#3: You can throw out all the other evidence. The woman saw him do it. What else do you want?

#12 [*Torn.*]: Well, maybe . . .

#3: Let's vote on it.

FOREMAN: Okay. There's another vote called for. Anybody object?

#12 [*Suddenly.*]: I'm changing my vote. I think he's guilty. [*He looks down at the table, ashamed. #8 turns his head toward #12, angry, upset, but helpless. #3 smiles slightly.*]

#3: Anybody else? [*He looks around the table challengingly.*] The vote is eight to four.

[*There is a pause.* #12, *tormented, gets up and walks to the window.*]

#11 [*To* #3.]: Why is this such a personal triumph for you, this one vote?

#3 [*Grinning.*]: I'm the competitive type! [*To all.*] Okay, now here's what I think. I think we're a hung jury. Let's take it inside to the judge. [*There is no answer to this.*] Well, I want to hear an argument. I say we're hung. [*He turns toward* #8.] Come on. You're the leader of the cause. What about it?

#8 [*Quietly.*]: Let's go over it again.

#3 [*Annoyed.*]: We went over it again! [*Indicating* #12 *with a wave of his hand.*] Batton, Barton, Durstine and Osborn up there is bouncin' backwards and forwards like a tennis ball. . . .

[#12 *stands at the window. He turns around.*]

#12 [*Hurt.*]: Say, listen . . . what d'ya think you're saying here? You have no right to . . .

[#4 *has his eyeglasses off and is polishing them.*]

#3 [*To* #12.]: I apologize on my knees. [*To* #8.] Come on! Let's get out from under this thing. I'm sicka arguing with you already.

#4 [*To* #3.]: There's no point in getting nasty about it. You keep trying to make this into a contest.

#3 [*Grudgingly.*]: Okay.

#4: Maybe we can talk about setting some kind of a time limit.

#7: Once around to the dealer.

[#4 *looks witheringly in his direction. Still polishing his glasses, he turns around to the wall clock and peers up at it.*]

#4: It's um . . . [*He squints and then puts on his glasses.*] . . . quarter after six. [*He turns back to the table, takes off his glasses and lays them down on the table. He looks tired now. He closes his eyes and clasps his fingers over the marks left by his eyeglasses at the sides of his nose. He rubs these areas as he speaks.*] Someone before mentioned seven o'clock. I think that's a point at which we might begin to discuss the question of whether we're a hung jury or not.

[#9 *is looking closely at* #4, *and obviously has thought of something tremendously exciting.*]

#9 [*Leaning forward.*]: Don't you feel well?
[*#4 looks up at #9, annoyed.*]

#4: I feel perfectly well . . . thank you. [*To all.*] I was saying that seven o'clock would be a reasonable time to . . .

#9 [*Excited.*]: The reason I asked about that was because you were rubbing your nose like . . . [*#9 notes #4 glaring at him.*] I'm sorry for interrupting. But you made a gesture that reminded me . . .

#4 [*Interrupting.*]: I'm trying to settle something here. Do you mind?

#9: I think this is important. [*#4 looks at him for a moment, then shrugs and leans back, relinquishing the floor.*] Thank you. [*He looks around the table for a moment, then back at #4.*] I'm sure you'll pardon me for this, but I was wondering why you were rubbing your nose like that.

#3 [*Annoyed.*]: Ah, come on now, will ya please!

#9 [*Sharply to #3.*]: At this point I happen to be talking to the gentleman sitting next to you.
[*#3 looks annoyed. During these next lines he sighs deeply, gets up from the table and strolls to the water cooler. #9 to #4.*] Now, why were you rubbing your nose?

#4: Well, if it's any of your business, I was rubbing it because it bothers me a little.

#9: I'm sorry. Is it because of your eyeglasses?

#4: It is. Now could we get on to something else?

#9: Your eyeglasses make those deep impressions on the sides of your nose. I hadn't noticed that before. They must be annoying.

#4 [*Angrily.*]: They are annoying.

#9: I wouldn't know about that. I've never worn eyeglasses. [*He points to his eyes and smiles slightly.*] Twenty-twenty.

#7: Listen, will you come on already with the optometrist bit!

#9 [*Firmly to #7.*]: You have excellent recuperative powers! [*#7 looks disgustedly at him. Now #9 turns to #4, quietly.*] The woman who testified that she saw the killing had those same marks on the sides of her nose. [*#4 digests this. There is a silence in the room for* *a moment. Then we hear a slow babble of ad lib conversation. #9 stands up, very excited.*] Please! [*The conversation continues.*] Please! [*It quiets down.*] Just a minute, and then I'll be finished. I don't know if anyone else noticed that about her. I didn't think about it then, but I've been going over her face in my mind. She had those marks. She kept rubbing them in court. [*He demonstrates.*]

#5: He's right! She did do that a lot.

#7: So what if she did?

#9: This woman was about forty-five years old. She was making a tremendous effort to look thirty-five for her first public appearance. Heavy makeup. Dyed hair. Brand-new clothes that should have been worn by a younger woman. No eyeglasses. Women do that. See if you can get a mental picture of her.

[*#3, at water cooler, glares at #9. He begins to stride toward the table. He ends up standing behind #5, shouting across at #9.*]

#3 [*Loud.*]: What d'ya mean, no glasses? You don't know if she wore glasses. Just because she was rubbing her nose . . .

#5: She had those marks. I saw 'em.

#3: So what! What d'ya think that means?

#6 [*Standing up to #3.*]: Listen, I'm getting so sick of your yelling in here . . .

#5 [*Jumping up, to #6.*]: Come on. Cut it out.

[*#6 looks at #5 and then turns away from #3.*]

FOREMAN: Listen, I saw 'em too. He's right. I was the closest one to her. She had those deep things, what d'ya callem, uh . . . you know . . . [*He massages the spot on his nose where they would be.*]

#3 [*Shouting.*]: Well, what point are you making here? She had dyed hair and marks on her nose. I'm asking ya what does that mean?

#9 [*Quietly.*]: Could those marks be made by anything other than eyeglasses?

#4 [*After a pause.*]: No. They couldn't.

#3 [*To #4.*]: Listen, what are you saying here? I didn't see any marks.

#4: I did. Strange, but I didn't think about it before. . . .

#6: Now that we're talking about it, I saw them. I mean it never occurred to me . . .

[*#3 steps back, thinking. #9 leans back and opens his bottle of pills. He slips one tiny pill under his tongue. He suddenly looks very old and very tired. #8 looks warmly at #9. #9 drops the stopper of his bottle. #8 picks it up for him, smiles at him, hands it to him.*]

#3: Well, what about the lawyer? Why didn't he say something?

#8: There are twelve people in here concentrating on this case. Eleven of us didn't think of it either.

#3: Okay, Clarence Darrow. Then what about the district attorney? You think he'd try to pull a trick like that, have her testify without glasses?

#8: Did you ever see a woman who had to wear glasses and didn't want to because she thinks they spoil her looks?

#6: My wife. Listen, I'm telling ya, as soon as we walk outa the house . . .

#8 [*Off, interrupting.*]: Maybe the district attorney didn't know either.

#6: Yeah, that's what I was just gonna say.

[*#3 is stopped by this momentarily. He stares around the room.*]

#3: Okay. She had marks on her nose. I'm givin' ya this. From glasses. Right? She never wore 'em out of the house so people'd think she was gorgeous. But when she saw this kid kill his father, she was *in* the house. Alone. That's all.

#8 [*Across to #4.*]: Do you wear your glasses when you go to bed?

#4: No, I don't. No one wears eyeglasses to bed.

[*There is silence, save for the sound of the rain. No one moves.*]

#8: It's logical to say that she wasn't wearing them while she was in bed, tossing and turning, trying to fall asleep.

#3 [*Angry.*]: How do you know?

#8: I don't *know*. I *guessed*. I'm also *guessing* that she probably didn't put on her glasses when she turned and looked casually out of the window. And she herself said that the murder took place just as she looked out, and the lights went off a split second later. She couldn't have had time to put glasses on then.

#3: Wait a second . . .

#8 [*Strong.*]: And here's another guess. Maybe she honestly thought she saw the boy kill his father. I say that she saw only a blur.

[#3 *walks furiously over to* #8.]

#3: How do you know what she saw? [*He turns to the others; loud.*] How does he know all these things? [*He turns back to* #8.] You don't know what kind of glasses she wore! Maybe she was farsighted. Maybe they were sunglasses! What do you know about it?

#8: I only know that the woman's eyesight is in question now.

#11: She had to be able to identify a person 60 feet away, at night, without glasses.

#2: You can't send someone off to die on evidence like that.

#3: Don't give me that.

#8: Don't you think that the woman might have made a mistake?

#3 [*Shouting.*]: No!

#8: It's not possible?

#3: No! It's not possible.

[#8 *turns away and walks down toward* #12. *He speaks to* #12's *back.*]

#8: Is it possible?

#12 [*Quietly.*]: Yes.

[#8 *walks around the room to* #10, *who still sits slumped in the chair. He stands over* #10.]

#8 [*Softly.*]: Do you think he's guilty?

[#10 *shakes his head tiredly, giving in completely.* #8 *turns to the table.* #3 *stands behind* #9.]

#3: I think he's guilty!

[#8 *walks toward the table.*]

#8: Does anyone else?

#4 [*Quietly.*]: No. I'm convinced.

#3 [*Angrily to* #4.]: What's the matter with you!

#4: I have a reasonable doubt now.

#9: It's eleven to one.

[#3 *glares angrily at all of them.*]

#3 [*Loud.*]: Well, what about all the other evidence? What about all that stuff . . . the knife . . . the whole business.

#2: You said we could throw out all the other evidence.

[#3 *glares at* #2, *speechless. He stalks down toward the* FOREMAN's *end of the table, not able now to sit down with the others. He stands with his back toward them. There is a long pause. The others all watch him and wait. #3 doesn't move.*]

#7 [*Very subdued.*]: Well, what d'we do now?
[*There is another long pause.*]

#5 [*To #3.*]: You're alone.
[*#3 whirls around furiously.*]

#3 [*Loud.*]: I don't care whether I'm alone or not. It's my right!
[*#8, who still stands behind #4, speaks softly but firmly.*]

#8: It's your right.
[*They all wait. #3 watches them as if at bay. #8 and the other members of the jury watch him. #3 stares back at them.*]

#3: Well, what d'ya want! I say he's guilty.

#8: We want your arguments.

#3: I gave you my arguments!

#8: We're not convinced. We want to hear them again. We have as much time as it takes.
[*#3 stands there, frustrated, for a moment. Then he begins.*]

#3: Everything . . . every single thing that came out in that courtroom, but I mean everything . . . says he's guilty. Do you think I'm an idiot or something? Why dontcha take that stuff about the old man . . . the old man who lived there . . . and heard everything, or take the knife, what, just because he . . . found one exactly like it? That old man saw him. Right there on the stairs. What's the difference how many seconds it was? What's the difference? Every single thing. The knife falling through a hole in his pocket . . . you can't prove that he didn't get to the door. Sure, you can hobble around the room and take all the time you want, but you can't prove it! And that stuff with the el! And the movies! Now there's a phoney deal if I ever saw one. I betcha five thousand dollars I'd remember the movies I saw the night I killed my father . . . as if I ever would! I'm telling you, every single thing that went on has been twisted and turned in here. That business with the glasses, how do you know she didn't have them on? The woman testified in court . . . and that whole thing about hearing the boy yell. . . . Listen, I've got all the facts here! You

guys . . . [*He pauses and looks around, then, shouting.*]
Well, what d'ya want? That's it! [#8 *waits.* #3 *looks
furiously around.*] That's the whole case! [*No one answers.*] Somebody say something. [*No one does.*] You
lousy bunch of bleeding hearts!

[*No one moves. Everyone watches.*] You're not gonna
intimidate me! [*There is no answer.*] I'm entitled to my
opinion!

[*There is no answer. And suddenly he strides swiftly to
#8, stands in front of him staring at him with utter
hatred.* #3 *clenches his fists and stares at* #8. #8
stares impassively back. It seems as though #3 *must
inevitably hit* #8. #8 *waits for it, hands down.* #3
*half-raises both fists, stands there tensely, his face con-
torted in silent rage. Then suddenly he turns to the table
and bangs both fists down on it, and thunders.*] All right!
[*Softly now.*] Not guilty.

[*He suffers silently. We begin to hear the quiet noise of
chairs being moved and footsteps shuffling about the
room. We hear a knock on the door and the door being
opened. Everyone is up. The* GUARD *stands in the doorway. Silently the jurors get their belongings and begin to
walk toward the door. Only* #3 *and 8 are left now.* #8
*walks to the door. He stands in the doorway and looks
back at* #3. *Then he steps out of the room.* #3 *still
stands at the table, head down. The* GUARD *looks at him.*]
GUARD [*Politely.*]: Let's go, mister.

[#3 *looks up. Then slowly he goes for his coat. He gets
it, puts it on, and slowly walks toward the door. The*
GUARD *steps outside. As* #3 *passes the table he stops,
then walks over to it. The knife is sticking in it. He
reaches over, pulls it out. He holds it up in front of him
and looks at the doorway. Then, with a last burst of
anger he flips it into the table. It quivers there. He turns
and walks out, slamming the door. The knife quivers in
the table in the empty room; and the sound of the rain
continues as before. Rain beats against the window.*]

[*A revolving door. The door to the courthouse building,
seen from outside. Rain beats against it. It begins to turn
now, and the jurors start to emerge. One by one they
walk into the rain, each reacting with his own maneu-*

vers. One turns up his collar. One pulls down his hat. One holds a newspaper over his head. They begin to move down the steps in groups and singly now. #8 is alone, rain beading his face. He raises his collar, looks around, and then walks off. The others begin to spread out now. Some turning left, some right, some going straight ahead, spreading out silently in all directions, never to see each other again. And finally they are gone, and the rain beats down on the empty steps. Fade out.]

THE FINAL WAR OF OLLY WINTER

by Ronald Ribman

ACT I

[*The sky above Vietnam, 1963. The camera fades in on the interior of a U.S. Air Force helicopter. The steady rhythmic sound of the blades can be heard. An American* PILOT *is at the controls. The others are:* OLLY WINTER, *a Negro master sergeant of the U.S. Army, a Vietnamese* LIEUTENANT, *and a half dozen Viet troops.*]

PILOT [*To* OLLY.]: We've just picked up the Mekong. [*The* PILOT *points out the window.* OLLY *looks down and watches the river flow by for a second.*] You've got about five minutes. I'm swinging east.

VIET. LIEUTENANT [*In Vietnamese to his men.*]: Check your weapons.

[*They do so.* OLLY *reaches out and inspects the men's weapons and then leans back and stares out of the window. The terrain flys by the way objects fly by the window of an express train. The camera holds on a close-up of* OLLY.]

[*Flashback to the interior of a subway train. The camera is on* OLLY. *He is now ten years of age, seated in the subway train staring out the window. He is dressed in black. The camera pulls back and we see Olly's* SISTER, *about fourteen, and his* MOTHER *who are also dressed in black. The* SISTER *and the* MOTHER *sit stiffly looking ahead. Nobody speaks. The train pulls into a station and stops. The camera focuses on an advertising poster showing a group of men, women and children—all Caucasians. In the train a very* FAT MAN *enters carrying a child, age about five. The* CHILD *is holding two balloons. They sit down opposite* OLLY. *The* FAT MAN *has a gold watch on a chain. He keeps pulling out the watch from his vest pocket, opening it, and then snapping it shut audibly.*]

OLLY *looks at the little* BOY *who has been sitting so primly—as indeed all have been sitting, except* OLLY. OLLY *seems to be the only one alive. The* BOY *gives him a big warm friendly smile.* OLLY *smiles back.*]

[*The picture dissolves into a cemetery scene.* OLLY, *his* SISTER *and* MOTHER, *and a Negro* PREACHER, *who is reading from the Bible, are near the grave. Two* GRAVE-DIGGERS *stand to one side. Since* OLLY *is a child, the people and objects seem big.*]

PREACHER: Now this I say, Brethren, that flesh and blood cannot inherit the kingdom of God; neither doth corruption. Behold, I show you a mystery. We shall not all sleep, but we shall all be changed. In a moment, in the twinkling of an eye, at the last trump; for the trumpet shall sound, and the dead shall be raised incorruptible, and we shall be changed. For this corruptible must put on incorruption, and this mortal must put on immortality. So when this corruptible shall have put on incorruption, and this mortal shall put on immortality, then shall be brought to pass the saying that is written, Death is swallowed up in victory. O Death, where is thy sting? O grave, where is thy victory? The sting of death is sin; and the strength of sin is the law. But thanks be to God, which giveth us the victory through our Lord Jesus Christ. Amen.

[*Throughout the reading,* OLLY's *attention is elsewhere than on the* PREACHER's *word. He looks up in the tree directly over the preacher. The tree is full of birds. In the middle of the* PREACHER's *reading, one of the birds in the tree relieves itself. The dropping falls on the* PREACHER's *hand. He wipes it off and continues, almost without a pause. Nobody notices but* OLLY. *The* MOTHER *is crying profusely.* OLLY *stands there scratching his nose until his* SISTER's *hand comes out of nowhere and slaps his hand down to his side. She whispers something to him.*]

[*The reverie ends and the scene shifts to a jungle clearing.* OLLY *leads; the* LIEUTENANT *and his men follow.* OLLY *signals a halt. He motions the* LIEUTENANT *forward.*]

OLLY: That's it. [OLLY *points toward a rice paddy. The* LIEUTENANT *pulls out a map. He keeps staring at the map trying to find the rice paddy. He cannot, but he will annot.* OLLY *reaches over and points on the map.*] That's the paddy, Lieu-

...es, that is correct.

...e paddies two and three.

... *looks at the map. He won't admit that ...and the paddies.* OLLY *points, without comment, ...ae positions of paddies two and three. One of the men says something to another man and there is a slight laugh. The* LIEUTENANT, *thinking that they might be laughing at him, whirls around.*]

VIET. LIEUTENANT [*To his men, in Vietnamese.*]: Be still! [*The men stop laughing. The* LIEUTENANT *turns back to* OLLY.]

OLLY: Okay. We'll start flushing Charlie out in this one. When you start coming through, don't stay too far apart or they'll come back through the holes. [*The* LIEUTENANT *looks at him without saying anything.*] I'm going around the flank as far as here . . . [*He points on map to upper left corner of the paddy.*] . . . the far left corner of the paddy. That'll give a base of fire to your front and left. Now, one man should be left over there. . . . [*He points to a spot on the lower right corner of the paddy.*]

VIET. LIEUTENANT: Why?

OLLY: He'll cover your rear and the right flank.

VIET. LIEUTENANT: It would be better if all the men crossed together.

OLLY: No, it would not be better. You leave one man there . . . [*He points again to the lower right corner of the paddy.*] . . . and don't start across until I'm in position and signal.

VIET. LIEUTENANT: I am in command. You are just the adviser.

OLLY: That's right. I'm an adviser and that's my advice.

VIET. LIEUTENANT: Sergeant, America always see the leopard in the jungle and then puts a gun in another man's hand and pushes him toward the leopard. Americans do not care if we die. Well, this is my jungle. All the men cross together. When America send soldiers to fight, then you give me advice. America send ten thousand soldiers to fight in jungle and we win war by end of 1963. Kill

by end of 1963. [*The* LIEUTENANT *walks*
OLLY *over to his men. He issues a number of*
mands.] All right. Let's go. We will all cross toge

OLLY [*Under his breath.*]: You stupid bastard. . . .

solve to another part of the jungle. The camera fo
OLLY *as he heads along the edge of the swamp. He*
far enough in the swamp so that he cannot be seen
the paddy, but not far enough in so that he canno
what is happening in the paddy. The LIEUTENANT, *intent*
on asserting his authority, has not waited for him to get
into position. He has begun to cross the field. OLLY
glances over and sees what is happening.] Not yet—you
stupid, stupid bastard—not yet. [*Before he can get into
position there is a burst of automatic fire from the direct
front.* OLLY *watches the Viet soldiers being cut down as
they cross the field.* OLLY *opens fire in the direction of
the enemy, but it is useless. He has only brought the
automatic fire down upon himself. The bullets cut a
swath in the jungle about him.* OLLY *falls down into the
mud and lies there until the fire ceases. He raises his
head. A* GUERRILLA *comes out into the rice field to see
if the Viet troops are dead. While the* GUERRILLA *is in-
vestigating,* OLLY *gets up and races in the direction of
the machine gun. Suddenly he stops as he hears the
sound of someone coming toward him from the front.
He flattens himself on the ground and waits. After a few
moments, a* GUERRILLA *is seen stalking toward him
through the jungle. The* GUERRILLA *has come to see if
they have hit* OLLY *with their fire. As he passes,* OLLY
*springs upon him and grabs him about the neck. He
shoves the* GUERRILLA's *face down into the mud. In the
agony of killing,* OLLY *stares away, his mouth open, con-
torted. The killing finally done,* OLLY *gets up and continues circling toward the machine gun position. When he
is about twenty yards from the gun, he sees that there is
an enemy* SOLDIER *manning it. This* SOLDIER *is watching
another in the field. If* OLLY *can kill the* SOLDIER *at the
gun quietly, he will be able to shoot the other one in the
field.* OLLY *slowly begins moving toward the machine
gunner, but when he has come within ten yards, the*
SOLDIER *hears him and whirls around.* OLLY *is forced to
shoot. The* SOLDIER *falls over the machine gun.* OLLY

runs as fast as he can toward the edge of the swamp to
try to get a shot at the SOLDIER in the field, but it is
too late. He is already gone from sight. OLLY goes back
to the machine gun and, turning it on the rice paddy,
begins spraying the field until the weapon is empty. He
waits a few moments after the gun is empty, but there
is no return fire. He pulls the bolt out of the machine
gun and throws it into the swamp. Then he enters the
rice paddy some twenty yards to the left of the machine
gun emplacement. It is impossible to tell if he has hit
the GUERRILLA or not. Three quick shots ring out and
splash into the mud. It has become a question of who
gets who first. When OLLY raises his head, he can hear
the GUERRILLA splashing toward him, but the GUERRILLA
is low in the field and cannot be seen. OLLY looks down
at his weapon. It is covered with mud. He pulls the bolt
open and begins cleaning out the mud as best he can.
The sound of the splashing gets closer and closer. Both
the GUERRILLA and OLLY see each other at the same time.
OLLY's weapon is still packed with mud. It won't fire.
OLLY finds himself looking down the enemy's gun barrel.
The GUERRILLA pulls the trigger, but the gun jams. OLLY
races forward as fast as he can. The GUERRILLA drops his
weapon and takes a swipe at OLLY with a machete. OLLY
ducks and the blade cuts the air over his head. OLLY stabs
the GUERRILLA in the chest with his knife. The GUER-
RILLA sinks into the mud, OLLY stabbing a few more
times. As the GUERRILLA falls backward, his hat falls off.
It is a young girl. OLLY stands staring at her as her face
slowly slides under the mud. The camera moves upward
above OLLY until the view contains the clearing and (?)
in the middle surrounded by the dead. OLLY stands with
his arms out from his side; his arms jerk and aimless(?)
move as if trying to push the scene away. All the w(?)
he cannot seem to find lie in the spastic movemen(?)
his body.]
[Flashback to a school playground. OLLY, (?)
is surrounded by a group of young boys (?)
push him from the back whichever wa(?)
throw pebbles and pieces of stick (?)
boys goes into the center of the (?)
ing OLLY in the chest. He push(?)

won't fight. *The boy returns to the edge of the circle, but the rest won't let him return. They insist he fight with* OLLY. *They begin to chant:*]

- BOYS: Olly is a mama's boy, Olly is afraid to fight.

[*They chant this over and over. A* BOY *hits* OLLY *in the face.* OLLY *falls to the ground. He lies there a moment. The chanting stops. They are waiting to see what* OLLY *does.* OLLY *reaches out and grabs a stone. He swings the stone wildly and hits two or three of the boys. The rest run.*]

[*Jungle clearing. The camera view is still from above. The view moves in close on* OLLY's *face. As he begins to walk away, the scene fades out.*]

ACT II

[*A small clearing in a mangrove swamp.* OLLY *has his poncho spread out in front of him on the ground. The parts of his gun are spread out on the poncho. He has been cleaning his weapon and is now in the process of putting the rifle together. He puts it together mechanically, with the sure skill of one forever used to putting weapons together.*]

[*Flashback to an apartment stairway. Superimposed on the scene of* OLLY *putting his rifle together is a scene of* OLLY *as a boy of ten climbing a flight of stairs. He carries a small schoolboy's briefcase in his hand. On the way up, he pauses to stroke a cat sitting on the steps. The focus narrows to his hands—the hands of an adult putting together a mechanical device—the hands of child stroking a living creature. The child raises his eyes. The stairway seems to loom a mile long. At the top of the stairs is a single shut door.*]

[*The scene shifts back to the mangrove swamp.* OLLY *snaps the last piece of his weapon into place. He slides the bolt forward on a round and the bolt cracks into place with a sharp reassuring sound. He repacks and refolds his poncho and moves out. A road appears.* OLLY, *covered by the heavy brush and vegetation, stands looking out at the road. He hears the sound of some walking. He falls to one knee, points his rifle in rection of the sound. After a moment a young* VI ESE GIRL *moves into view. She walks until she lel with* OLLY *and then she senses something and looks into the swamp at* OLLY. *For a just stand there looking at one another. weapon pointed at her. He gets to his step toward her. She backs up a ste on the road, keeping his gun leveled at her.*]

OLLY: Come here. Come here. [*She doesn't move. He starts walking toward her and she starts backing up.*] Come here. [*He motions to a spot in front of him, but she gives no sign that she understands or intends to obey. To himself.*] All right, the hard way. [*He runs at her. She turns to run, but he is too fast. He overtakes her. Pulling her off the road, he holds her down and searches her. He practically pulls her clothes off.*]

GIRL [*In Vietnamese.*]: No . . . No.

OLLY [*As he is searching her.*]: I don't figure on getting knifed in the back by you or anyone else, lady. Where's the rest of your friends? How many knives you got? Where are the rest of your friends? Across the road? [*Finally convinced she is not armed, he lets her up. For a long moment she stands more or less naked in front of him. She looks at OLLY with the look one gives another when a grave mistake has been made. It is almost as if she stands there accusing him, and waiting for an apology. OLLY more or less realizes he has made a mistake, that his anger directed toward the girl is anger at himself for having been forced to kill the girl guerrilla, for having more or less been tricked into doing it, for the war that makes people do such things.*] All right. Put on your clothes. [*He is embarrassed, but unwilling to give up the tone of anger in his voice. She still stands there. He bends down and picks up some of the clothes he has torn off. He throws it over to her. The clothes strike her, but she does not pick them up. They fall to her feet. She stares at him and he stares back. Then he goes over and picks up her clothes and hands them to her. She takes them and holds them up in front of her exposed body, but she still makes no effort to dress herself. He goes over to her and begins to put on her clothes. At first she doesn't move, then she begins dressing herself. As soon as she does this, he moves away. He stands looking away while she dresses. Muttering to himself.*] Stay out of the war. Stay home with the children. You women have no business in these wars. 'posed to be home. [*He becomes sullenly quiet ... finishes dressing. After she has finished, he ...*] All right. Let's fall out on the road.

[OLLY *points to the road and repeats himself.*] The road. [*She understands and goes out on the road. He remains in the jungle a few feet.*] Okay, lady, take off. [*She doesn't move.*] Move out. [*She still doesn't move even though he gestures with his arms.*] You go your way. I'll go mine. [*She does not move.* OLLY *begins walking through the brush and trees that parallel the road. The* GIRL, *still on the road, begins to walk in the same direction. She keeps staring over at him as they walk.*] Lady, will you stop staring at me. You're telling the whole world I'm in here. [*He walks on. She parallels him on the road and keeps staring at him.*] Oh, what the hell! [*He comes out of the jungle toward her. She backs up about fifteen feet. He looks at her and then continues walking down the road. She begins following, but keeps her distance. Every once in a while he looks back. Once he stops, she stops, then he gives up and goes on. She follows.* OLLY *stops. A few feet ahead on the side of the road is a mangy-looking dog.* OLLY *approaches the dog. When he is near the dog, it slinks off into the underbrush.* OLLY *moves on. The* GIRL *follows. Now the dog reappears out of the brush and moves to the road behind the* GIRL. OLLY *stops. The* GIRL *stops and the dog stops.* OLLY *moves on. The* GIRL *follows and the dog follows. Led by* OLLY, *the three move forward.* OLLY *stops. The* GIRL *and the dog stop. The camera swings ahead of* OLLY. *The road ends. In front and to all sides the jungle surrounds them.* OLLY *takes out his map and machete. The map indicates that the road continues, but obviously it doesn't.*] That's great. [*He walks into the jungle, but the girl doesn't follow. She squats on the road and so does the dog.* OLLY *looks back.*] So long, lady. [*He presses on, slashing his way through the thick vines. The jungle is almost impenetrable. He does this for about twenty y〈...〉 and then it simply becomes too swampy. He can 〈...〉 lift his boots out of the mud. He turns aroun〈...〉 gust and heads back to the road. The* GIRL a〈...〉 are still sitting there. He stares at her. She 〈...〉 to the right.*]

GIRL [*In Vietnamese.*]: This way.

OLLY: Yeah? Suppose I go the other w〈...〉 the heavy brush at the left. The car〈...〉

chopping at it and going a few steps, he gives in and returns to the road. Again the GIRL *points to the right.*] Okay. [*He moves in that direction. The* GIRL *and dog follow.* OLLY, *still followed by the* GIRL *and dog, moves into a clearing.* OLLY *looks at the* GIRL. *She points left. He moves left, with the* GIRL *and the dog following. They break through the high, thick brush to see the road. The* GIRL *looks at* OLLY *and gives him an "I told you so" look.*] Okay. Okay. [OLLY *stops at the edge of the road and sits down. He opens up his pack and starts rummaging through the contents. The* GIRL *and the dog become very interested in the whole operation, and* OLLY *becomes increasingly uncomfortable under their hungry gaze. He finally pulls out some of the rations and begins opening the wrappings. He is about to take a bite, but their stares bother him.*] What are you staring at? Didn't you ever see anybody eat before? [*He takes a defiant bite and begins chewing. Then he touches the insignia on his sleeve.*] This is the American Army, not the Salvation Army. [*As they still stare he speaks, to himself, mostly.*] Man, this is what comes from all those foreign-aid programs. [*Then he speaks directly to the* GIRL *and dog.*] What the hell were you eating before I came to this stinking hole? [*He takes another few bites.*] I just got enough food here for me, understand? For me. [OLLY *eats some more.*] They figure it out that way. Down to the last candy bar. [*The dog starts licking his chops.*] All right, damn it. [OLLY *fishes around in the sack and pulls out a small tin, a can opener, a spoon, and some C-ration biscuits. He holds them out toward the* GIRL.] Here. You'll be sorry you ate it. [*She doesn't approach.*] Well? . . . Oh ye gods! [*He gets up and starts walking to the* GIRL *with the food. She begins backing up and the dog begins backing up, his tail between his ... .*] What are you backing up for? Will you stop ... . All right. All right. [*He puts the food down on ... und and returns to his original spot. The* GIRL *... rward and picks up the food.* OLLY *watches her. ... looks at the can both top and bottom. She ... g it. She realizes that there is food inside ... know how to get it out. She looks at the ... begins banging the spoon on the can.*

OLLY *lets out a cry of disgust.*] You don't bang on it.
You eat with it. [*She keeps banging at the can.*] Man,
you are truly ignorant. [*He gets up and walks toward
her. She backs away holding on to the food. In fact, she
clutches it to her.*] Look, I ain't gonna take it back. I
wanna open it for you. Put the can on the ground. [*He
gestures, but she just stands there clenching the can.*]
On the ground. Put it on the ground. [*She stares at the
ground.*] Stop staring at the ground. Just put the can
on the ground. I'll open it and then I'll come back here.
You understand? [*He points to the spot where he was
sitting. She just looks at him.* OLLY *puts his hands on his
hips.*] Man, you are truly ignorant. . . . Okay, the hard
way. [*Suddenly, unexpectedly, he runs at her. She turns
to run but he overtakes her. He grabs her and tries to
take the can away. She holds on to the can for dear life.*]
Will you give me the can? I'll give it back. I just want to
open it. [*He wrenches the can out of her hands. She
bites his hand and breaks away, clasping her hands
around her clothes.*] Look, lady, I'm not going to pull
your clothes off again. [*He goes back to where he
originally put the can down. He looks around for the
can opener. He finds it and opens the can.*] I'm
gonna show you one of the great moments in Western
culture. It's called "opening the can." [*To himself.*]
Can't get through at all. It's like talking to a brick wall
. . . talking to a brick wall. [*He makes motions on how
to use the spoon. He puts the opened can down and
goes back to his original position. She comes forward
and picks up the can, smells the contents.*] It ain't poison,
lady. It just smells that way. [*She starts eating. Her eyes
peer at him over the can of food. She uses her fingers
and throws the spoon away.*] Man, whatya think I gave
you a spoon for? You know what you look like ea
that way? A nervous duck. Quack, quack. How
you don't speak English. *Parlez-vous français?*
sie Deutsch? You wanna know something?
country is illiterate. I ain't never met so ma
people till I came here. And I've seen
people. You name me one person
that don't speak English or can't use
what comes from American aid.

that's the trouble. Take the American pioneer. Who sub-
sidized them? Nobody, that's who. What you gotta do
is be self-sufficient. You get rid of this jungle, see, and
you set up factories and stores. You get outta those
crazy clothes and put on real clothes. This ain't the gay
nineties. Nobody wears dresses down to their ankles.
This country gotta westernize itself. Get some decent
morals. You gotta adapt, move with the times. You
gotta put on shoes. [OLLY *points to his feet.*] Shoes. You
run around barefoot you get germs on the bottom of
your feet. Little bugs. [*She gets up and goes to the dog.
The dog backs up a few feet. She puts down what is left
in the can for the dog and then returns to her original
spot. The dog returns and smells at the can before eating.*] Dogs don't eat fruit. [*The dog starts to eat the fruit.*]
Even the damn dogs are illiterate here. [*The dog finishes
eating.* OLLY *shoves the paper wrapper in his pocket
and stands up.*] All right. Everybody finished eating?
Now back up because I'm gonna pick up the cans. [*He
comes forward and the* GIRL *and dog back up.*] That's
right. Everybody back. [OLLY *picks up the cans and
throws them into the mangrove swamp. They start off
down the road.* OLLY *is in front, the dog and the* GIRL
side by side some five yards to the rear.]
[*The scene dissolves slowly revealing birds of prey circling in the late afternoon sky. The camera returns to
OLLY and his companions, who are still on the road.
OLLY watches the birds, then looks off into the brush at
the side of the road. He motions for the GIRL to remain.
He moves off into the brush. OLLY chops his way into
view. He stops, listens. There is the sound of a small
baby crying. He moves on. OLLY pushes through. The
camera swings to the clearing and discovers the bodies
of a Vietnamese man and woman. They are lying face
down. Strapped to the woman's back is a baby. OLLY
... s and looks at the desolate scene for a few seconds.
... ry buzz of flies is the only sound. The buzz seems
... louder and louder. He kneels down beside the
... d pulls the baby out of the sling. There is the
... omeone coming through the brush. OLLY
... , ready to shoot, but it is only the GIRL
... he looks stoically at the dead man and*

OLLY: I thought I told you to stay on the road. [*He looks at the baby in his arms.*] That's it, baby, cry, cry. The world stinks. [*The baby continues to cry.*] What am I gonna do with you? I got fifty miles to walk. [*He begins to walk back to the road. The GIRL gestures toward the bodies of the two dead people and then points to the ground and makes digging motions.*]

GIRL [*In Vietnamese.*]: You must not leave them this way.

OLLY: Bury them! You gotta be outta your mind. I got fifty miles to go and this country is full of guerrillas. [*He continues walking away. She grows more insistent. She exposes a cross dangling around her neck and holds it in front of him. She points to the cross and then to the ground.*]

GIRL [*In Vietnamese.*]: The dead must be buried.

[*He opens the collar of his shirt and shows his dog tags.*]

OLLY: Atheist. You understand? I ain't required to give Christian burials.

GIRL [*In Vietnamese.*]: The dead must be buried.

OLLY: Lady—you think they care? You really think they care? All right, all right. Let's bury the whole world. Let's spend our time digging up the ground. This is my last war, lady . . . if I get outta here . . . [*He moves his entrenching shovel and begins digging.*] . . . alive. I'm gonna get married and settle down in Yonkers. Spend my pension money at the track. Get a house with a cement yard, don't want to see any more grass, any more jungle, don't even wanna hear birds, just dry cement. That's civilization. No grass buildings. Cement buildings from Yonkers to the Battery and the only guerrillas I wanna know from are in the zoos. Man, that's what this place is. One gigantic zoo. You know that? This place is from one million B.C.'ville. Damn savages running loose from one end of the jungle to the other. W than Central Park. Al Capone wouldn't've lived They'd'a cut him down in a week.

[*Slow time dissolve to OLLY finishing the sec The GIRL is seated with the baby, feeding it. a moment in his digging.*]

OLLY: You're eating my dessert. I was savi sauce. I ought to open up a restauran make a fortune. [*He stops digging and* side of the grave. *The girl motions at the grave and then makes digging motions.*] I know it ain't deep enough. I'm resting.

GIRL [*In Vietnamese.*]: Deeper, deeper . . . dig deeper.

OLLY: Yeah, I know what you want. I'm taking a ten-minute break. You get a ten-minute break every hour in the American army. That's the American way. You heard of the Bill of Rights? Article One says you get a ten-minute break every hour. [*She hands him the child and climbs into the grave. She starts digging.*] Now what do you want to do that for, lady? I told ya I'd finish. I just wanna rest for eight more minutes. I got that much coming to me. [*He looks at the baby. The baby has a sour look on his face. To* GIRL.] Okay you wanna dig? Dig. Dig to China. [*The baby's nose starts to run.*] Hey! Wait a minute. [OLLY *fishes in his pocket for a handkerchief, and wipes the baby's nose. The baby reaches over and grabs his nose.*] You don't want my nose, believe me, you don't. It won't get you anywhere in this world. [OLLY *looks at the baby. Suddenly the expression on his face changes. The baby has evidently gone in its pants.* OLLY's *expression is one of surprise. He withdraws his hand, brings it up to his nose and smells it.*] Oh man, what did you do that for? [*To girl.*] Okay, that's it. Ten minutes are up. [*He pulls her out of the hole with one arm and points to baby's behind.*] You take care of this. I'll dig. Wet, wet. [*She holds on to shovel.*] Oh no. I'll dig. [*He jumps into the grave as she takes the baby. He smells his hand.*] Oh man. [*He rubs dirt into his hand, smells it again, and returns to digging.*]

[*The scene dissolves to gravesite. It is several hours later at night. The* GIRL *is sitting by a tree with the baby. The dog sits nearby.* OLLY *throws the last few shovels of earth ... the graves. He walks over to the* GIRL. *She and the ... are asleep. He doesn't say anything to awaken her. ... urns back to the graves and silently closes his en-... g shovel.*]

... e's gotta be a better way of doing things. Dig ... oles in the dirt. People gotta be more than ... dirt. [*Addressing the dead people.*] So long ... don't know where you've gone to, but I hope it's better than what you had. [*He sits down at a nearby tree and places the rifle across his legs.*] Hope it's better than what you had. [*The scene fades out.*]

ACT III

[*It is early morning.* OLLY *is asleep against a tree. The rifle is spread across his lap. The sounds of birds calling in the trees wake him up. He slowly opens his eyes and then, remembering where he is, springs to his feet. He looks about him, but the* GIRL *and the baby are gone.*]

OLLY: The food! Took the food! [*He runs over to his knapsack and looks through it, expecting to find his food gone, but it is all there.*] Where's the other applesauce? [*He starts looking around. Finds empty applesauce can. He is disappointed.*] Oh man, she took the applesauce. [*There is the sound of someone coming through the brush. He points his rifle at the brush. It is the* GIRL *returning, the baby on her back, some wild fruit and flowers in her hands. She empties the fruit by the knapsack, puts the baby down, and looks at* OLLY.] Whatta they got, a supermarket in there? Where did you get this stuff?

GIRL [*In Vietnamese.*]: I picked it off a tree. [*He holds up one of the fruits—a pomegranate. She goes over to a bush, points at it, and then motions further into the jungle.*]

OLLY: What is this? [*He lifts it up and tries to take a bite, but of course, the skin is too tough. The* GIRL *starts giggling.*] What's so funny? It's as tough as a baseball! [*She takes the pomegranate from him, puts it on a flat ? and suddenly pulls a knife out from under her ?*] You had that on you all the time? Oh man. [*? ?ptly slices the pomegranate into four quarters ? him one. He watches her just as adeptly slip ? ?ck up her sleeve.*] You oughta join the Mafia. [*? ? time she looks at him as if she is really ? ? understanding.*] Never mind. [*To dog.*]

Have a biscuit? [*He tosses a biscuit which the dog wolfs down.* OLLY *has the pomegranate in his hand.*] How do you eat this thing? [*He takes a bite and starts crunching . . . since the pomegranate is all pits he has a tough time. She watches him with an amused expression on her face. When he swallows it, valiantly, she starts to giggle again. She picks up one of the sections and taking a bite sucks out the juice.*] How the hell can you eat it when it's all pits? [*She spits out the pits.*] It sure ain't the kind of fruit you eat in company. [*He makes another try at it and this time spits out the pits.*] Yeah, that's better. [*They pick up the other quarters of the pomegranate and really enjoy themselves eating it. She picks up another fruit, slices it and they eat it. He thinks a moment, then points to himself.*] Olly. My name is Olly. Olly.

GIRL [*With some difficulty.*]: Olly.

OLLY: Yeah, yeah. [*He points to her.*] What's your name?

GIRL: Olly. [*He looks at her hopelessly.*]

OLLY [*Shakes his head.*]: No. No, that's my name. [*He thinks some more, then lifts her cross up.*] What did the Christians name you? [*She smiles and nods her head.*]

GIRL: Jesus. [*She continues nodding her head.* OLLY *looks at her and then raises his hands despairingly over his head. She thinks he is pointing at the heavens and becomes convinced he is talking about the Christian God.*] Jesus. [*She points to sky and then to her cross.*]

OLLY: Okay, great. You're Jesus. How can we lose? Now, let's get out of here. [*He starts collecting the fruit and putting his odds and ends in his knapsack. He clears out all the debris in the area. She takes some of the flowers and sprinkles them over the graves.* OLLY *watches her.*] That's it lady. Give 'em lots of flowers. Lots of leaves, flowers, and dirt. [*Then he starts walking. He walks a few feet expecting her to follow, but she doesn't. She just stands in the clearing, the baby at her feet. He gestures for her to follow, but she doesn't.*] C'mon. Don't stand there like a wooden Indian. Look, I'm going south. [*He points with his finger, south. She looks at him and then points east.*]

GIRL [*Vietnamese.*]: This way.

OLLY: I don't want to go east. I want to go south. [*He gestures again to the south. She points east with equal vehemence.*] Wait a minute. [OLLY *pulls out his map and puts it on the ground.*] Look, lady, we're here. [*He points to the map. She seems to understand.*] That's right, where my finger is. And this . . . [*He points to a spot further south.*] . . . is where I wanna go. South.

GIRL [*In Vietnamese.*]: This way. [*He points again to the south. She points to the east. He looks at the map. Eastward is a village called Plei Ia Hue.*]

OLLY: There's nothing there but this Plei Ia Hue.

GIRL: Plei Ia Hue. [*She nods her head up and down and points to the east again.*]

OLLY [*Shakes his head.*]: No. I have to go south. You don't want to go there. Between here and that village they got half the Vietcong army. Behind every bush, bang, bang. They'll kill you before you get five miles.

GIRL [*Speaking rapidly in Vietnamese.*]: The child must be brought there. They will take care of him at Plei Ia Hue.

OLLY: Whoa. Just whoa a minute. Lemme think. [*He does not, of course, understand a word of her rapid conversation, but stands still, thinking. She looks at him hopefully.*] Okay. You got to go to Plei Ia Hue and I gotta go south. I think you're crazy because you ain't never gonna get there. But this is a democracy. Everybody makes his own mistakes. Here . . . [OLLY *pulls out some of the fruit and a few cans from his knapsack.*] You go your way and I'll go mine. Understand? [*She understands and just looks at him with a great look of disappointment on her face.*] Don't look at me like that, lady.

GIRL [*In Vietnamese.*]: The child must be taken to the village.

OLLY: Here, take the food, fifty-fifty. [*He hands it to her but she doesn't move to take it.*] Okay, I'll leave it here. [*He puts it on the ground.*] Well, so long. I hope you make it. [*He backs up, looking at her for a few feet and then he turns around and starts walking away. She watches him. There is a sound in the brush a few feet behind her. As the GIRL turns in the direction of the sound, the long thin tube of a gun barrel begins nosing*] *itself out of the brush. The dog barks. The* GIRL *gives out a kind of half shout, half scream and throws herself at the* GUERRILLA. *She knocks him off balance. He hits her in the face. She falls down.* OLLY *whirls around and fires. The* GUERRILLA *screams, raises his hand to his temple and falls down.* OLLY *rushes over. The* GIRL *is pulling herself to her feet. The soldier is unconscious. To girl.*] Stay down. [*He pushes against her shoulder as she tries to get to a sitting position. The blood streaks down her left cheek.* OLLY *goes over to the* GUERRILLA *and throws his rifle away. He searches the unconscious* GUERRILLA *and finds a knife. He puts the knife in his belt. He examines the wound for a second and then turns back to the* GIRL. *He takes out a first aid bandage and presses it against her cheek. Then he listens for further activity. There is none.*

GIRL [*In Vietnamese.*]: Kill him. [*She takes out her knife and wants to stab the soldier.* OLLY *restrains her.*]

OLLY: A little Christian love, Christ, Christ! [*The Vietcong* SOLDIER *begins stirring. He tries to sit up but can't. He stares at* OLLY *wide-eyed.* OLLY *presses a rifle against his throat. There is a long moment when the Vietcong* SOLDIER *just lies there looking at the end of the rifle.* OLLY *is making up his mind. The blood flows down the side of the* SOLDIER's *face.*]

GIRL [*In Vietnamese.*]: Kill him. He and others like him have destroyed our village. He killed those people. [*She points to graves and then at the* SOLDIER.]

OLLY: I know they killed those people. Everybody kills everybody. The world's greatest outdoor sport. [*The* SOLDIER *turns to face her. She looks at* OLLY. *He tosses a bandage at the* SOLDIER *and motions for him to use it to stop the flow of blood along his temple. The* SOLDIER *does so. The dog goes from one person to the other wagging his tail.*]

GIRL [*In Vietnamese.*]: If you do not kill him, he will kill you.

VIETCONG [*To* GIRL *in Vietnamese.*]: We will catch up to you and your lover and will kill you both.

[*She runs at him with her knife, but* OLLY *again stops her from using it.*]

GIRL [*To Vietcong in Vietnamese.*]: Murderers.

VIETCONG [*In Vietnamese.*]: Imperialist! Slut!

OLLY: Hold it. Just hold it right there. First of all, where is the baby? [*He makes a cradling motion with his arms.*] The baby. [*The* GIRL *understands, and gets very excited. She runs around in the brush for a few seconds and returns with it. To* Vietcong.] Get up.

VIETCONG [*In Vietnamese.*]: You slut.

GIRL [*In Vietnamese.*]: You murdered the parents of this baby. Deny it. Go ahead deny it.

VIETCONG [*In Vietnamese.*]: We did not see the child. They gave aid to the American Imperialists.

GIRL [*In Vietnamese.*]: Liar.

OLLY: Look, I don't know what this is all about, so just keep quiet for a minute. [*They both look at him.*] That's it—quiet. [*To* GIRL.] Now first off, I want to thank you for saving my life. [*To dog.*] Thanks to you, too.

GIRL [*In Vietnamese.*]: I cannot understand.

OLLY: Right. Right. I'll take you to that village. You got that much coming to you.

GIRL [*In Vietnamese.*]: You must kill this soldier.

OLLY: You'll understand in a second. [*He motions to all three and then toward village.*] We are going to Plei Ia Hue. [*The girl begins to nod her head.*] That's it. Now walk. [*He points to village. The* SOLDIER *begins walking.*] Man, I just know I ought to blast you right now. I just know it. [*To the* GIRL, *who is standing still at the moment.*] Well, come on. You're getting your guide. [*She picks up her possessions and follows. Followed by the dog, the three disappear in the thick brush. The camera picks them up moving out of the brush, confronting a morass of mud. It is almost evening.*] Okay, hold it. Stop.

GIRL [*In Vietnamese.*]: This way. [*He stands there looking at the mud. The* GIRL *grows impatient and motions to the other side.*]

OLLY: Yeah, I know where we have to go lady, but that's all mud out there. Wait a second, I'll get a stick. [*She starts to head into the mud, he grabs her arm.*] Wait. Wait. That's it. Stay there. Don't move. [OLLY *watches her as he backs up looking for a stick. He picks one up.*] Okay. [*He goes over to the edge of the morass and pushes the stick in. It goes down a distance. He pulls it*

*out and looks at the mud dripping off. He has a very
disgusted look on his face. The idea of marching through
several feet of mud doesn't appeal to him.*] Swell. Okay,
let's go. [*He picks up the dog and gives it to the* SOLDIER.]
Here. Carry something. [*Holding his rifle high,* OLLY
*slides into the mud. He probes ahead with the stick,
they follow him into the mud.*] This is very familiar
mud to me, lady. When I look at it real close, I can
see it's the same mud I went through in World War II.
This is Italian mud. After they were done using it in
Italy, they shipped it to Korea. Soon as the Korean
thing was over they shipped it here. Soon as we cross it,
they're gonna come and pick it up and ship it to the
next war location. They never get a war going until the
mud's in place. [*Wearily, one by one, they pull themselves out on a dry bank.* OLLY, *disgustedly, throws
the stick back in.*] All right. This is as far as we go today.
[*They look at him not understanding.*] We're sacking out
here. [*They still look at him.* OLLY *makes eating and
sleeping motions.*] Eat. Sleep. Here. [*The* GIRL *takes the
baby out of the sling and* OLLY *begins emptying his food
supply. She motions toward the baby's mouth.*]

GIRL [*In Vietnamese.*]: The baby is hungry.

OLLY: There's nothing here that he can eat. [*She takes
some of the fruit and begins mashing it up. When the
fruit is mashed, she begins to feed it to the baby.* OLLY
takes out some of the food and begins eating. The SOL-
DIER *looks at him.*] Man, don't they give you any food?
You guys look like you've been livin' on chicken bones
for the last ten years. [OLLY *hands him some of the food.
The* SOLDIER *won't touch it. He shakes his head furiously.*] You on a diet, man? Too proud to eat? Well, it's
provided for in the Geneva Convention. You gotta feed
prisoners. Geneva Convention, you understand?

VIETCONG [*Shakes head and repeats.*]: Geneva. [*He takes
the food.*] Geneva! [OLLY *opens a second can.*]

OLLY: You understand that. Sure. Just don't overstuff
yourself. You don't wanna get too used to eating, 'cause
when we get out of here you're gonna go back to eating
tree leaves. What you guys wanna do is lose the war.
Then you'll be eligible for American aid. [*The* GIRL
finishes feeding the baby and reaches over for some

food.] Help yourself. [*He throws some food to the dog and then looks at all of them eating.*] That's it, everybody eat. When you get done with this, we'll use my diner's card.

VIETCONG [*In Vietnamese.*]: What is he saying?

GIRL [*In Vietnamese.*]: I don't know.

VIETCONG [*In Vietnamese.*]: Why is he fighting a white man's war?

GIRL [*In Vietnamese.*]: Because you are murderers.

VIETCONG [*In Vietnamese.*]: We are not murderers. We are liberators. You are helping the imperialists enslave your people.

GIRL [*In Vietnamese.*]: You are seeking to enslave our people. [*They angrily turn away from each other.*]

OLLY: What was that all about? [*They both look at him.*] You two just naturally gotta hate each other, don't you?

VIETCONG [*In Vietnamese to* GIRL.]: Why does he keep talking when I do not understand?

GIRL [*In Vietnamese.*]: Because you are stupid.

VIETCONG [*In Vietnamese.*]: You do not speak English either, so if I am stupid, you are stupid.

GIRL [*In Vietnamese.*]: You are a murderer.

VIETCONG [*In Vietnamese.*]: You sleep with one that seeks to exploit our people. [*She leaps to her feet and runs at the* SOLDIER. OLLY *stops her.*]

OLLY: What the hell is it you keep arguing about?

GIRL [*In Vietnamese.*]: Murderer!

VIETCONG [*In Vietnamese.*]: Betrayer of the masses.

OLLY: All right. Now the both of you hush up. [*As if they understood everybody keeps quiet.*] That's better. We just don't talk the same language. But that doesn't mean we have to act like goddam savages all the time. [OLLY *sits back and lights up a cigarette. He offers the* VIETCONG *a cigarette. He takes it.* OLLY *goes to light it, but the* SOLDIER *lights his own. The three sit in a circle, the men smoking, and looking at each other.*] Okay. That's better. Now I'm gonna tell you something. Man, do you know why you're fighting in this jungle? [*The* SOLDIER *looks puzzled.*]

VIETCONG [*In Vietnamese to* GIRL.]: What is he saying?

GIRL [*In Vietnamese.*]: How many times do I have to tell you, I don't speak English. [*The* SOLDIER *sits back, frustrated and sneering.*]

OLLY: The first thing you gotta understand is that nobody —you hear me—*nobody* really wants this country. That's the first thing.

VIETCONG [*In Vietnamese.*]: Why do you keep talking when we don't understand? Are you crazy?

OLLY [*Rather angrily.*]: Just listen. [*More calmly.*] Like I say, nobody wants this country. The United States doesn't want it. What the hell would we want it for? Rice? Who the hell wants your rice? What the hell we got to be imperialistic about? The Chinese keep filling you with a lot of hogwash and you keep swilling it down. Man, you think I love being in this jungle? That I came here all the way from Yonkers, New York, to eat your lousy fruit and get shot at in the back? You think I wanna be here? You think I don't get tired of these stinking endless wars? You gotta be outta your mind.

VIETCONG [*In Vietnamese.*]: Are you crazy? Stop talking to me. I don't understand what you are saying.

GIRL [*To* GUERILLA *in Vietnamese.*]: Well, listen anyway.

OLLY: That's it—shut up. Which brings us to the question why I'm here. [*There is a pause while he collects his thoughts.*] There should be a reason for me being here. [*He pauses again.*] I'm here to take helicopter rides. To see stupid lieutenants who don't know their tails from their elbows get killed. I'm here because I ain't in Yonkers. But there are other less obvious reasons, less obvious. Somebody's got this thing all figured out. Somewhere somebody's got charts and papers which makes all this killing worthwhile. Well, leave it go. This is my final war, man. I'm going to get a house in Yonkers and settle down. Watch the trotters run right from my window. In my backyard get a hothouse going for commercial flowers. [*To* GUERILLA.] How old are you?

VIETCONG [*In Vietnamese.*]: What do you want? I don't understand you.

OLLY: How old are you? [*The boy raises his hands over his head in exasperation.*] Twenty?

VIETCONG [*In Vietnamese to* GIRL.]: He's out of his mind.

OLLY: So you're twenty. That's a good age to fight a war. Young. Walk all day and never get tired, man. I was fighting when I was twenty. Yeah, I was fighting the Germans, just about when you were getting born. Think about that, man. In some stinking swamp somewhere right now some woman is giving birth to a kid so you can fight him in twenty years. Yes, sir. They got one coming up for you, but not for me. This is my final war. [*He gets up and walks a few feet away.*] You and the rest of them can blow your stupid heads off, man. I'm gonna sit in front of my TV, drinking beer and watching old war movies. I don't even know what I'm doing here. Who needs this place? The hell with their charts and papers. You could die from their charts and papers.

[*The three sit in silence. Scene dissolves to the river bank at night.* OLLY *leans against a tree. The* GIRL *and the* SOLDIER *appear to be asleep. The* GIRL *opens her eyes and getting up, comes over to* OLLY. *She indicates that he is to go to sleep and that she will watch the prisoner.*]

GIRL [*In Vietnamese.*]: You sleep—I'll watch. [OLLY *just shakes his head. She sits down next to* OLLY *with her eyes wide open, indicating that if they will not take turns, she will watch, too.*]

OLLY: You sure get determined about things, lady. Stubborn like my sister. You know what she once did? Claimed the gas meter was crooked. That it was going around even when there was no gas coming in. So she shut off all the gas in the house, the gas heater, too, and this was in January, and still the meter went circling around. Man, before she was done, she had them all in court. She was some woman, my sister. [*He looks at the* GIRL.] That was a long time ago, before you were born. The house is tore down now. I went back to see when I came back from Korea. There was a beauty parlor there that straightened out kinky hair. [*He touches her hair carelessly. She looks at him and his hand drops to his side, almost with embarrassment. Then almost angrily:*] People I know spend a lot of money to get rid of their kinky hair. Fake out the world. [*Then calmly.*] The world is moving. Sit here quiet and I feel it. Round and round. The old houses come down, sisters die, little babies sit in the clearing and don't know what happened to them. You eat crazy fruits you never seen before, sleep in jungles, you open your eyes and it's twenty years later and nobody knows your name. [*The girl brushes off insects. He gives her his poncho from his pack and over her mild protests puts it around her shoulders.*] Take it, I don't get wet or buggy any more. [*She rests back against the tree and in a few moments her eyes shut and she is asleep. He looks at her and half smiles. There is a gurgling sound from the baby and* OLLY *gets up and goes over. He picks the baby up and carries it back to where he was sitting. He sits down, the baby cradled in his left arm, the rifle held in his right. The* GIRL's *head falls against his shoulder.* OLLY *sits still for a time and then shuts his eyes. Some time passes by. The moon moves a bit further in the sky. The Vietcong* SOLDIER *slowly opens his eyes. He does not move but looks over at* OLLY, *who is apparently asleep and decides this is his chance. A few feet from where he is stretched out is a stone the size of a man's fist. The* SOLDIER *moves his hand until he has the stone. He slowly gets to his feet and silently walks over to* OLLY. *He obviously intends to smash* OLLY *over the head with the stone. He creeps closer and closer until he stands perhaps five feet in front.* OLLY, *scarcely opening up his eyes, swings the rifle around so that it points at the* SOLDIER's *chest. For a long second there is a pause.* OLLY *slowly opens his eyes half way, and looks at the* SOLDIER. *The* SOLDIER *drops the rock.* OLLY *just stares at him.*] Man, nobody puts nothing over on me. [*The* SOLDIER *returns to his spot and goes to sleep.* OLLY *looks up at the full moon gliding through rows of thin clouds. As he stares at the moon, we faintly begin to hear the voice of Billy Eckstine singing a popular song of the 1950's, "My Foolish Heart."*

"The night is like a lovely tune,
Beware, my foolish heart,
There's a line between love and fascination
That's hard to see on an evening such as this
For they both give the very same sensation
When you're lost in the magic of a kiss . . ."

[*As the song becomes more audible, we move into a close-up of* OLLY's *face. The camera moves past* OLLY *and dissolves into a flashback of an American beauty parlor.*

[*A Negro* WOMAN, *covered by a white smock up to her neck, is having her hair straightened by a Negro* BEAUTICIAN. *The music comes from a small portable radio on the* BEAUTICIAN's *table. The* BEAUTICIAN, *working in a fury of activity, keeps dabbing a small sponge into a dish of ammonia and then working the sponge through the* WOMAN's *hair. He keeps pulling at her hair to straighten it as he works.*]

BEAUTICIAN: Keep your head back, Mrs. Pierce. [*He shuts off the radio.*]

MRS. PIERCE: It *is* back. My scalp hurts, Mr. Joseph.

BEAUTICIAN: You're purposely moving your head to make me distraught, Mrs. Pierce.

MRS. PIERCE: I'm not. I'm still. I'm very still.

BEAUTICIAN: If you do not keep your head back, the ammonia will run in your eyes. We don't want to burn your eyes. It wouldn't do if we burned your eyes.

OLLY: What happened to the house that used to be here?

BEAUTICIAN [*Not looking up.*]: Try next door. I can't say.

MRS. PIERCE: Ouch.

BEAUTICIAN: I can't stand being made distraught, Mrs. Pierce. I can't straighten your hair if you don't keep still.

OLLY: There was a house here. My sister's house. [*The* BEAUTICIAN *pulls* MRS. PIERCE's *hair and furiously continues working on it.*]

BEAUTICIAN: Oh, this is going to be straight. Very straight. [*He suddenly looks up and stares straight at* OLLY.] Try next door. [OLLY *turns away as the camera dissolves into another scene revealing a porch on which three women sit in a circle around a metal lawn table playing cards. The table is littered with ashtrays, soda pop, cigarette butts, chips. The woman shuffling the cards is in her late sixties, thin, bony. On her left sits a fat woman, younger, heavily lipsticked. On the right of the shuffler sits a woman in her fifties, smoking. She is in a bathing suit; the other two women wear cheap housedresses. Both the smoker and the* FAT WOMAN *wait impatiently for the shuffler to finish shuffling. The* SHUFFLER *seems never to finish.*]

FAT LADY: You've shuffled enough. Deal the cards. [*The* SHUFFLER, *arthritic, cannot shuffle normally. Something always goes wrong with the shuffle. She continues shuffling.*] That's enough shuffling.

SHUFFLER [*Defensively.*]: It's not enough. [*She shuffles some more. The* FAT LADY *watches for a few seconds as the* SHUFFLER *ineptly handles the cards. Suddenly, she pulls the cards out of the* SHUFFLER'*s hands.*]

FAT LADY: Enough. Enough. [*She begins dealing the cards out.*] We can't wait all day.

OLLY: There used to be a building next door. What happened to it?

FAT LADY: They tore it down.

THE SMOKER [*Looking at her hand.*]: This is going to be a good hand for me. [*To the card players.*] I could knock right now. How would you like it if I knocked right now?

OLLY: My sister lived there. I can't find my sister. I've been away in Korea.

SHUFFLER [*Suddenly, angrily to* FAT LADY.]: It was my deal. Everybody's supposed to deal, not only you.

FAT LADY [*To* OLLY.]: I think she died. Nobody told ya? [OLLY *stands there silently shaking his head, over and over.*]

SHUFFLER: That's my soda. Who told you to drink my soda?

SMOKER: Those are my cards. Who told you to use my cards?

SHUFFLER: You can drink the soda if ya want to, but you have to ask.

SMOKER: Well, I'm not going to ask.

FAT LADY [*To* OLLY.]: Check with Mrs. Keating in Seagate. She cleaned house for Mrs. Keating. Go down to the Neptune Avenue gate and let the gatekeeper let you in. [*The camera again fades into a scene revealing a private community surrounded by a seven-foot fence topped with barbed wire. A gatekeeper appears at the entrance as the voice of the* FAT WOMAN *is heard off-screen:*]

FAT LADY: The gatekeeper will let you in. Just go right in through the gate.

[*As* OLLY *stands there at the gate, the* GATEKEEPER *moves toward him.*]

GATEKEEPER: Hey, you got a pass?

OLLY: A pass?

GATEKEEPER: Yeah, a pass. [OLLY *shakes his head.*] Ya need a pass to get in. Who you wanna see?

OLLY: Mrs. Keating.

GATEKEEPER: What about?

OLLY: About my sister.

GATEKEEPER: What about your sister? [*A bright red convertible drives up to the gate. A blonde about twenty-five is at the wheel. The guard turns from* OLLY *to greet the woman and open the gate.*] Good afternoon, Mrs. Sloan.

MRS. SLOAN: Good afternoon, George. [*She drives through.*]

OLLY: Look, I just want to see this Mrs. Keating for a minute.

GATEKEEPER: What's this about your sister?

OLLY: Why do you have to know about my sister or why I want to talk to Mrs. Keating?

GATEKEEPER: Nobody gets in here unless they live here or a resident wants them in here.

OLLY: I've got to talk to Mrs. Keating.

GATEKEEPER: What's your name?

OLLY: Olly Winter.

GATEKEEPER: And your sister?

OLLY: Mary Winter.

GATEKEEPER: Just a minute. [*He starts walking back to the gatehouse to phone.* OLLY *accompanies him. Another convertible drives up full of kids, teenagers, on the way to the beach. They toot the horn.*] Hi, Mr. Jackson. [*They drive through, horns blaring. In the gatehouse, the* GATEKEEPER *looks up* MRS. KEATING's *phone number.*] Augusta Keating?

OLLY: I don't know her first name.

[GATEKEEPER *looks at him for a second and then begins to dial.*]

MAID [*Answering the phone in the house.*]: Keating residence.

GATEKEEPER: This is George Lewis down at the gate. May I speak to Mrs. Keating, please.

MAID: Hold on, please.

GATEKEEPER [*To* OLLY.]: Your sister worked for Mrs. Keating?

OLLY: She cleaned house.

MRS. KEATING [*On phone.*]: Hello, this is Mrs. Keating.

GATEKEEPER: Mrs. Keating, this is George down at the gate.

MRS. KEATING: Yes, George.

GATEKEEPER: Mrs. Keating, there's a colored guy down here who wants to speak with you. His name is . . . wait a minute . . . [*To* OLLY.] What's your name?

OLLY: Oliver Winter.

GATEKEEPER [*To* MRS. KEATING.]: Oliver Winter.

MRS. KEATING: I don't know any Oliver Winter.

GATEKEEPER: He says his sister worked for you. Cleaned house.

MRS. KEATING: Oh, yes. What does he want?

GATEKEEPER: Something about his sister. Shall I let him in to speak to you?

MRS. KEATING: I'll speak to him on the phone.

GATEKEEPER: Yes, ma'am. [*He hands the phone to* OLLY *and stands right by his side listening to every word.* OLLY *is annoyed that the* GATEKEEPER *will not even show a minimum of regard for his privacy.*]

OLLY: Mrs. Keating, I'm trying to find out what happened to my sister. I've just returned from Korea and I find the house my sister lived in is no longer there, and the ladies who lived next door say she may have died.

MRS. KEATING: Oh, my. Yes, it's true. She was working for me and she had a stroke. I'm sorry. Surely somebody notified you.

OLLY: No, Mrs. Keating. Nobody told me till today.

MRS. KEATING: She cleaned for me on Mondays and Fridays. She was in my kitchen when she had a stroke. I called the ambulance and they told me later she died in the hospital. She never mentioned any relatives.

OLLY: When did she die, Mrs. Keating?

MRS. KEATING: On Friday . . . no, it must have been Monday because I remember the laundry had just been hung . . . yes, it was on Monday, in the summer of 1951. I'm sorry. [*Hesitatingly.*] I hope they buried her all right. [OLLY *slowly puts phone down. He leaves the gatehouse, and catching hold of the wire fence in his fingers stands there with his face pressed against the wire. Gasps of almost mute sound come from his throat. . . .*] [*The camera fades back into the scene at the river bank in Vietnam. It is night.* OLLY *continues to gasp, his face pressed against the tree. The baby is still in his arms. The* GIRL *is awake and so is the* VIETCONG. *They both* are looking at him. After a moment, he turns to them.]

OLLY: All right, let's get started. [*He recovers his composure and rises, picking up his gear. Accompanied by the others, he starts walking along a jungle path.*]

[*The scene shifts back to the gravesite where four Vietcong* SOLDIERS *are looking down at the two graves. They speak to each other. Two are inspecting the area carefully. The* OFFICER *takes a map and places his finger decisively on it.*

SOLDIER [*In Vietnamese.*]: They went south.

OFFICER: Nam? [*He looks at map.*] Plei Ia Hue!

ACT IV

[OLLY *gradually comes upon a group of small houses forming a village. Some children move hurriedly in from the jungle path. They move across the scene, shouting and pointing back toward the path. After a moment, the dog runs in from the path, followed by* OLLY, *the* GIRL *and the* VIETCONG. *By now, there are a number of village people gathered watching them. Presently the village* CHIEF ELDER *moves up to confront the travelers.*]

CHIEF ELDER [*In Vietnamese.*]: Good day. Welcome to our village.

GIRL [*In Vietnamese.*]: Good day. Thank you for your welcome. The American soldier only speaks his own language.

CHIEF ELDER [*To* OLLY *in English.*]: Good day, my dear sir.

OLLY: Good day to you, my dear sir.

CHIEF ELDER [*To* VIETCONG *prisoner in Vietnamese.*]: And who are you?

VIETCONG [*In Vietnamese.*]: I am a soldier in the army of liberation. I am being held prisoner by this tool of the capitalists and I demand to be released. If you aid the American in keeping me prisoner you will all die and your village will be burned to the ground. [*The people in the crowd become very frightened. They gather to one another. The* CHIEF ELDER *becomes upset.*]

OLLY [*To* CHIEF ELDER.]: What did he tell you?

CHIEF ELDER: He is of the Vietcong, your prisoner?

OLLY: Yes.

CHIEF ELDER: You must release him, dear sir.

OLLY: I can't release him. If I let him go, he'd bring the Vietcong here.

CHIEF ELDER: Ah . . . ah . . . [*The* CHIEF ELDER *confronts the* GIRL.]

GIRL [*In Vietnamese.*]: The American found me on the road after my village was destroyed in a battle between the Vietcong and the Government. He fed and took care of the child when he found its parents dead. Even though the soldier that you see here tried to kill him he would not take his life. He is a person of compassion. [*She follows the* CHIEF *over to the group and the discussion goes on. The* GIRL *is obviously explaining what has taken place . . . how they met . . . about herself . . . the baby . . . the soldier. As she speaks, she motions at* OLLY *and the crowd studies him. From the tone of her voice and from her expressions and the crowd's response, it is clear that she is painting a very favorable portrait of* OLLY. OLLY *looks around him as they talk. A bit beyond the village is a waterfall.* OLLY *longingly looks at it. Finally, the* CHIEF *comes back.*]

CHIEF ELDER [*To* OLLY.]: You are a brave soldier. This one . . . has told us of your deeds. [*He points to* GIRL *and offers a little bow.*]

OLLY: Thank you. [*He returns the bow.*]

CHIEF ELDER: This one comes from village to north that give aid and comfort to Americans and Government soldiers. Vietcong attack village, kill soldiers. Soldiers kill Vietcong. Everybody kill whole village. Village now dead. [*The* CHIEF *points to* GIRL.]

OLLY: The girl's parents? Mother and father?

CHIEF ELDER [*To* GIRL *in Vietnamese.*]: Are your parents alive?

GIRL [*In Vietnamese.*]: They were killed in the village.

CHIEF ELDER [*To* OLLY.]: They were killed in the village she say. If you hold this soldier prisoner they will destroy this village. We do not wish our village to be dead.

OLLY: If I release him he will go back to the Vietcong and tell them that I am here and they will come for me and then they will destroy your village anyway. [*The* CHIEF ELDER *thinks a moment. He goes over to group and they talk for a moment. The* CHIEF ELDER *calls out three men armed with long knives. The four of them return to* OLLY.]

CHIEF ELDER: You have all traveled a long way together. To think in the sun is not too wise. Come, cleanse yourself of the earth of your journey. Come. Wash. Talk.

OLLY: What about him? [*He points to Vietcong* SOLDIER.]

CHIEF ELDER: He will cleanse himself, too. All cleansed.

VIETCONG [*In Vietnamese.*]: I wish to be freed.

CHIEF ELDER [*In Vietnamese.*]: We will speak of that at the waterfall. [*To two of the men.*] Escort our guest to the waterfall. [*The two lead him off. The third comes over and when the Vietcong* SOLDIER *is out of earshot, the* CHIEF ELDER *gives instructions. In Vietnamese to another* ELDER.]: Guard him well. He must not escape. Post sentries around the village. Signal if anyone comes.

OLLY: He must not escape.

CHIEF ELDER: He will not escape. The men of the village will watch to see if anybody comes. Go, wash, talk.

[*The* GIRL *gives the baby to a village woman.*]

[*The scene shifts to a pool in the jungle. The camera is on the surface of the water.* OLLY's *face comes up. The camera moves to include the whole scene. The* ELDERS *sit below a shady tree, chattering about something. In the background, seated squatlegged beneath a small waterfall is the Vietcong* SOLDIER. *He enjoys the washing, but his petulant expression belies it. The dog runs in and out of the waterfall.*]

OLLY [*To* PRISONER.]: Go ahead, man, sit like a brass Buddha in a rainfall.

ELDER [*In Vietnamese.*]: I don't understand how he can be black and be an American.

CHIEF ELDER: They do not understand how you can be black and be an American.

OLLY: Tell them Americans come in all colors.

CHIEF ELDER: Ah, that is most unusual. [*To the others in Vietnamese.*] Americans are not all white in color. They come in other colors, too.

ANOTHER ELDER [*In Vietnamese.*]: Brown, too?

CHIEF ELDER [*To* OLLY.]: Our color, too?

OLLY: Oh, yes.

[*The* CHIEF ELDER *translates to other* ELDER, *who nods his head.*]

CHIEF ELDER [*To* OLLY.]: We must decide what is to be done. What do you wish to be done?

OLLY: I do not wish any harm to come to your people. But I have a long journey to make and the Vietcong must not know that I have been here. If they find out, they will come after me and kill me before I reach safety.

CHIEF ELDER: Yes. What is to be done about the soldier?

OLLY: Three things. One, I could just kill him and bury him where he would not be found but I do not want to do this. Two, I could take him with me.

CHIEF ELDER [*To* OLLY.]: I think this course is best.

OLLY: But to bring him with me on a journey that will take many days will be very difficult. He will have many chances to escape.

CHIEF ELDER: That is true. What is to be done?

OLLY: The third way would be if you could hold him for a few days, that would be all the time I need to escape. Three days.

CHIEF ELDER [*To* OLLY.]: When he is released he will inform Vietcong and they will destroy us for what we have done.

OLLY: Not if the decision were his. Not if I tell him that unless he agrees to remain here I will be forced to kill him. Let him make the choice.

[*The* CHIEF ELDER *translates this to the others. They talk among themselves and come to a decision.*

ANOTHER ELDER: Let soldier make decision.

CHIEF ELDER [*To* OLLY.]: We say this. Let soldier make decision. We will do as he agrees to do.

OLLY: Good enough.

[*There is a splash in the pool behind* OLLY. *The* GIRL *has entered the pool. She comes to the surface at a respectful distance from the* ELDERS *and looks over toward* OLLY. *The* CHIEF ELDER *looks at the* GIRL *and then at* OLLY.]

CHIEF ELDER: She has suffered much misfortune. It is a bad thing to have no parents and no husband. [OLLY *looks quizzically at him. The* ELDERS *start to leave.*] We will see what the soldier wishes to be done. [*The* ELDERS *head toward the waterfall.* OLLY *watches as they talk to the Vietcong* SOLDIER. *The* SOLDIER *continues to sit like a Buddha staring straight ahead.* OLLY *turns to look at the* GIRL, *who stands a few feet from him, her eyes fixed upon the surface of the water. She has some flowers in her hand.* OLLY's *hand, hesitantly at first, reaches out slowly to touch the flowers.*]

OLLY: This is a hell of a bathtub. . . . [*She does not smile and the smile goes from his face. He touches the flower.*] There are no flowers like this in America. [OLLY *cups her face in his hands, and lifts her head.*] No flowers like this. Oh lady, if there were just a little world for you and me, I would plant flowers all over my yard, keep the sun in my house all day. [*The* GIRL *lowers her eyes. The scene fades out.*]

[OLLY *and the* CHIEF *enter a hut and confront the Vietcong* PRISONER.]

OLLY [*To the* CHIEF.]: Ask him what his decision is.

CHIEF ELDER [*In Vietnamese.*]: You have heard the choices given to you by the American. What is it you wish me to tell him?

VIETCONG [*In Vietnamese.*]: I am a prisoner of war.

CHIEF ELDER [*To* OLLY.]: He says that he is a prisoner of war.

SOLDIER [*In Vietnamese.*]: Why does he give me choices? Why does he not shoot me as the Americans shoot other prisoners of war?

CHIEF ELDER: He asks why you have made him choices. Why you do not shoot him as Americans shoot other prisoners of war.

OLLY: Americans do not shoot prisoners of war.

CHIEF ELDER [*In Vietnamese.*]: American says Americans do not shoot prisoners of war.

SOLDIER: Bah.

CHIEF ELDER: He says . . .

OLLY: Yeah, I can hear what he says.

SOLDIER [*In Vietnamese.*]: If I wish to leave when the American is gone and you attempt to hold me, this village will be destroyed.

CHIEF ELDER [*In Vietnamese.*]: Yes, that is why we will not keep you against your will.

SOLDIER [*In Vietnamese.*]: Does the American know that you will let me go if I wish to go?

CHIEF ELDER [*In Vietnamese.*]: Yes.

SOLDIER [*In Vietnamese.*]: I do not understand why he does this.

OLLY: What is he saying?

CHIEF ELDER: He asks if you understand that he will be free to leave once you are gone. I say yes. He say he do not understand why you do this.

OLLY: Tell him I do not wish to kill him. That if he will give his word to remain I will believe him.

CHIEF ELDER [*In Vietnamese.*]: The American says that
he does not wish to kill you. That if you will promise
to remain he will believe you.

SOLDIER: It is then a matter of honor?

CHIEF ELDER [*To* OLLY.]: He says is it then a matter of
honor?

OLLY: Yes. Tell him it is a matter of honor.

CHIEF ELDER [*In Vietnamese to* SOLDIER.]: It is so. It is a
matter of honor.

SOLDIER [*In Vietnamese.*]: Ah. [*He turns around and begins pacing about the hut, talking to himself.*] A matter
of honor. A matter of honor.

OLLY: What's he saying?

CHIEF ELDER: He is thinking.

SOLDIER [*In Vietnamese.*]: Ah. [*To* CHIEF ELDER.] I am a
man of honor. [OLLY *looks to the* CHIEF ELDER *for a
translation.*]

CHIEF ELDER: He say he is a man of honor.

OLLY [*Sarcastically, but kindly.*]: Yeah—now, is he going
to stay? [*The* CHIEF ELDER *holds up his hand as a sign
for* OLLY *to have patience. The* SOLDIER *walks about for
a second or two and then reaches a decision.*]

SOLDIER [*In Vietnamese.*]: I will stay for three days. A
matter of honor.

CHIEF ELDER: He will stay for three days.

OLLY: Good enough. [*He starts to leave.*]

SOLDIER [*In Vietnamese.*]: You must tell him, Elder, that
I regret trying to hit him in head with rock, but a prisoner of war must try to escape.

CHIEF ELDER [*To* OLLY.]: He says he is sorry he try to hit
your head in with rock, but it is for enemy to hold
prisoner but it is for prisoner to escape.

OLLY: Tell him I understand.

CHIEF ELDER [*In Vietnamese.*]: It is as you say. He understands.

SOLDIER [*In Vietnamese.*]: Ah. [*He bows his head slightly.
OLLY and the* CHIEF ELDER *bow back and leave the hut.*]

CHIEF ELDER [*To* OLLY.]: He has much respect for you.
[OLLY *seems about to say something, but does not. The*
GIRL *stands in the distance looking at them but does not
approach. The* ELDER *looks from* OLLY *to the* GIRL *and
then back to* OLLY.] She is girl of much grace and plea-

sure. [OLLY, *momentarily distracted, doesn't catch it. He is staring at the* GIRL.]

OLLY: Huh? Yeah.

CHIEF ELDER: She bring much happiness to a house. Like a fire that take away all dark corners from the house.

OLLY: Yeah, she should get married. She'd be a real fire in the house.

CHIEF ELDER: That is observation of much wisdom, but there is none here to marry with her.

OLLY: There must be many men who would want to marry her in this village. The ones with the knives?

CHIEF ELDER: All married.

OLLY: All of them?

CHIEF ELDER: That is so.

OLLY: Where are all the young men?

CHIEF ELDER: At war—some the Government take away. Some the Vietcong take away. We do not see our sons any more, I think. She does not please you? You perhaps find her distasteful?

OLLY: No. No. I find her very tasteful. I mean I like her very much. [*The* CHIEF ELDER *smiles knowingly and motions to the* GIRL *to come over.*]

CHIEF ELDER [*To the* GIRL *in Vietnamese.*]: Come here. He say he like you very much. [*The* GIRL'S *face lights up.*]

OLLY: Hey, man, what did you say to her?

CHIEF ELDER: What you yourself have said.

OLLY: What?

CHIEF ELDER: That you like her very much.

OLLY: Oh, man.

GIRL [*In Vietnamese.*]: I am ready to leave with the American.

OLLY: What did she say?

CHIEF ELDER: She is ready to leave with you.

OLLY: Now, wait a minute. Oh, man.

[*The scene shifts to a jungle trail.* OLLY *walks ahead, followed by the* GIRL *and then the dog.*]

OLLY: They didn't make that guy Elder for nothing. [*He imitates the* CHIEF ELDER.] "That is an observation of much wisdom. . . . You perhaps find her distasteful?" Man, if he threw in some cheap jewelry, he coulda sold me the whole jungle. Another ten minutes and I woulda owned this whole jungle. [*He looks quite contented as he forges on ahead through the jungle.*]

[*The camera fades in on the village. The Vietcong* OFFI-
CER *who appeared at the gravesite confronts the* CHIEF.
All speak in Vietnamese.]

OFFICER: The Americans have been here?

CHIEF ELDER: Yes.

OFFICER: What did they want?

CHIEF ELDER: Nothing. [*The guerrilla* LEADER *raises his
hand as if to strike the* ELDER. *The old man does not
flinch. The guerrilla* LEADER *thinks better of it and puts
his raised hand down.*]

OFFICER [*Repeats.*]: What did they want?

CHIEF ELDER: There was only one. He came to bring us
this child from another village. [*He points to the baby
being held by a woman.*]

OFFICER: I do not believe you, old man. What else did he
want?

CHIEF ELDER: He left a prisoner.

OFFICER: Where is this prisoner? [*The* CHIEF ELDER *begins walking to the hut. The guerrilla* LEADER *and a few
of his followers walk after him. The rest of the guerrillas remain in the square with the inhabitants. The
Vietcong* OFFICER *and* CHIEF *enter the hut. The Vietcong* PRISONER *snaps to attention.*] What are you doing
here?

SOLDIER: I attempted to kill the American, but was taken
a prisoner. He bandaged my wounds. I had to give my
word to remain here for three days or else be shot.

OFFICER [*To* CHIEF ELDER.]: Is this true? [*The* CHIEF ELDER
nods his head. The OFFICER *stands unbelieving for a moment. Then he turns back to the* SOLDIER.] You are a
fool. There is no question of honor with the Americans.
They are fascist imperialists.

SOLDIER: This one was not. This one was a black man.

OFFICER: Then he is a trained dupe of the imperialists.
Where did he go?

SOLDIER: South.

OFFICER: Come. [*The* OFFICER, CHIEF *and* SOLDIER *move
through the open doorway. To the* CHIEF ELDER *and the
people of the village.*] You have been repeatedly warned
against helping the enemy who would enslave you. How
many times must you be told who your enemies are? If
we fight and we die to save our land from the aggressors

and you give aid to those who kill us, are you not our enemies as well? Do you not betray us? This time an example must be made. Who made the decision to help the American? [*The* ELDERS *look at one another but none speak.*] If you do not tell me, you will all be shot.

CHIEF ELDER: What was done for the American was done by me alone.

OFFICER [*To the other* ELDERS.] Is that true? [*They say nothing.*]

CHIEF ELDER: Tell them that what I say is true.

ONE OF THE ELDERS: It is true.

OFFICER: Then we will be just. We have no wish not to be just. [*He takes out his automatic pistol.*] For aiding the enemy in time of war, for crimes against his own people, it is my order that your Elder shall be shot. [*To the* ELDER.] Do you wish to say anything?

CHIEF ELDER: Can anything be said to prevent my death?

OFFICER: No.

CHIEF ELDER: Then what shall I say?

OFFICER: I am sorry, old man. Your execution is a military decision done without rancor. [*He gently pushes the* ELDER *to his knees. There is a loud report. The pistol is fired.*]

[*The camera fades in on the jungle trail. It is early morning.* OLLY *and the* GIRL, *still followed by the dog, move wearily through the thick brush.* OLLY *turns around and sees that she cannot walk much farther.*]

OLLY: Okay, let's take ten. [*He moves to help her and they move forward to a small clearing. He gestures for her to sit down. She protests that she is not really tired . . . that she can go on. But it is only pretense and* OLLY *sees that she cannot.*] Yeah, sure. I'm the one that's tired. The way I figure it, another day or so and we can make it— if they haven't gotten in front of us. Sun'll be up soon. You know what I'm going to do when we get out of here? Teach you the English language all by myself. We'll start with the alphabet. There's a way of singing out the letters that lets you get them down real quick. [*He sings.*] "ABCDEFG . . . HIJKLMNOP" I'll get one of those first-grade readers from the American school in Saigon and we'll start in with that. . . . This is a house. This is a big house. This is a big brown house. . . .

You'd be surprised how easy English is once you get the alphabet down. I want to get a garden started. Lots of flowers. There's money to be made in hothouses. There aren't too many people who want to go into gardening. With a good hothouse you can make a nice income. And you live in a beautiful world because it's all flowers. [*The* GIRL *tries to keep awake but her eyes shut. He looks and smiles at her. His arm is around her and she sleeps against his shoulder.*] Well, no rush. When you're married, you can stay put, not have to keep moving around. [*The words "moving around" remind* OLLY *of something. He says "around" slowly, and then just sits back against the tree.*]

[*The scene fades and dissolves into a flashback of* OLLY's *childhood apartment.* OLLY, *a boy of ten, is peeking out the bedroom door. His* MOTHER *is arguing with the* LANDLORD. *The* LANDLORD *is yelling.*]

LANDLORD: You'll have to . . . move. You'll just have to move. I'm not going to accept part payment of the rent, Mrs. Winter. Part payment doesn't pay my taxes or the coal that gets shoveled into the furnace. I can't go over to Uncle Sam and say, "Listen, I'm only getting part rent on 4D so let me only pay part of my taxes." Oh, no, Mrs. Winter, it doesn't work that way. It just don't. This is the second month you ain't paid now. Your husband died, okay, I'm sorry, but sorry don't pay my taxes.

[*Again the scene dissolves into a flashback of the cashier's office in a hospital.* OLLY's MOTHER *and* OLLY *are listening to the* CASHIER. *The* CASHIER *picks up four crumpled dollar bills that have been placed by* MRS. WINTER *on her desk.*]

HOSPITAL CASHIER: Four dollars a week, Mrs. Winter? Four dollars? Do you have any idea how long it would take you to pay your husband's hospital bill at four dollars a week?

[*The* CASHIER *begins tapping away on the keys of an adding machine and then stares at* MRS. WINTER *and* OLLY *while the machine takes over with its shifting, clicking, whirring sounds. The machine, impossibly enough, seems to go on and on, as if giving an interminable mechanical answer to the question.*]

[*The scene dissolves and fades into a funeral office.* OLLY *and his* MOTHER *are listening to the* FUNERAL DIRECTOR.]
FUNERAL DIRECTOR: You should have had him cremated. You could have saved over a hundred dollars. Most people don't realize how much money they can save by cremation. They seem to feel that cremation isn't as sacred as burial, but let me tell you, Mrs. Winter, that in God's eyes it is the soul that counts, not how a man's mortal remains are disposed of. More and more people are being cremated each week rather than go through the expense of a casket burial. But your husband had a fine Christian burial, Mrs. Winter, and there is one hundred and forty dollars outstanding. Surely if he were alive he would want to feel that the sarcophagus in which he is sleeping out eternity has been paid for. Surely, Mrs. Winter, he would tell you that.

[*The scene shifts to the stairway leading to* OLLY's *apartment.* OLLY *lets go of the cat he had been stroking and moves up the stairs. School books are under his arm. He reaches his landing, opens the door to his apartment and goes in. His* MOTHER *is sitting on the floor, her head resting on the oven door. The camera zooms in quickly to focus on his dead* MOTHER.]

[*The camera brings in the jungle trail.* OLLY's *eyes are wide open and his cheeks are streaked with tears. The* GIRL *is silently looking at him with a look that shows awareness of the bitter problems that haunt him. For a long moment they look at each other. It is one of those moments in which either a love relationship begins or not. She reaches out and with her fingers, wipes dry his cheeks.* OLLY *remains immovable, unable to react, still under the weight of his memory. She is resting on her knees in front of him. The* GIRL *gives a soft cry as her face suddenly registers shock. There is a sound of a shot. She pitches forward and* OLLY *instinctively moves to catch her. As he does so, he is hit. They both slip to the ground.* OLLY *and the* GIRL *lie in the middle of a circle of Vietcong soldiers. The dog, for some unknown reason, is running in furious little circles around and around. . . .*]

> "Brilliant . . . easily the best of the
> several recent books about
> the treatment of women in films."
> —*Washington Post*

WOMEN AND THEIR SEXUALITY IN THE NEW FILM

by Joan Mellen

A bold exploration of the treatment of women and their sexuality in modern films. The author analyzes many significant recent films and shows how female sexuality, lesbianism, and sexual politics have influenced the new film. She includes provocative appraisals of Bergman, Bertolucci, Buñuel, Mike Nichols, Eric Rohmer, Visconti and others. Among the films she explores are: *Cries and Whispers, Carnal Knowledge, Klute, Last Tango in Paris, The Heartbreak Kid, Tristana, My Night at Maud's* and others.

This book contains forty revealing photographs of scenes from the films.

9342—16   **LAUREL EDITIONS $1.25**